ESKIMOS WITHOUT IGLOOS

*Social and Economic
Development in Sugluk*

ESKIMOS WITHOUT IGLOOS

Social and Economic
Development in Sugluk

NELSON H. H. GRABURN   *University of California, Berkeley*

Little, Brown and Company
BOSTON

Preface

This book concerns the history and sequence of changes among a group of Eskimos along the south coast of the Hudson Strait who called themselves Takamiut, "the people of the shadow," because of their northerly position on the Ungava Peninsula (see Figure 1 facing page 1). There are now three settlements in this huge area — Ivujivik, Sugluk, and Wakeham Bay — and all are phenomena of recent times. Sugluk is the focus of this book because it was the largest of the three when I visited in 1959, 1964, and 1968.

Sugluk is the Anglicized name for one of the two large inlets in the coastline that the Eskimos call Salluit, "the Sugluks, or the Narrows (Inlets)." Therefore, Sugluk is the name of a place rather than of a group of people. In the minds of white men, it has become identified with the cluster of white agencies that have settled in the area within recent years, and it has attracted a sizeable Eskimo population (over 300). These Eskimos now call themselves Sallumiut, "the people of Sugluk," but this is a recent phenomenon for most of them, as we shall see.

Sugluk has only recently become a community of Eskimos exhibiting any kind of solidarity. For most of the history of the area, the only communities for the indigenous population were those small seasonal camps, family-based and very flexible, that grew and diminished during the annual cycle. This book is therefore concerned with the creation of a new community — one which is very recent and in many ways completely unlike anything the Eskimos had previously known.

The emphasis is on changes that have been brought about by the coming of "civilization" to this area, traditionally one of many small communities, leading to a realignment of the population into one large community. Although it may appear that initially most of the changes were in the economy and technology, their ramifications and consequences have led to revolutionary changes in many other areas of life. Particularly, the realignment of population distribution, primarily due to economic changes, has had great effects on most of the important areas of social life. Thus, the Eskimos have embarked on a path of change both irreversible and itself ever-changing.

I wish to thank those institutions and people who enabled me to carry out research among the Eskimos. For the 1959 and 1960 fieldwork I was supported by the Northern Coordination and Research Centre of the Department of Northern Affairs and Natural Resources, Ottawa, and I would particularly like to thank Messrs. Vic Valentine and Martin Greenwood for all their help. My second visit to the area, in 1963–64, was supported by the Cooperative Cross-cultural Study of Ethnocentrism, and I would like to thank the co-directors, Professors Donald Campbell of Northwestern University and Robert Levine of the University of Chicago, for their generous aid and advice.

The analysis and writing up of the results of this fieldwork have been generously supported by a number of institutions to whom I am most grateful: 1959–60, The Canada Council, Ottawa, and the McGill Carnegie Arctic Fund, Montreal; 1965–66, The Institute of Social Sciences and the Committee on Research, both of the University of California, Berkeley.

Too numerous to mention are those many anthropologists, fellow teachers, and students whose advice and criticism have, I hope, contributed to the value of my researches and of this particular book. The inhabitants of the whole of Ungava and southern Baffin Island have helped in their many ways to educate me in the ways of the North and without their cooperation all my work would be nil.

"Sallumiulimat nakutsaritsingai!"
To all the people of Sugluk, thank you.

Contents

Figure 1

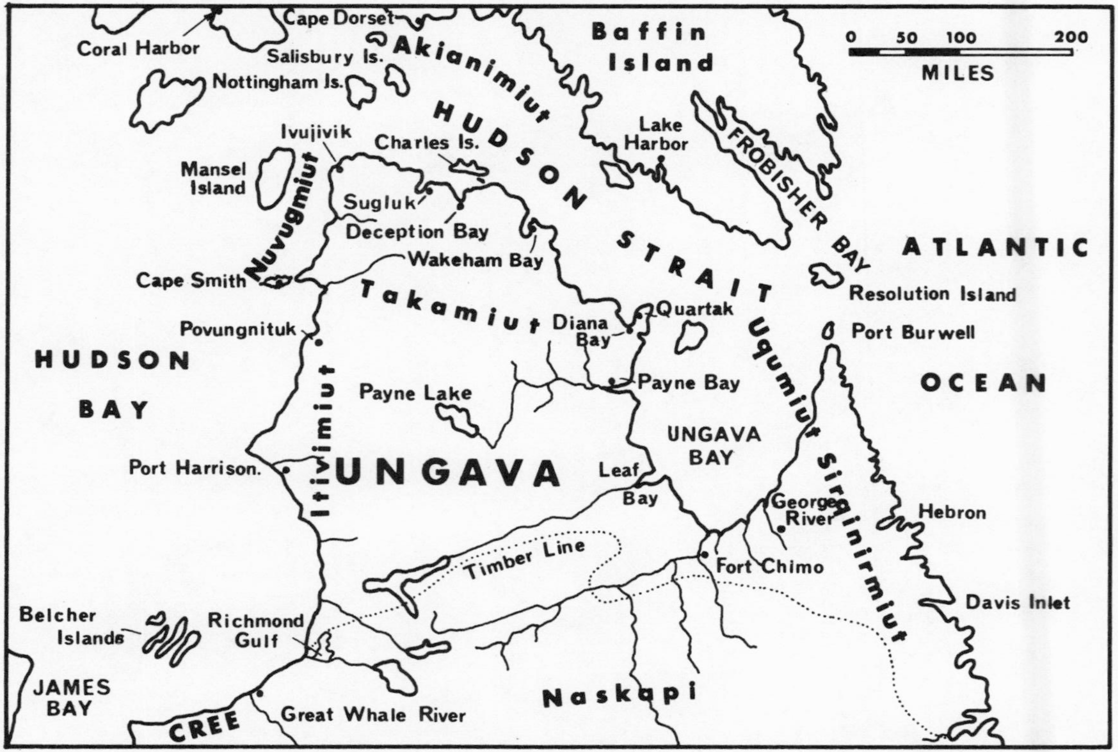
Coral Harbor
Cape Dorset
Salisbury Is.
Nottingham Is.
Akianimiut
Baffin
Island
0 50 100 200
MILES
HUDSON STRAIT
Lake
Harbor
FROBISHER BAY
Ivujivik
Charles Is.
Mansel
Island
Nuvugmiut
Sugluk
Deception Bay
Wakeham Bay
Cape Smith
ATLANTIC
Resolution Island
Takamiut
Quartak
Diana
Bay
Port Burwell
Povungnituk
HUDSON
BAY
Payne Lake
Payne Bay
OCEAN
Uqumiut
UNGAVA
BAY
Itivimiut
Port Harrison.
UNGAVA
Leaf
Bay
Sirqinirmiut
George
River
Hebron
Timber Line
Fort Chimo
Davis Inlet
Belcher
Islands
Richmond
Gulf
JAMES
BAY
CREE
Great Whale River
Naskapi

CHAPTER ONE

Eskimos in a
Changing World

This book is about the people of Sugluk, a settlement on the south side of the Hudson Strait. The Sallumiut (the inhabitants of Sugluk) belong to a larger group, the Takamiut, who inhabit the whole of the northern part of the Ungava Peninsula. In recent times the people of Sugluk have grown in numbers and Sugluk itself has become the most important settlement in the area.

A JOURNEY TO ESKIMOLAND

The first time I visited Eskimoland I went by ship. This is the best way to gain time to change the images one has formed about the Arctic. Sailing from Montreal, we took eleven days to reach Sugluk via the Gulf of St. Lawrence, the Labrador coast, and the Hudson Strait. Each day the weather got colder and daylight lengthened. It was June and the long evenings began to merge imperceptibly into the early dawns. The ship carried a number of Eskimos from

1

the tuberculosis sanatoria "down south" back to their scattered settlements. Although I was to work with these people I did not rush to acquaint myself with them all. Day by day I met a few more — those who were younger and came on deck more often (the rest stayed in their improvised living quarters in the forward hold). A few spoke a little English and the older children were the least shy in talking to strangers. The three interpreters got to know me but none could make out my purpose in asking questions that few white men ever did. Interest in the family and kinship was something even the missionaries rarely showed. Soon I became known as *Apirku,* "the questioner," because my English names were unpronounceable in Eskimo.

Luckily I met one or two residents of Sugluk on the ship who were later able to introduce me to their families when we arrived there. People from other settlements chatted about places I was to visit only years later. None of them ever forgot our short conversations, though, and those, too, were good introductions in later years. When the ship reached the Hudson Strait, fog and low clouds closed in and the sea was more ice than water, slowing the ship. The land, what little could be seen, was partly covered with snow and the rocks that showed through were gray and brown and cold. The shoreline was solid with ice, the hills rugged and monotonous. No trees, bushes, or grass were visible and even the waters appeared devoid of the fauna that I had read about. The Eskimos grew more excited every day. This was familiar territory and they were able to name and talk about places and things that the rest of us did not even notice. Furthermore, they were talking about all the people whom they had not seen for so long, as though they were re-entering the world after a long trip in space.

Finding a settlement in this huge and endless Arctic land is like looking for a needle in a snowbank. Even today, when the settlements are composed of hundreds of people and the white man has erected many large buildings, all but the very largest towns seem lost in the enormity of the coastline and the massiveness of the land forms. In the past, when the Eskimos wandered over the land in small family bands, evidence of humanity was a

2

mere speck — with only one person in tens and, in some places, hundreds of square miles. Yet the Eskimos knew this land and all its significant features. They were able to meet other groups where the probability of doing so by chance is one in a million. Rarely did they get lost and their ability to communicate about location and space must be among the most highly developed in the world (Graburn 1961).

The ship, after visiting an island where the white man had established an outpost for weather observation, struggled along the Hudson Strait. One afternoon we entered a huge bay, with cliffs more than a thousand feet high guarding the entrance, which I was told was Wakeham Bay. A local storm blew up with winds of a hundred miles an hour. The ship hove to and the helicopter was unable to take off. I wondered how the Eskimos on land were faring in their small summer tents. At last, when the wind died down and the clouds of spray subsided, we were able to make out a cluster of white dots and squares in a small part of a minor bay within the inlet we had entered. This was the settlement — a few Eskimo tents and a large mission building. I was lucky enough to get a helicopter ride ashore and, while the local population were being ferried out to the ship for their annual medical exams, I talked to the resident missionary. I marveled at the size of his establishment and the modern paraphernalia under his control: he and his assistant had a greenhouse for growing vegetables, and his personal boat had a cabin and could carry twenty tons of cargo. On all sides of the mission were the low, white Eskimo summer tents. Only one Eskimo, a leading convert, had a wooden house. All the Eskimo dwellings together could have been placed inside half the mission — the dwellings of a hundred compared with that of two. It was like a small kingdom, isolated by hundreds of miles from the nearest other humans. I asked myself, "Are all settlements like this?"

Two days later we sailed into an equally large inlet where, similarly situated on a small piece of flat land lost in the vastness of the bay, was Sugluk. Again the small white tents covered part of the ground but the larger square buildings of the white man were far more evident. There was not one complex, as in Wakeham Bay, but five, each dwarfing the dwellings of the Eskimo majority. Each complex stood on its own ground and had its own color scheme so that one could identify the resident agency from far off. I was later to learn that the types of buildings and the color schemes are virtually universal throughout the eastern Arctic.

Here, then, were two overtly different settlements. The Eskimos in each, however, looked and acted like the Eskimos on the ship, who came from many settlements throughout eastern Arctic. I was to find later that only a few years previously Sugluk had looked like Wakeham Bay and only a few decades before it had been smaller and less important. Such is the speed of change in this area; settlements rise and fall and the Eskimos migrate from one to the other according to the fortunes of hunting and the economy. Like other anthropologists who have visited the area, I have tried to show how and why these changes have come about and where they are leading.

Ashore in Sugluk I was confused by the number of people I met in a short time. All the whites were busy with the mail they had received from the south and the Eskimos, at first apprehensive about their medical exams, were later occupied with the hard work of unloading supplies from the ship for the coming year. After a night in the Anglican missionary's house I moved into a small Eskimo tent alongside the many Eskimo tents near the shoreline. Even while my household was being set up, many Eskimos came to stare and to help although I was hardly able to communicate with them. Sooner than I expected many heard that I had brought some food from the ship and I learned that the community had been short of many vital foods. Within the first week at least 120 Eskimos came to visit and to share my food. I tried to learn all their names but they crowded in faster than memory could handle. Some came as families but most were small groups of men, women, and children; many were mothers with babies in their parka pouches and little ones at their side.

We did our best to talk. I learned a little Eskimo and some knew a few words of English. Even without any English many would take over tasks or try to advise me on unfamiliar problems, such as dogs coming in at night and stealing food. From the moment of my arrival there was no privacy, which I found absent all over the Arctic. I was "working" twenty-four hours a day, it seemed. Yet I soon neglected the few books I had brought with me; they seemed irrelevant. I never had to worry about boredom or what to do next; it was always a matter of which of many things to do. Living itself was time-consuming — cooking, fetching water from a distant stream, keeping things in order, and the like. Very soon my supply of foods ran low and the tables were turned; for most of the summer I spent my time visiting Eskimo households and sharing in their foods and drinks and conversations. I found that just as I had not excluded them, so they never excluded me from such sharing at any time of day or night. These were the most fascinating few months of my life and I began to understand why the Eskimos had occupied a special place in the interest of the white man ever since their discovery centuries ago.

THE ESKIMOS OF THE EASTERN CANADIAN ARCTIC

The Eskimos whom I met and got to know at Sugluk and Wakeham Bay and, later, at more than ten other settlements in the Hudson Strait and Hudson Bay area numbered more than a thousand. They were fairly typical of the contemporary small, but widely spread, group of hunters we know as Eskimos. They know themselves as Inuit, "The People," and are the only people indigenous to the hundreds of thousands of square miles of tundra and coastline that stretches north beyond the treeline of North America.

The Eskimos inhabit an area greater than that of any other tribal people. From Siberia in the west to the eastern shores of Greenland the Eskimos have inhabited most of the coastline and the hinterland tundra for hundreds, if not thousands, of years. Although their lands encompass tens or hundreds of thousands of miles of coast and possibly more than a million square miles of "barren lands," they have never numbered more than 100,000. Of these, between 10,000 and 15,000 inhabit the larger portion of this vast land — the central or Canadian Arctic. And of these, 2,000 or 3,000 are found in the Baffin Island area and another

2,000 or so in Arctic Quebec, or Ungava, along the shores of the Hudson Bay and Hudson Strait. Sugluk is here, on the south coast of the Hudson Strait — one of scores of tiny settlements strung out far from each other in order to make the most of the meager resources.

This book is the story of this one settlement, which has grown in size and importance in the past few years, drawing people from surrounding areas. Through no collective wish of the Eskimo nor conscious plan of the white man, there is this unintended phenomenon, a settlement of more than three hundred people gathered together for a number of reasons the roots of which we shall try to find in the following pages.

In many ways, the life of the Eskimos is better known, described, and even filmed than that of most aboriginal peoples. Hundreds of people have gone to their land and thousands of reports have been written about these relatively few people. It used to be said that there was one anthropologist for each settlement in the Arctic, but now I am beginning to wonder whether it is not more nearly one per family! Why? It is not the hugeness of their land, or their not too great numbers, or even their minor place in world history and economy.

Here are two main reasons for the popularity of the Eskimos in the scientific and lay literatures. First, and most important, the Eskimos were and are an "exotic" people. They have customs and a way of life that differ remarkably from those of the "civilized" observers and, for the most part, from any other peoples. These are different not because Eskimos are a special breed of humanity but plainly because they *must* live in these ways in order to survive. I think it is fair to say that no other people could survive independently in the Arctic environment without adapting to the Eskimo ways. The Eskimos have evolved a technology and a social organization that have enabled them to adapt as successfully as possible to the strange Arctic environment. To be sure, many white men now live there in both Siberia and Arctic North America, but only when constantly supplied and aided by compatriots "down south." Throughout their history the Eskimos have been bothered little by economic or other competition from neighboring groups — that is, from the Indians to the south. The reason is, perhaps, not only that the Indians did not like the look of the barren tundra lands, but also that they would not have been able to survive the year round in the foreign environment — all they could do was make occasional raiding forays in the summers.

The remarks above are not meant to indicate that I am a complete environmental determinist in explaining why cultures are the way they are. The Arctic does, however, limit very severely the ways in which a people may construct their culture to best solve the problems of existence. Also, the Arctic presents unique opportunities for developing a different and specialized way of life — given the abundance of sea mammals and a shoreline surrounded by ice for more than half the year. The Eskimos' particular adaptations have often been described and will be reviewed here. The patterns of Eskimo life are not quite the *only* ones that would allow existence in the North. Before the present population arrived, other "proto-Eskimos" were in this area, known to archaeologists as pre-Dorset and Dorset peoples and to the Eskimos as Tunit. We do not know exactly how these earlier peoples lived. They had many of the same characteristics as the modern Eskimos, though they lacked some of the more important ones. Their population density was probably lower than that of the Eskimos who took over from them, presumably driving them out as the Eskimo myths indicate.

Apart from the interest that their cultural and technological uniqueness aroused, a second reason for the wealth of information on the Eskimos was their geographical position. For centuries the Eskimos' land lay in the path of the many explorers seeking the famed "Northwest Passage" to the riches of Asia. These men, except for Frobisher with his "fool's gold," thought little of the riches of the Arctic area, and even less of the Eskimo inhabitants, who treacherously slaughtered many of the visitors.

Later still, the Hudson Strait and Hudson Bay became the gateway to the rich fur trade with the Indians in the interior of Canada and, in the past hundred years, to the enormous agricultural production of the Canadian prairie provinces. In the last century and the earlier part of the present one, whaling flourished, and sail and steam ships annually frequented the Hudson Bay and Davis Strait, pursuing baleen for profit. Eskimos were sometimes hired for manual labor or for pilotage. The white crews were usually given shore leave at the end of the summer to indulge themselves with the Eskimo women, and it is said that every crewman became a petty trader when with the natives. It is only in this century that much serious thought has been given to the trade or lands of the northern Eskimos themselves; during this period the flow of writings and interest in the area has grown enormously.

In the past two decades, world history has pushed Eskimoland into prominence. During World War II, the eastern Arctic lay directly in the path of the Great Circle flying routes between North America and Europe. A number of air bases and radio stations were built, some of which have since been shut down. The Cold War has made the Arctic the most immediate "front line" between Russia and North America, leading to the construction all across the Arctic of the DEW-line (Distant Early Warning) radar sites and, more recently, BMEWS (Ballistic Missile Early Warning System) antimissile bases. Once more the Eskimo is under the gaze of "civilized" man, whose reasons for coming to his land have nothing to do with the native populations.

The most significant developments are yet to come, in the exploitation of the enormous mineral resources of the Arctic mainland and archipelago. In a very small way this exploitation started more than seventy years ago. Large-scale operations are only just under way; their effects will be described later in more detail.

This second reason for the abundance of information on the Eskimos, then, involves the special geographical position of their homeland, particularly of the eastern Canadian Arctic and Greenland Eskimos. That the white man wanted much of the resources of their lands and seas does not make the Eskimos unique; the same could be said of the Indians of the United States or the Bantu of South Africa. As distinguished from these, however, the Eskimos are far enough away from white civilizations to survive without too rapid change and degradation. Moreover, until recently, the white man was not able to survive for long in the area himself, allowing a cultural recuperation for the Eskimos between summers. The Eskimos, then, have been near enough to be known and studied but, until recently, a little too far from us to be completely overrun.

The exoticness of the Eskimo has long been attractive to the white man. Generally we are led to believe that the "natives of the North" are peaceable, happy-go-lucky, friendly peoples — models of unaggressiveness and primitive "communism." This reputation has embellished both lay literature and scientific investigation. As we shall see in later chapters, this peaceful reputation did not always accord with the view held by the visiting whites nor by any means was it always deserved. These centuries of white interest and activity in the North have left their mark on the Eskimos, even though originally much of it had nothing to do with them.

Sugluk, one of many settlements in the eastern Arctic and one of ten or more in the Hudson Strait alone, is not particularly special. It is fairly typical of the many middle-sized settlements that have grown, unplanned, in this century, leading to relatively great changes in the kind of life the Eskimos are able and want to live. This book, therefore, is a case study — a study of one of many settlements. I hope that it will clarify the processes of change not only among the Eskimos but also among the many other peoples in the world whose ways and thoughts are being irreversibly charted by forces far beyond their power.

APPROACHES TO THE STUDY OF CHANGE

In studying change in the Sugluk area, we must consider both economic and socio-cultural change; in fact, they are well-nigh inseparable here. I have chosen, where appropriate, to use concepts from many theoretical positions.

The Arctic presents a very special ecology, and, though such ecological determinism may not hold for other areas, the Eskimo way of life is overwhelmingly influenced by this environment. Before the coming of the white man, with his essential economic connections with the outside world, the Eskimos probably adapted themselves as much as their environment permitted. Their tech-

9

nology made use of almost every resource available to a nonindustrial society, and their social organization was modeled on an annual cycle that promoted the splitting up and coming together of groups according to the seasons and the abundance of game. Their economic system, simple though it was, reflected the group form at the various points in the annual cycle and the flexibility and necessary interdependence of all family and age groups.

In studying and delineating change, we can of course point out almost exactly those changes brought in by the agents of civilization. Knowing the Eskimo culture and proclivities, we can see the initial effects of these introductions and the uses and attitudes that were elicited. Acceptance and rejection of "traits" is only an initial stage in change.

Far more important have been the ramifications of change. The interests and intentions of the agents of white institutions have by no means had their "common factors" (Malinowski 1945) in Eskimo life, nor have they directly affected only their opposite numbers among Eskimo institutions. A functionalist approach, however, is unavoidable. It will be seen again and again that changes in one area of life have profound, often unintended or even disastrous, effects on areas of life that appear to be completely unrelated. I shall try to elucidate the chains of cause and effect.

Economics will be treated here in the "substantive" sense (Polanyi 1957); I will not assume that economizing or maximizing of material goods for personal gain necessarily entered into aboriginal transactions. In fact, I shall characterize the system as dominated by reciprocity (Service 1966:9–26) and try to illustrate how the Eskimos' thinking about economic transactions has changed since they became involved, through traders, in the white man's market system. In addition, the Eskimos have divided their economy into two "spheres of exchange" (Bohannan 1955), their traditional economy and the new — each with its own very different rules and content. Finally, I hope to show that, just recently, ever-changing economic circumstances have begun to break down this division.

The story of Sugluk and its area is arranged historically and is divided into "stages," or time periods. I do not believe that the acculturation of the Eskimos or of all peoples necessarily goes through a predetermined or a similar sequence of changes. I do hope to show that, where similar contact conditions prevail, as in most of the eastern Arctic, a similar sequence of changes is likely to be seen. Such parallels in acculturation have been shown even for widely separated peoples under similar influences (Murphy and Steward 1956). The idea of stages of change in the eastern Arctic was suggested to me by Asen Balikci, both in personal communications and in his own analyses (Balikci 1960b:65–92). As successfully used by Balikci and his followers, and I hope here, this concept demonstrates a sequence of adaptive reactions, by no means permanent of course, to the sequence of white innovations and new conditions entering the area. As I hope to demonstrate, the present picture of Sugluk is no end point but a temporary adaptive stance, born of Eskimo culture and previous influences, which changes almost from year to year according to new conditions.

CHAPTER TWO

The
Natural
Environment

CLIMATE

The natural environment of the North is dominated by the severe and unique climate. It is not enough, however, to describe the conditions of the area immediately surrounding Sugluk; the Eskimos have always been travelers and events occurring hundreds of miles away affect their lives. Climatic and environmental conditions must be seen from the point of view of the inhabitants of the area, rather than in absolutes. The opportunities and limitations of the North have shaped much of Eskimo culture and recent changes in the environment continue to do so.

The northern limit of the trees runs approximately from Richmond Gulf on the west to Leaf River on the east (see Figure 1). North of this is the true Arctic. The ground is frozen all year, although this permafrost is nearer the surface at higher latitudes. These barren lands have long been the Eskimos' exclusive habitat, the tree line forming an ecological boundary with the Indian territories to the south.

The Seasonal Cycles. The Eskimo word for "year" is the same as that for "winter," *ukiuk,* which is the major climatic feature of the region. There are freezing nights at all seasons, but the frost is not cold enough to freeze over the fresh water lakes until late September, and although there are no strict divisions between the Eskimo seasons this is one of the markers of autumn. Soon after, the snows come and the Eskimos are able to use their sleds. By early November it is freezing nearly all the time. By late November the sea itself begins to freeze, forming that huge offshore mass of ice called *tuvak.* The large lakes are also frozen over by then but fast-running streams and rivers and those parts of the sea subject to strong tides and currents may not freeze until much later, if at all. It is not until December, usually, that enough snow is piled into banks and hardened by the wind to provide material for igloos. At Sugluk, the sun never fails to rise each day of the winter, but in midwinter it is very weak and appears for only a few hours. Temperatures may drop to 50° below zero in January and February but lower temperatures are found only inland, for the sea is a warming influence. Occasionally, winds from the south and the southwest blow strongly in the winter, causing blizzards. Even more rarely, warming winds melt the snow and igloos and, combined with waves and tides, break up the tuvak, causing great difficulties for Eskimos traveling by sled over sea ice.

Most of the snow falls in this area between November and April and totals less than 100 inches a year. Because it very rarely melts in winter, the actual depth of the snow on the ground continues to rise until May. In most places this great depth lies on the sea ice as well as the land, so that igloos can be built almost as easily on the ice floe as on the shoreline.

Spring, *upingaksak,* "almost summer," starts in late April when the sun has risen high enough to begin to melt some of the snow and streams begin to flow. To the Eskimos it is an ecological rather than a meteorological season; the birds are beginning to return and seals and caribou are in advanced pregnancy. By late May igloos are almost uninhabitable. The sun is in the sky more than twelve hours a day, and on some days temperatures rise above freezing. But snow and ice do not melt very fast at these temperatures; the Eskimos say that only very warm winds or, better, rain finally get rid of the snow, causing streams and rivers to swell. The thick ice of the large lakes and the sea does not melt until much later; pools of water may stand on it and holes form through it but only the waves and tides break it up into smaller blocks that are carried out to sea.

Summer, *upingak*, is signified by a quick growth of plants. By July the average temperature rises into the thirties, and it is light day and night. At Sugluk the tuvak of the Inlet begins to break up in late June, but these huge floes do not go out to sea until blown by a suitable wind. Rain may start in May, but reaches its maximum from July through September, at which time the winds are mostly from the west and northwest. Winds from the south, often local, sometimes rise to over 100 miles an hour, causing great damage to Eskimo tents and boats.

Winds and Tides. The Eskimos when hunting or traveling are very conscious of wind, *anuri*, and draw their conception of direction from the major winds in the area. The most common winds are from the southwest, west, and northwest, though the northwest predominates in late fall and is at its least in early summer. The other major wind directions are north, northeast, and east. West and north winds predominate in the fall and winter, whereas the more easterly winds are strongest in the spring and summer. South winds are uncommon throughout the year, but are most frequent in midwinter. Fogs occur in spring, when there is little wind around the rugged coastline.

Near Sugluk the shore slopes very gently and tides go in and out about half a mile. To the Eskimos the tides are more important for their action on the ice than on the water. The tuvak always floats on deep water and is therefore separated from the shore by constantly broken tidal ice floes. At high tide these loose blocks float and are easy to traverse; at low tide they are aground and present a steep and crevice-ridden pathway to the sea. In inlets like Sugluk, however, the tides often have a rise and fall approaching 30 feet, especially at spring tides or when backed by the wind. Where the shoreline is steep, part of the sea ice clings to the rock and may be left high and dry at low tide. These "ice cliffs" are sometimes useful as paths for sled travel but may be dangerous in the spring.

FAUNA AND FLORA

The Eskimos divide the living things in their natural environment according to several principles. They do have a classification that divides animals from plants much as we do, but it is equally important whether the species lives on the land or in the water and whether it is edible or not. We shall be guided by their classifications.

Generally speaking, beings that we would call animals are known as *umajuit*, but this does not include human beings, who are *inuit*. Human beings live, *inujuk*, whereas animals live, *umajuk*, although both share something to make them live, the heart, *umati*. Most animals are also known as *niqiksak*, "that which is able or about to be food."

Land Animals. The caribou used to be the most important land animal to all the Eskimos in this area. Until this century there were three main migratory caribou herds in the area. In the summer all these herds moved north, arriving in early April and leaving in November, and were hunted by the Eskimos. One herd traveled up the east coast of Hudson Bay as far north as the Hudson Strait at Ivujivik and Sugluk. Another herd went north near Fort Chimo in the spring and reached the Diana Bay and Wakeham Bay areas for the summer. In all these herds there were hundreds of thousands of caribou. They supported much of the Eskimo population and were the mainstay of the subarctic Indians during the winter when the caribou were south of the tree line.

In the Takamiut area caribou were plentiful until the first two decades of this century, when they began to be scarce, and in the last decade the Eskimos of Sugluk say that they are so distant that they are not worth hunting at all. Many authorities have claimed that excessive slaughter by the Eskimos and Indians since they acquired repeating guns has been the reason for the decline, but this is problematical:

[the caribou] . . . were eventually depleted by wanton slaughter of the animals at the time of migration. . . . Fires which swept the

15

country and destroyed the lichen on which the caribou grazed also speeded the decline of the herds. . . . Forest fires were apparently common at the time of the caribou decline, [some] . . . caused by the carelessness of the Indians in the use of signal fires. . . . Such extensive fires, besides reducing grazing areas, could halt caribou migrations and caused the loss of herds from unsatisfactory winter food conditions. . . . Winter rainfall and frozen over food supplies . . . could also work to deplete the herds by starvation. (Wright 1944:193–194)

Since this statement was made the situation seems to have changed. When I was in Chimo in 1964, the George River herd started to come back in huge numbers, estimated at more than 40,000. They passed north and summered in the Payne Lake area. The Sugluk and Wakeham Bay Eskimos also reported seeing caribou and their tracks when inland trapping. The Povungnituk and Great Whale Eskimos are also getting many caribou in recent years. Some Arctic residents have said that a population cycle may account for the fall and rise in numbers of caribou over the years, much as the Arctic fox population varies in four-year cycles.

The caribou rutting season comes in the fall, and in the spring migration north the males and females may separate. The fawns are dropped in May and June but are able to walk and keep up with the herd as it grazes on the abundant lichens and mosses.

Caribou skin used to form most of the clothing and bedding of the Sallumiut. The horn is very workable and the large stag horns were used for such articles as spears, arrowheads, and drumsticks. Most useful perhaps were the back sinews, which were used as thread for sewing clothes and boots. The meat of course was food for both humans and dogs and the back fat was a great delicacy. The greatest delicacy of all, however, was the warmed-up contents of the stomach, consisting of half-digested lichens and moss.

Arctic foxes were of little economic value to the Eskimos until the white man wanted to trade for their skins. Foxes in the area vary in color; the one with the greatest value these days turns snowy white during the winter.

Since foxes depend primarily on the lemming for their food, the four-year fox cycle in fact reflects the lemming population cycle. Foxes are not gregarious animals and so are thinly distributed over wide areas. Although they generally stay on the land in the spring, they may go out on the sea ice after newborn seals. It has even been said that they will attack adult seals and other large animals when they are very hungry (Payne 1886:114).

In the past, the Eskimos spent little time hunting foxes, although they did at times set crude traps. The fur was considered not very useful, because it falls apart quickly under Arctic conditions. The flesh, however, was eaten with some relish.

Wolves are relatively rare in this area and are generally found in small packs harassing the caribou herds. With the scarcity of caribou, wolves have declined in this century. Wolves eat all sorts of small animals and birds and occasionally dogs, in addition to caribou; they may even eat fish.

The Eskimos used to hunt wolves when they were near the caribou; their fur is one of the best for trimming the hoods of parkas, because it remains fairly ice-free.

Arctic hares, rather large animals, have snowy white fur all year. They are often found in small groups not far inland. Though the Eskimos used to snare the animals and now shoot them, the hare population does not seem to have declined. The skins, used only as trimming, are perishable like the fox's, but the meat is considered quite edible.

Wolverines, always rare and solitary animals, seem to have declined even further in the last few decades. Very strong, and vicious when cornered, they were formerly found around the coasts, where they continually raided Eskimo caches, pushing aside even the heaviest rocks. The fur is the most favored for trimming parka hoods, and for this reason, and to protect their food, the Eskimos kill wolverines whenever possible.

Lemmings and mice are the smallest animals found in this area. The former, the main food of foxes and the Arctic owl, are very abundant and burrow through the surface of the ground and under the snow. These rodents are of no direct economic use to the Eskimos. The children "practice" hunting on them by stoning them or by shooting them with bows and arrows. Ermine or weasels are also found but are of little significance.

Other Eskimos hunt and trap land animals which do not come

as far north as Sugluk. The Sugluk Eskimos, however, know about them, have names for them, and would recognize them. Among the more important are otter, beaver, marten, and lynx. Brown bears are known to these Eskimos but are seriously hunted only by the Indians to the south.

Polar bears hardly qualify as land animals since they live most of their lives on the sea ice. They are said to be getting rare but they probably were never very common in the area. A few are shot near Sugluk most winters. Polar bears are seen most often in the winter, because in the summers they migrate north or spend their time on the sea ice. They feed mainly on fish and seals; but they are extremely strong, weighing up to 2,000 pounds, and have been known to attack walrus. These bears are known to be more common around Mansel Island in Hudson Bay, possibly because the island is uninhabited.

The Eskimos never have gone out of their way to hunt polar bears unless they were close by. Occasionally, the bears, when hungry, come right into settlements and even break into igloos. Although Eskimos are very frightened of them, I do not know of a single fatal attack on a man in this area. The skin of the polar bear makes very good bedding, and in the Takamiut area it is not uncommonly used for trousers. The flesh is eaten by men or dogs, but the liver is known to be poisonous. In recent times most skins have been sold to white men.

Sea Mammals. Sea mammals, *puijii,* "the ones which show," also qualify as niqiksak and as *imaqsiut,* "inhabitants of the water." Their generic name differentiates them from fishes; they have to come up to breathe and therefore "show their noses." They are by far the most important fauna to the Eskimo of the eastern Arctic.

The common ringed seal is the most abundant sea mammal in the area. It is present all year and breeds in the sea ice in the late winter. The coastline between Cape Weggs and Cape Wolstenholme is said to have approximately 5,000 seals, which should yield approximately 400 each year without harming the population. The area west of this as far as Cape Smith is said to contain 8,900, and the area to the east as far as Diana Bay, 20,400 (Mac-

Laren 1958:28–31). Thus, both Ivujivik and Wakeham Bay are in far better seal-hunting areas than Sugluk.

The meat of the seal is the mainstay of the Eskimo diet, and its skin can be used for clothing, boots, tents, or for covering skin boats and kayaks; even the intestines are eaten and considered tasty. Though these seals weigh up to 200 pounds much of this is fat, which is used for seal-oil lamps, so there may be only about 30 pounds of meat on each. Much of the remainder is used as dog food.

The young of this seal, up to one year, are by far the most valuable for trading these days. They are at first pure white and are called "silver jar." They may be hunted at their "nests" in the tuvak ice of the late spring.

The ringed seal lives under ice in the winter and comes up to breathe at holes in the tuvak that it keeps clear, or at cracks and leads. In the spring the seal likes to lie on the ice and sunbathe; in the summer its curiosity often causes it to come too close to humans for its own good. Unfortunately, in the late summer the seal has less fat and sinks when shot if not quickly harpooned.

The bearded or square-flipper seal is by far the largest seal in the area, weighing as much as 800 pounds, a 600-pound animal being far from rare. Although it rarely winters near Sugluk, it is common in late spring, and basks on the larger offshore ice floes. In the summer it swims closer to shore in search of the sea-run fish that are its main food. The young, until from two to three years old, have a coloration different from the adults' unspectacular gray-brown hair coat. There are said to be 6,600 of these seals along the south coast of the Hudson Strait between Quartak and Ivujivik, with a safe annual yield of about 350 adults (MacLaren 1958:54).

The products of this seal are most useful to the Eskimos. It supplies a lot of meat, for both human and dog consumption, and its hide is very tough. Formerly, the hide was used for covering skin boats, kayaks, and tents, and it is still used for the soles of winter and waterproof boots. When cut spirally, one skin may provide as many as 100 yards of very strong line useful for tent ropes, dog traces, harpoon lines, and many other purposes.

The harp seal breeds farther south down the Atlantic coast but abounds in the Hudson Strait in late spring. It generally does not bask on ice floes but swims playfully around in groups. It is of medium size and may weigh 350 pounds. More difficult to hunt, it is less frequently caught than the two seals discussed earlier. It is used much as the bearded seal is, though line and boot soles are rarely made from the skins, which are very silky and have a beautifully distinctive harp-shaped black marking in their backs. They are the prime seal skin of the commercial market.

The fresh-water seal is extremely rare in the Hudson Strait area. It lives most of its life in huge inland fresh-water lakes, such as Lake Minto and the Seal Lakes. Occasionally one or two make their way down the Leaf or Nastapoka rivers into the sea. They are thought to belong to the same species as the ringed seal that remained in the inland lakes as the land gradually rose after the last ice age. The skins are the softest and most beautifully marked of all, and bring top prices when traded. However, because of their rarity they are of minor significance for trade or indigenous uses.

Walrus are gregarious animals and only one herd frequents the Hudson Strait. This large herd, which does not always keep together, is thought to winter in northern Hudson Bay and Fox Basin (see Figure 1). In the spring it passes eastward down the Strait. Few are caught by the Eskimos because they pass far out to sea, at a time when ice usually prevents the Eskimos from taking to their boats. After spending the summer in the Ungava Bay region around Akpatuk Island, they return in the fall and may be found off Charles and Nottingham islands. It is at Nottingham Island in late September that the Eskimos from Ungava and from southern Baffin Island gather to hunt them.

The meat is usually used for dog food at Sugluk, although elsewhere some of the flesh is allowed to become gamy by being kept all winter under fat and is considered a great delicacy. The contents of the stomach when fresh are similarly relished. The very thick skin is almost useless except as an extra layer on the bottom of boot soles and generally it is eaten by the dogs. The ivory tusks are the important products; these can be made into harpoons and spears, can be cut into strips for sled runners, and have many other uses.

Walrus eat clams, which they pry from the sea bottom with their tusks, and they feed together in herds. They quite often come up onto the shore and may be hunted there or in the coastal waters. They are very powerful animals, the bulls sometimes weighing more than a ton. When wounded, they may attack a boat or kayak, and they vie with the polar bear for fierceness and for the terror they inspire. This fear is reflected in Eskimo mythology and art.

The white whale or beluga, a "porpoise," is native to the Straits. It is found swimming in schools near the coast and in bays in the summer, always searching for its sole diet, fish, at the mouths of streams and rivers. It generally travels in schools of from ten to one hundred, the biggest groups being found in the larger rivers or bays. Large numbers also may be found when the beluga are being pursued by the killer whale.

This whale is hunted in great quantity and provides much meat for the Eskimos. It may weigh up to two tons but usually runs to less than one. A large proportion of this is meat. The skin, which is tough, rubbery, and has an oily taste, is pure white in adults and is eaten both raw and cooked. Formerly it had commercial value, but now it has none. The very long back sinews are used as thread in making waterproof boots and for other things. This thread is much like that made of caribou sinew.

The narwhal is very similar to the white whale except that it has a single long ivory tusk. It is very rare in the area.

The killer whale, a large, ferocious whale, is sometimes seen in the Strait. It chases white whales and others, as well as seals and even walrus. It has no commercial value and the Eskimos fear it too much to hunt it. It is said to have sometimes turned over hunting boats, though guns may scare it off.

The huge baleen whales (Right and Greenland) used to be common in the Straits, but the commercial whaling of the last century eliminated so many that they are not often seen. A long time ago, apparently, the Eskimos used to hunt them, and those which washed up on shore and were stranded were eaten with glee by dog and man alike. Their skin is said to be as good as that of the white whale. Some use was also made of the baleen itself.

The Eskimos have heard of the sperm whale, which they call "there are teeth," though none are found in the Straits.

Fish. Fish do not come to the surface to breathe, and this distinguishes them from the sea mammals. They are not classified by their location in fresh or salt water.

The Greenland shark is occasionally found in the Straits and may even eat the sea mammals already caught by the Eskimos. It is commercially fished in Greenland. The Takamiut do not bother to go after it, they told me, because they would not be able to follow since a fish doesn't have to come up to breathe.

Cod are found all through the Straits but they are never large. When fishing for other fish, the Eskimos often catch them. They are eaten though not relished. Sea sculpin are small fish that abound near the shore in the spring and summer. They are fished from the ice and eaten with relish in spite of their thousands of bones.

Three species of lake trout live in the inland lakes all year and are very good eating. In the past, they were speared but they are now caught by hook or net. One species may weigh as much as fifty pounds and the other two up to twenty-five. Whitefish is another lake fish, less common than the trout. It is said to be almost identical to the Great Lakes whitefish.

Arctic char or salmon trout, a beautiful fish, is found in both small and large lakes and rivers. It winters in the lakes and descends to the sea in June, where it is very common along the coastline. It makes its way up to the lakes again in the early fall. Weighing up to thirty pounds, it is probably the largest item in the Eskimo fish diet in spring and summer. It forms the basis of the commercial cooperative fishing that is starting in the area. The Atlantic salmon, also migratory, is most common in the large rivers of Ungava Bay and eastward. It is the other mainstay of local commercial cooperative fishing.

Many smaller fish are sometimes used as food but they are too numerous to mention and are insignificant.

Among the imaqsiut (water-dwellers) are some other important species.

Mussels, common in the area, are eaten by the Eskimos. They are gathered at low tide in the summer, and in winter and spring the women climb down among stranded ice blocks at low tide and gather the various molluscs in the cavernlike spaces underneath. Clams are less common and more difficult to gather than mussels but are relished by the Eskimos.

There are smaller species, such as the many varieties of barnacle, plankton, crabs, shrimps, and sea lice. These form the diet of the larger fishes but the Eskimos do not gather or eat them.

Although they are "plants," we shall consider the seaweeds here because the Eskimos do not classify them with land plants. Both bladder and thong seaweed are found in great quantities around the coast in summer and fall. The Eskimos gather and eat both kinds. Sometimes they are called *piaraliksak*, "potential for there being a baby," because they are supposed to increase fertility in women and are eaten in quantity by childless wives.

Birds. Hundreds of species of birds, *tingmiat*, "the flying ones," live in or visit the area. They are too numerous to mention but are important to the Eskimos. I shall consider only those found in abundance and will classify them according to their migratory habits.

The raven, one of the few birds found all year, lives in the cliffs and hills and lays its eggs in March. The Eskimos do not eat the raven except when very hungry; they rarely get a chance to raid its nests. An eater of carrion, the raven frequents Eskimo haunts, and occasionally gets caught in fox traps.

The snowy owl also stays in the area and nests in rugged places. It is part of the cycle involving the lemming and the fox and depends heavily on the former for its food. This link is mythologically recognized by the Eskimos, both the owl and the fox having the same "guardian spirit." When it is caught the owl is eaten; its flesh tastes rather like that of the fox. Its skin may be used for making bags, and its wings (like those of similar large birds) are used as igloo brooms.

The ptarmigan is migratory but only as far south as the tree line. It winters around Chimo and in early spring migrates north, reaching its breeding grounds near the Hudson Strait in May. In the winter it is pure white with two black tail feathers, but it changes to a speckled brown in the summer. Usually found in large flocks, ptarmigan are easily slaughtered, forming a useful human food, especially for Eskimos traveling by sled inland when there is little else to eat. The eggs are also eaten, but, although the ptarmigan nests on level ground, they are hard to find.

Both the snow goose and the Canada goose migrate to this area in large numbers, the former being the more abundant. They nest in marshy areas along level parts of the coast and near lakes. Both are eagerly shot by the Eskimos, and their eggs are eaten in quantities.

Many species of ducks visit the area: king eider, eider, and others. They arrive in May, breed in June, and leave for the south again in September and October. They, too, nest in places near water. All ducks and their eggs are eaten by the Eskimos. The king eider is most numerous in this area, and its Eskimo name, *mitirk*, is almost the generic name for ducks.

A number of species of loons and divers inhabit this area. They arrive somewhat later than the ducks and are far less numerous. They are eaten occasionally; their skins are used for pouches, their wings for igloo brooms. They build their nests on very small islands in the lakes, and these are difficult to raid, but the eggs are eaten when obtained.

Swans arrive with the geese but are less common and more solitary. They breed along the coasts of Hudson Bay south of Ivujivik and on Mansel Island, and they are eagerly hunted by the Eskimos, because they provide so much meat.

Murre are medium-sized water birds that breed only at Digges Strait near Ivujivik, where they cover the cliffs for several miles. There are millions of birds there, their numbers undiminished by the constant Eskimo raids. The flesh is solid but fairly tasty. The large eggs are taken from the cliffs in June, but luckily these birds lay more eggs each time their nests are raided. Although all murres are based on these cliffs, they scatter far in search of food and some stragglers are found all along the coast of the Hudson Strait, although not much farther east than Sugluk.

Guillemots, the smallest of the auks, breed in a number of places in the Hudson Strait and Bay. These breeding places are widely separated and the nests are often at the bottom of holes, making them difficult to raid. Both flesh and eggs are eaten when obtained.

Gulls are also migratory but arrive earlier than the other birds. They are very common over the whole coastline and nest on many islands and cliffs. The Eskimos do not eat the flesh because, they say, the bird eats carrion like the raven. Its nests, however, are raided for the eggs, and the young are sometimes kept as pets.

Terns are less common than the gulls. They and their eggs are considered edible.

The birds of prey, the eagle and the hawk, may be native to the area, but only the latter is common. Both are eaten when obtained, but this is rare.

Snow bunting, a little sparrowlike bird, is looked upon as the harbinger of spring. Everyone perks up and looks forward to the arrival of the more important migratory birds when it arrives. It and its eggs are rarely eaten.

Many, many other small species such as sandpipers, plovers, larks, chats, and the like visit the area. None are of great significance to the Eskimos, despite their large numbers.

The majority of my informants stated that, generally speaking, the Eskimos never ate any *qupikuit*, "insects," except lice and the larvae of warble flies. The very idea filled them with disgust; indeed, now that most of the Eskimos know about germs (from the white man), they identify disease-causing "microbes" as *qupikuapik*, that is, little *qupikus*. But members of this class are not insignificant, as we shall see. I shall mention only the most important.

The warble fly lays its eggs on the backs of caribou, and the grubs burrow under the skin; later in the spring the grubs emerge and fall to the ground to pupate. When the caribou is killed the back fat and skin may be covered with these insects, and in some areas the Eskimos eat them. The skins so penetrated have scarred places where the holes were, reducing their value to the Eskimos and whites. The flies and grubs bother the caribou greatly, driving them almost mad with itching, thus distracting them and making them easier to hunt.

Lice formerly were found on all Eskimos but are rare now. It is said that in the past many Eskimos ate them, but now the thought disgusts all but a few. Lice were removed by searching and picking. The Eskimos identify the flea as "the white man's louse," and say it is cleverer than its Eskimo counterpart because it jumps! Various other kinds of lice are found on seals and birds and are similarly identified by their primary host.

Intestinal worms are found in the bearded seal and others. The Eskimos know that they will become ill from eating them but will not die. Maggots are common but not eaten.

Mosquitoes swarm in great numbers for about three weeks in July and August. They are extremely bothersome to the Eskimos, who may go hunting out to sea to get away from them. They are said to bother caribou, too, and to make them nervous. In southern Baffin Island the caribou sometimes climb up onto the glaciers in summer to get away from these and other bothersome insects. These mosquitoes seem to be very large and tough and they can bite through more than half an inch of clothing.

Blackflies are not found near the coast but formerly bothered the Eskimos severely when they went inland to hunt caribou in the summer. They are said to have caused the death of both men and caribou with their multiple stinging, which results in serious loss of blood, and pain, which leads to total distraction.

Plants. There is no general category of plants for the Eskimos. Those which lie close to the ground are often known as *nunat,* "the ground thing(s)."

In the late summer many of the small ground-hugging plants produce edible berries which are gathered in abundance by the women and children. They are distinguished mainly by the color of their fruit, which may be black, blue, or red.

Other plants are eaten occasionally including plantains, flower petals, and parts of a certain small tree.

Recognized as important to the caribou, but not eaten by the Eskimos, are some lichens, mosses, and mushrooms. The Eskimos say that nothing in their land eats grass.

All the smaller bushes and larger plants mentioned above may be used for making fires when there is no wood. These would be used for cooking when the Eskimos were inland hunting caribou or fishing, before the days of portable stoves and lamps. Other plants have some special but very important uses. The dwarf willows, which are the largest plants in this area, are collected in late summer, stripped of their leaves, dried, and tied together into small mats. These are light, easily rolled up, and portable. They are used as the underbedding of igloos, being placed directly on the snow under the caribou or bear skins. They serve as an important insulation against the cold and damp.

Equally important is the dried or fossil moss that the Eskimos use for lamp wicks. It is found everywhere in light brown lumps on the edges of swampy ground. Although the lamps would work with other wicks, this is the only kind used in the area. The moss is taken home, dried, and crumbled to a powder that is spread along one edge of the lamp to soak up the oil.

Trees and Wood. In many areas of the Arctic, including much of the land of the Takamiut, driftwood was the major source of wood. The Takamiut knew that wood came from trees, *napaktuk*, "it stands erect." Often, the Takamiut and even some of the inhabitants of southern Baffin Island would make the very long journey to the northern tree line near Chimo and Leaf Bay to cut wood and take it home.

Wood was used for many essentials among the Eskimo: frames of kayaks and umiaks, handles of harpoons and spears, bows and arrows, tent poles, sled runners, and cross beams. Because wood was so important and so rare it was not burned in fires for cooking or heating unless there was nothing else. The Eskimos preferred to use the soapstone oil lamps or the various bushes and plants already mentioned.

Another product of trees, the resin, was chewed by both Indians and Eskimos. It was also occasionally used for hafting axes and harpoons.

27

Sugluk is one of the many inlets where the sea of the Hudson Strait indents the coastline of Northern Ungava, the northernmost part of the Labrador Peninsula. It lies at about 65° North by 75° West, about 100 miles east of Ivujivik and 200 or more miles west of Wakeham Bay (see Figure 1). The present settlement is about 6 miles from the mouth of the 14-mile inlet on one of the few patches of level ground. The rolling hills in the area rise to 1,000 feet or more. At the entrance to the inlet lies Sugluk Island which has long been a favorite spring camping ground for the Eskimos and their predecessors.

Inland from Sugluk there are rolling hills, increasing in altitude to the Povungnituk range, 100 miles to the south. Beyond that, but still within the area traveled by the Takamiut, are huge lakes set in a plateau that drains mainly to the east and west through several large rivers.

Along the coast to the west of Sugluk, the cliffs increase in height and the inlets become more spectacular, culminating in Eric Cove, which is surrounded by the cliffs of Cape Wolstenholme, over 1,000 feet high. In rough weather this coastline affords some shelter but it has never been very popular with the Eskimos. From Eric Cove westward the land becomes less rugged and the coast more complex. Islands and bays richer in fish and sea mammals support the Eskimos of the Ivujivik area.

East from Sugluk, the coastline is simpler and the land forms less massive. About forty miles east is Deception Bay almost identical in form and size to Sugluk Inlet. It was inhabited by Eskimos and at one time had permanent white habitation, but all have moved to Sugluk. Inland of this huge bay the recent find of millions of tons of asbestos has stimulated immense industrial activity that may bring a huge mine and further civilization to the area. Beyond Deception Bay the coast is simple and relatively unproductive for Eskimo hunters until the more complex coast near Wakeham Bay is reached. All these inlets have been inhabited from time to time, but past and present Eskimo populations have always flourished at Wakeham Bay and the incredibly complex coastline to the east.

Beyond the Wakeham Bay area there is little habitation until one reaches Diana Bay and Quartak. Here, again, hunting and fishing are very good because of the coastline and the many islands. These people are the easternmost of the Takamiut and are also much in contact with the people of Ungava Bay with its shallow coastline and huge river mouths. The river mouths are important because of the huge runs of fish that in both past and present have been of great economic value to the Eskimos. Nothing like them is found in the Takamiut area.

Across the Strait, the land is only a hundred or so miles from the Takamiut land. The Strait, however, can be crossed only via the chain of large islands between Cape Wolstenholme and Cape Dorset, and this crossing is rarely made.

A number of significant facts stand out among those presented here. The Arctic environment, while harsh and cold, is very special and by no means monotonous. There are limits, of course, to the quantity of any species that can be slaughtered, but the wild life is enormously varied. It may be said that the natural environment gives the Eskimos special opportunities as well as severe limitations.

The area and the useful species are divided between land and sea and the latter are divided between migratory and residential. The year is divided into winter ice and snow and summer streams and abundance, which is reflected in the annual cycle and the social organization of Eskimo life (see Chapter Three). Styles of life and technology are very different at different times of the year. Game and resources are so distributed as to require the coming together and splitting of groups, and migrations and trading.

Within the limits of a nonindustrial civilization, the Eskimos have adapted remarkably well to this environment. They are extremely knowledgeable about all the important species and make use of almost everything that is present, often in most ingenious ways. The only exception is their failure to eat the rather uncommon mushrooms that they deem suitable for the caribou; they were horrified when I ate them, although I knew that no species in the area is poisonous. The Eskimos rationalize this omission in their diet by saying the mushrooms are riddled with "bugs."

Sugluk in May 1964, looking out over Sugluk Inlet. The small wooden buildings in the foreground are the Eskimo's winter houses, the larger structures are those of the white man's agencies (Catholic Mission, Anglican Mission, Federal Government, and Hudson's Bay Company).

A winter and spring sealing camp on an island east of Wakeham Bay, including igloos and a dog team and sled. (1964)

CHAPTER THREE

Traditional Takamiut
Eskimo Culture

PREHISTORY

The area along the south coast of the Hudson Strait has probably
been occupied by Eskimolike peoples for more than 2,500 years.
These earliest inhabitants of the area left remains, which are
called pre-Dorset and Dorset by archaeologists. The Eskimos
identify all "prehistoric peoples" as Tunit and identify archaeologists as "Tunit hunters." At one early Dorset site at Sugluk itself
there are remains and a skull said to be about 2,000 years old. The
skull and other remains in the area resemble those of present-day
Eskimos (Oschinsky 1960). It is probable that the Tunit had
most of the Eskimo cultural equipment but lacked dogs; this
meant that they had to pull their smaller sleds by hand which
would have restricted nomadism and inland hunting. They were
probably unable to make as efficient use of the natural resources
of the areas as the Eskimos who followed them. From a count

of known camp and house sites I estimate their population to have been approximately 400 at the very most, between Cape Hopes Advance and Nuvuk (beyond Ivujivik) inclusive. I estimate that the Eskimo population in this area during the last century was approximately 600–650 (Stupart 1886; Hawkes 1916:22).

The Dorset people, whoever they were, were probably ousted by the people who bore the Thule culture. The spread of the latter culture was gradual and in southern areas may not have reached the previous inhabitants until the time of first European contact. In the Takamiut area, however, the Thule people arrived, from Baffin Island (as did the previous Dorset people), about A.D. 1350 (Taylor 1964:203). Taylor describes the Thule culture:

. . . better suited to the environment, completed replacing the Dorset culture . . . and was a main cultural and biological ancestor to the historic Central and Labrador Eskimo. . . . Thule culture presents a fully developed Eskimo pattern. . . . the main differences between Thule culture and the modern Eskimo . . . include a marked decline in whaling in the latter. (*Ibid.*:194)

The Eskimos explain how the Thule people took over the land from the previous inhabitants, though the archaeologists do not. The most common story follows:

The Eskimos came to the land (from the north) and found the Tunit living there in stone houses, without dogs or a knowledge of cooking. They did not make war on them but had little to do with them at first. At that time there lived in the land a huge giant named *Sikuliaksujuituk*, "he who cannot go on new ice," being so heavy. This giant's sister was married to a Tunit man and they had two children who were also very large. The Tunit killed the giant because he used to steal so much of the game they caught, and the two nephews took revenge. Together they would get hold of a Tunit and drill a hole with a bow drill in his skull and were therefore known as the *Ikutajut*, "the drillers." Thus they methodically killed the Tunit, who were naturally very scared. Some say the Eskimos combined with some of the Tunit to kill one of these nephews of the giant by tying him down at night and stabbing him while he slept. Even so he broke his bonds and killed more Tunit before he died. The Tunit were therefore even more scared of the revenge of the other and they all migrated out of the area, probably to the south. Some say that the Tunit are still "down South" and kept there by the white man as slaves because they are so strong. The whites are reputed to tell the Tunit that the giants are still there whenever the latter ask when they can go home! The Eskimos know that the other members of the giant family fled the land and have never been heard of again. (From a number of Eskimo informants)

However it really was, the Eskimos came to inhabit this land and have remained ever since. They never expanded their territory very far south beyond the treeline because the hostile Indians living there killed the Eskimos when they got the chance. Along the Atlantic coast of Labrador, the Eskimos spread in historic times far up the St. Lawrence River and even to Newfoundland, perhaps as part of a raiding pattern, developed since contact, to steal acquired goods from the Indians.

This chapter outlines the essentials of the presumed way of life of the Eskimos from their arrival in the thirteenth or fourteenth centuries until their first regular contacts with the white man in the last century. It is a reconstruction based on a number of sources. I interviewed a large number of people, many of whom were old — probably more than fifty of my informants were sixty or older — who lived in more than ten settlements. It was easy to cross check their stories, and in addition the most reliable informants are generally known. The data from the Eskimos can often be independently checked against the books and vice versa. Among them are the published works of Low, who explored much of the area (1897, 1898, 1902, 1906); Stupart (1886) and Payne (1888-89, 1895-96), who were at Stupart Bay during 1884 and 1885; Turner (1888, 1894), who was at Chimo during 1883 and 1884; and D'Anglure (1964), who was at Wakeham Bay in 1961 and who attempted to reconstruct the traditional social organization of the natives of that area. In addition, some inferences and comparisons are drawn from more general works and from some works about other areas of the eastern Arctic, such as those of Boas (1888, 1901, 1907), Hawkes (1916), and Munn (1922). For the most part, however, I rely on accounts given by my older informants throughout the area.

DISTRIBUTION

In the last century the total population of Eskimos along the coastline from Great Whale River to Cape Chidley was probably between 1,200 and 1,500, of whom the Takamiut comprised nearly

33

half. The numbers and distribution are not the same today; factors other than the capacity of the land to support inhabitants have become more important during this century.

The Eskimos categorize the population of this land mass by area. The inhabitants of these areas were often called "tribes" by early reporters, but in fact the categories were just convenient geographical labels and had no political character. In the area of Arctic Quebec the following groups are known (see Figure 1):

Qikirktamiut: the inhabitants of the Belcher Islands (*qikirtait*, "islands"); Itivimiut: the inhabitants of the east coast of the Hudson Bay, from Great Whale to Cape Smith (*itivi*, "the other side of the land"); Takamiut: from Nuvuk (near Ivujivik) to Cape Hopes Advance (*takak*, "shadow or darkness," appropriate from the northerly location of the group); Ungavamiut: the people of the west coast of Ungava Bay (*ungava*, "distant"); Sirqinirmiut: the people south and east of Payne Bay (*sirqinirk*, "sun"); Uqumiut: the people of the southeast (*uqu*, "warmth, heat").

The suffix -*miut* signifies simply "inhabitant of" and applies to smaller or larger areas; indeed, it is applied also to those who normally camp at a certain locality, e.g., Sallumiut, "the people of Sugluk." In addition, many of the areas overlap and the exact boundaries, which are of little importance, vary depending on whether one is a member of the group named or an outsider from one or another direction. For instance, the Takamiut are called Illumiut, "the people of the other of two sides," by the Eskimos across the Hudson Strait. The latter call themselves Sikusuilamiut, "the people of the land lacking in new ice," whereas the Takamiut call them Akianimiut, "the people across the water."

There are slight cultural and linguistic differences among the groups, and often within them. For instance, Turner notes that the language of the Itivimiut differs considerably from that of the people of Fort Chimo whom he calls Suhinimyut:

Their [Itivimiut] speech is very rapid and much harsher. . . . Many of the words are quite dissimilar, and even where a word has the same sound it is not unusual that its meaning is more or less different. . . . (Turner 1894:179)

Most of the cultural differences among the groups that Turner noted reflected the differential states of acculturation of the various groups whom he met trading at Chimo. Here we are most concerned with the Takamiut (*Tahagmyut* in Turner 1894; *Taqagmiut* in Graburn 1964) of the Hudson Strait, but it must be kept in mind that these groupings have indefinite boundaries and are of little significance in differentiating the major cultural features of the area.

THE ANNUAL CYCLE

The Eskimo year is divided into two main seasons, winter and summer, and further into a number of subseasons. Each season and subseason brings with it changes in social groupings, diet, technical equipment used, location, and weather. Thus, the annual cycle has always been a prime feature of Eskimo life.

In winter the Eskimos lived along the coastline in small villages, numbering in this area from 15 to 60 people, depending on the availability of resources. The village was located with an eye to the food supply, distances and ease of travel to other areas of game, and protection from the worst of the weather. In traditional times there were probably about three or four such camps between Cape Wolstenholme and Cape Weggs and another four or five in the Wakeham Bay area, which was richer in game. Although these campsites were generally occupied every year, there were other places of winter habitation and the same individuals or numbers of people did not always frequent the same camp. Two of these winter camps were regularly at Sugluk and Deception Bay.

The camps consisted of families, often related to each other, who lived in "permanent" snow-houses from November to February or March. These houses, bunched together like molehills near the shoreline, were often connected by under-the-snow passages or common porches and entrances. Also, in some of the larger villages, there was a larger snow house that could contain the whole population. In these meeting places, the shaman, *angakuk*, could perform and various "games" could be played, such as *illuriik* (song-contest partners) or *kataksatuk* (a grunting competition between women), to amuse the inhabitants during the long winter nights. Also, in this large house, the midwinter festival took place. The people in these often isolated winter camps exhibited a close social, economic, and recreational solidarity.

During the winter, game was scarce. The main hunting activity was for common seal at breathing holes or along the floe edge. A few birds were eaten, and when possible, molluscs and seaweed were gathered under the ice. Although the caribou migrated south in the winter, there were always some stragglers from the herd, and men traveled inland short distances when this might have been fruitful. Caribou were even found near the coastline from time to time in the winter (Gordon 1887:47). Foxes and wolves were also occasionally taken.

Two additional sources of supply in the winter were fish and stored foods. In the summer and late fall, the Eskimos tried to preserve surpluses of food for the winter, such as dried meat and fish, blubber, and "preserved" meat. These stores were kept in little "rooms" off the igloo or cached near where they were obtained. Eskimos had to feed both themselves and their dogs, and if the dogs were to work hard they had to be well fed with foods containing fat — fish alone would not do. There were fish in most of the larger lakes all year, but in midwinter they were difficult to get because the ice was many feet thick. There may have been natural holes in the ice or holes made by the Eskimos with an ice chisel. If fishing was very good, a couple or even a large family might spend much of the winter encamped near the spot; but, as I have said, fish was not an adequate diet for either Eskimos or their dogs.

Food got very scarce toward the end of winter, when the stored food had run out and the ice was too thick to fish through and the floe edge was far out to sea. Starvation and near starvation were common, and the Eskimos grew restless waiting for spring and all the food to come. Payne remarks that during March at Wakeham Bay "most of the seals leave the coast. . . . It was a matter with many of life and death and every man looked out for himself and his family." (Payne 1888–89:214) When things got really bad the camp, or some of it, would split up, moving by sled to other nearby areas for possibly better hunting. Those who could not follow because of age or infirmity might be left to fend for themselves and occasionally cannibalism resulted. In 1884–85, the storehouse of the Ice Observation Station at Stupart Bay was broken into three times. A direct quote from one of my oldest informants about a journey in the Sugluk area, around the turn of the century, illustrates the hardships and desperation of these times (translation from the Eskimo):

The next morning, maybe it was dark, we were moving off again to another place. At last we got up over onto the land and unloaded our sled. . . . As for our long sled and big dogs we used the sled for a fire and cooked the dogs. Going on like this we had no sled left. My brothers, Tullik and Qullialuk, were adult men; our father had died long before. We tried to move on to another place. We were very hungry, going on day after day, we had no dogs, and we were trying to keep the wood from our sled for firewood [having no oil]. My brother had a wife, and they got a caribou at their place. So he brought us some small pieces of meat. Even then, it was not enough though we tried to save it for ourselves. Knowing we were very hungry, my brother tried to save the meat for us. My married older sister, Tullauak, and her husband also brought us some food, eating little themselves. They moved off again to another place — anywhere — to get some food. So we were not friends any more. My brother, too, left his wife and came to join us, so we had many "ex-relatives." . . . We kept on moving again. We used a polar bear skin dragging it along as a sled with no dogs left. Thus we spent two days and nights just dragging the bear skin. Then we got one ptarmigan at Pulik's place . . . people were abandoning their own children, just anywhere. Eating the one ptarmigan — that was hardly enough for everyone! We kept stopping for. a while all the time. My mother was cutting up her clothes to eat, hats, hoods and all. We kept on having this for food every time we stopped. We nearly didn't have any clothes left, just enough to keep us warm. It was caribou skin we were wearing and we had another small skin which we were dragging; it was not even big enough for a *qaa* [bedding skin]. Because we were always eating it, there was nothing left, in the end, except the flat bare ground!
Then, after two more sleeps, they found caribou though it was the middle of the winter. My brother kept on falling down [he was so weak] so we pulled him along on the skin. My brother, Tullik, used to eat a lot, and he was not used to having little food. He kept on trying to save some of it for us, not keeping enough for himself. Still, [normally] he would certainly never miss a caribou. Because he kept on falling down, he was being dragged along, and we circled the caribou to get him close, but he didn't even bother to try to get the caribou — he

wasn't able to because he was so thin. They went after one caribou, and the other disappeared straight away. The one we hit was wounded. However, there was a second chance at night, and in the morning we were glad to have something to eat. Indeed, the next morning, we got two more. . . . We moved on after we had eaten them and settled down to hunt some more, but we could still hardly walk from being so thin. My brother's oldest baby was saved. When there was no more left of those caribou, we started to get drowsy again from hunger. Someone who had caught one in the area went looking for where they had cached it, some being left over from before. After getting four more, we were eating again and nicely dressed once more! The family split up again, mother and daughter being left behind. . . .

We started running out of food again, we left my older sister behind and then our brother, Qullialuk, left us behind. He kept on saying he didn't have time to go back [to his mother and sister], and he never went back. He would have gone back if we had been very close to them still; we had left them two sleeps back. He nearly never made it back to us either! . . . We only had arrows then, not having got guns yet, big bows and arrows. They used to save people when my mother and Pulamak used to get caribou. . . . The first guns weren't very good and would only bang once in a while, and then only after a long time! . . .

Finally we arrived at Sugluk as the snows were beginning to melt, and we were not starved again. We stayed in Sugluk and that's where I grew up. [The lady now lives in Great Whale River. Recorded August 1964.]

The text above, which is part of a longer story, illustrates the continual splitting up and coming together of relatives, the never-ending moving on and searching for game, and the loyalties and hostilities revolving around food. It is a kind of life we and the younger Eskimos cannot even imagine.

It is possible that some Eskimos lived all year in inland camps. Some people only visited the sea at the inland tip of Leaf Bay and others were known to live near huge Payne Lake, trying to subsist off fishing and stray caribou. The Takamiut lived near the coast and visited these people and their lands on their annual visits to the interior, generally made during the spring and summer.

In the late winter the young seals were born and the Eskimos eagerly broke into the "nests" in the ice floe and clubbed them. They also used them as decoys and harpooned the mother seal as she came to see what had happened to her crying young. The winter camp group generally broke up at this time and smaller groups still living in igloos, although more temporary ones, went out to the floe edge to hunt seals there. The weather was better and there was more traveling; people often visited their relatives and friends in other camps, knowing roughly where they would be at that time.

Spring and summer brought an abundance of food for the Eskimos after the various migratory birds and mammals began to arrive in April and May. Whereas, in traditional times, during the winter the Eskimos had little food, in spring and summer the problem was which of the various food resources they should concentrate on. The locations of the various food sources were often far apart and required considerable travel in different directions.

The most important resources of the early summer were the caribou, which was inland; the walrus; the white whale, which migrated down the Straits and was found in bays as well as offshore; and the many kinds of birds, which nested in swampy areas and on many of the offshore islands. These were soon followed by the migratory fish that left the lakes for annual visits to the coast. Obviously, not all Eskimos could pursue all the game; the particular quarry for each family was determined by their own abilities and the distribution of game in their area.

D'Anglure, in a very perceptive analysis of the Eskimo's solutions to these problems in the area around Wakeham Bay, suggests that the ability to travel was the determining factor (1964:94–97). Those who were weakest or very young or old would stay near their winter camping grounds all summer. They would support themselves by fishing and some seal hunting. Those with more mobility left the coast in May and spent the summer far inland hunting caribou and fishing, returning only in the later fall. Conversely, those who had lived inland during the winter came to the coast for the summer, hunting seals and fishing with the group who did not move at all. Later, almost all would join in the late summer caribou hunt and then return to their winter quarters.

The most active and best-equipped Eskimo families tried to cover as many resources as possible. D'Anglure suggests the following circuit for Wakeham Bay (1964:97, my translation):

May: Inland to hunt caribou, which are advancing towards the coast.
June: Back to the coast and islands for spring hunting for seals and walrus and the gathering of birds and their eggs.
June–mid-August: From place to place along the coast, fishing and some sea-mammal hunting.
August–September: Those families with large umiaks would travel along the coast and up the mouths of large rivers; then go on foot inland to hunt caribou for skins and meat for the fall.
September–October: Back to the coast and out to the islands to hunt seals, whales, and especially walrus.
October–November: Back to the sites of the winter villages, until May.

He notes the major characteristics of these migrations as follows:

1. Dispersion and mobility were most important, because of the movement of the game.
2. Two types of habitat: inland, for fish and caribou, and the coast for sea mammals. Both resources were essential and complementary.
3. The best-equipped families made the longest migrations. The poorer ones remained on the coast or inland all year and tried to obtain by exchange those products that they could not get themselves.

Wakeham Bay was a typical but fairly well-off habitat and differed slightly from the area around Sugluk and Ivujivik. For the people who wintered in Sugluk and Deception Bay, the cycle was slightly different:

March–April: Move out to the floe edge for better seal hunting.
May: Inland for the first caribou hunt; some fishing and bird hunting.
June: Back to the coast and islands such as Sugluk Island, Siuraktuk (Deception Bay), and even farther beyond Cape Weggs, or to Angit and Qalliik to the west; visit birds' nests at all these places for eggs and young and older birds.
July: The ice goes out and travel is by boat now. Some of the poorer families move to inland lakes or the head of the inlets for spear and hook fishing, staying there all summer. Others move along the coast, walking, or in kajaks and umiaks travel to Charles Island for walrus and bearded seals, then return to the coast.
August: The more able-bodied go inland for the all-important caribou hunt, getting skins for new winter clothing and meat for food supplies. Others stay near the coast.
September: All are on the coast again. Many hunt white whale in the large bays along the coast, caching the oil for the winter and drying the meat for food.

September–October: The walrus pass the area on their way north. Eskimos with umiaks go to Charles Island to hunt them, and the more ambitious go to Cape Wolstenholme and over to Nottingham and Salisbury islands. There they meet the people of Ivujivik and South Baffin Island. They return as fast as they can before they get caught by bad weather and the ice.
November: Most get back to their winter camps but some winter in the Ivujivik area and return in the winter by sled.

The Sugluk people, then, had to travel far for really abundant supplies of food. They were not so well off as the people on either side of them. The three families whom Low found at Sugluk in the late summer of 1904 (Low 1906:66) were probably not active or strong enough to go inland for the caribou and were waiting for their relatives to return. He noted that they were in a state of destitution and had never seen a white man before. I suspect that their more active relatives were the ones who traded into Chimo at that time.

The people of the Ivujivik-Nuvuk area were more fortunate than those of Sugluk and in the murre rookeries had one great advantage over those at Wakeham Bay. Their annual cycle differed considerably from those described above because of their special geography and resources:

March–April: The families move from their winter quarters out to the Nuvuk Islands and farther down the coast to hunt basking seals and those at the floe edge.
May: The caribou, meanwhile, come north and are met by hunters along the coast and slightly inland, after which the people return to the coast. There is some fishing through the ice of small lakes.
June: Staying on the coast, the families spread out according to their abilities and camps are made on the nearby islands. Vast flocks of birds arrive and begin to nest between Nuvuk and Kovik. The birds are killed and their nests raided. There is little walrus hunting.
July: Some families stay in the northern area and hunt seals, and fish at weirs for char. Boat trips are made to the murre rookeries along Digges Sound; Eskimos climb the cliffs and take thousands of eggs. Murre abound all along the coastline and many are killed. Other families go farther down the coastline to Kovik, where the fish run is enormous and the bearded seals could be harpooned while basking on the broken-up ice floes. Some families go to Mansel Island to fish.
August: At the beginning of the month, those families in the north travel overland or by umiak to Eric Cove to hunt the white whales,

which arrive in large schools. The meat is dried and the fat stored and taken back to winter camps. The caribou are now not far from the coast (Low 1902:18D). Between Kovik and Nuvuk is one of the favorite breeding grounds of the caribou (*ibid.*: 71). Those to the south near Kovik also go inland to hunt caribou and might return north by foot or boat. Some remain at Kovik for the winter and others all year. (*Ibid.*:22D).

September: Hunting the remaining caribou, the Eskimos gradually return to the coast and there hunt the schools of harp seals that pass at this time. Some fishing goes on.

October: Those with umiaks are able to visit Nottingham and Salisbury islands for the walrus hunt. They have a shorter distance to return with their catch than those of Sugluk and Deception Bay.

The Ivujivik people, then, were split by their dispersed resources and might go south to Kovik, or remain in the area for the white whales and murre eggs, or try to do both. As in other camps, those unable to get around stayed near the coast and fished. It should be noted that Eric Cove was only occasionally visited.

The activities of early fall have already been described in the accounts above. There was a coming together of people, and the storage of foods for the winter. After most of the migratory game had disappeared, a gloom set in because no one knew what perils the winter would bring. In the preceding seasons, the Eskimos had been busy and traveled far. When hunting caribou inland they had met people from far-distant areas. Itivimiut and Takamiut and even some Ungavamiut used to meet at the headwaters of the rivers in the summer, and this was a time for rejoicing and exchanging news and even marriage partners. Some people went on to other areas and did not return to their kin in the fall.

About the fall Payne remarks:

The sea is once more covered with ice . . . kayaks are put away, and until the ice is firm, times are very hard; and now the caches are opened and a large hole is soon made in the small winter's stock of provisions. With empty stomachs and leaky wigwams, they exist until the latter part of December. (Payne 1888–89:215)

TECHNOLOGY AND HUNTING TECHNIQUES

The technology of the Eskimos was extremely specialized, perhaps more so than that of any other group of hunters and gatherers (Service 1966:11). One might say that there were a number of technologies, each appropriate for a particular season or kind of game. The emphasis here is on those techniques that were specialized for certain resources and on the effects they had on some aspects of the social organization. The next chapter deals with how changes in technology brought about changes in social organization and its relationship to resources.

Technology is treated in terms of the annual cycle as are certain aspects of the social organization. A review of the sequences of changes will make clear that technology, social organization, and the annual cycle are highly inter-dependent features of Eskimo life and changes in any one lead to changes in each of the others.

Winter. During the winter, all the Eskimos of this area lived in large igloos. These were constructed of snow blocks cut out of wind-hardened snow drifts with long snow knives usually made of ivory. A family igloo might be ten feet in height and 15 feet in diameter and would take two or three men a day or so to construct. The interior of the igloo was divided, as were all Eskimo dwellings, into a raised sleeping platform, *illiq*, at the rear and a floor next to the entrance. On the illiq were willow-twig mats covered with caribou and bear skin bedding, and clothes and women's things were also stored there. At one or both sides was a wooden frame supporting a soapstone lamp which burned seal and whale oil; caribou oil was used only in dire necessity or times of excess. At the sides, near the entrance, were the meat benches where food was stored. The outside entrance of the igloo was low, requiring those entering to stoop or crawl on hands and knees. This entrance led to a porch where the dogs usually slept, and some of the men's implements were kept; others were kept on the roof (out of the way of the hungry dogs) or outside. Sometimes little additional rooms were built on the outside to store extra food. The snow blocks of the igloo were about 3 by 1.5 by .5 feet. Light came in through a block of clear ice set into the roof. When the igloo began to melt in late April or May, it was not abandoned immediately unless it collapsed. The roof would be removed and covered with skins to form a half-igloo half-tent.

Travel in winter was by dog sled. Nearly all families had at least one dog, but only the richest had ten or more (Tuttle 1885:65). I asked one of my older Sugluk informants why the Eskimos then had fewer dogs than they do now, thinking that perhaps it was because they could not get so many large game animals before they had guns. He replied that it was not that they could not provide the food but that a strange sickness visited the teams every few years cutting down the numbers and causing great hardship. From his description, this sounded like the same disease that struck the dogs at Cumberland Sound in 1884 (Boas 1888) and at Frobisher Bay and Lake Harbour in 1960 (Graburn 1963). In good times, the dogs were well fed all year, eating what the Eskimos did, plus much of the offal and tough parts of game. The dogs were fed every evening when traveling, and less regularly at other times. The Takamiut fed their dogs at the entrances of their houses or tents, trying to make sure that all the team got enough, not just the strongest and most aggressive dogs. A man who was lazy or very tired might just throw all the food into the middle of the pack, but this was looked upon as bad because some dogs got very little and others might be injured in the resulting fights. As we have seen, eating dogs was a last resort in starvation, just before eating one's clothes.

If a dog became sick or would not pull, it might be cut loose from the team, and if it could not keep up it might be lost and die — like the Eskimos themselves in hard times. A dead dog would be skinned, and the flesh when cold would be eaten by the other dogs. The skin would be used for trimming the parka hood for which it was next best to wolverine and wolf skin.

The sleds in this area were as long as 8 to 12 feet in traditional times. The wood used either was driftwood collected along the shoreline at certain times in the summer or came from trees chopped down on caribou hunts in the south or on visits made expressly for the purpose. The wooden runners were attached to crosspieces about 2 feet long with sealskin line made from spirally cut bearded seal skins. Another short line went across the front of the sled and to the middle of this was attached the main central trace to the dogs, which was from 10 to 20 feet long. At the front end, this central trace was tied to all the individual lines going to the dogs. The lines to each of the dogs were of different lengths so that although they formed a fan formation when the dogs were running some dogs were always in front and others closer to the sled. The dogs were harnessed around the shoulders with harnesses made of seal skins with the hair left on. At night, these and the traces had to be stored on top of the igloo or the dogs would chew them. Most of the men in this area had whips from 10 to 16 feet long with wooden or ivory handles and walrus skin and bearded seal skin lashes. They were used to keep the dogs in line, and the handles were often used for breaking up dog fights.

The dogs usually trotted when on the trail, but they ran when going downhill or when other animals were nearby, notably polar bear or caribou. Unless there were a large number of dogs only one or two people could ride on an empty sled and all had to push in hilly areas. The sled driver would sit sideways on the front, turning it by calling the dogs and pushing or pulling the front of the sled in the direction he wanted to go. In flat areas, a sled might travel more than 30 miles a day but one heavily laden with game or with a large family might do only about 10, especially if they hunted on the way. There were two forms of sled runners. In the winter, the sled would be turned upside down and a coating of mud plastered on. After the mud froze, a layer of warm water would be blown onto the mud and when this froze it would be smoothed out by a patch of caribou or bear skin soaked in more water until the whole runner was coated in a smooth layer of ice. This provided the most friction-free form of travel in the very cold weather but the driver had to look out for protruding rocks or sharp or hard ice which would damage it. In the spring, when the snows were melting and the rocks were exposed, the runners would be shod with strips of ivory or bone pegged to the bottom. At this time a longer sled was more desirable for passing over the broken tuvak, but because few men had two sleds most families had one short sled shod with bone or ivory, which would do for both winter and spring conditions.

Sled travel was measured in "sleeps," a relative distance dependent on the terrain and weather. Each night, a small igloo would be built, the dogs unharnessed, all edible materials stored on top or inside, and the dogs fed. No porch was built, and it was generally cramped inside. Generally no lamp was lit unless a woman was along, and food was eaten frozen and raw.

In winter, sealing on the ice was the main occupation. Two methods were used: the hunter waited at the breathing hole or hunted at cracks or the sea edge. The former method, requiring great patience, is a well known procedure of the Eskimos but was less well developed in this area than in the Central and High Arctic (Balikci 1964:85). It worked better if a number of men covered the adjacent holes of an area so that the seal was bound to come up at one of the holes and be harpooned; the seal would then be shared among all. The sealing harpoon was medium sized and had a wooden handle fixed to an ivory forepart to which an ivory (or sometimes slate) head was attached by a line that was also tied to the handle. When the bubbles came up and the harpoon was thrown, the seal dived. The barbed harpoon head stuck in its flesh and remained attached to the line which the Eskimo had wound around his waist. Thus the animal was secured and the man would call to his friends to help pull it out. In areas of smooth tuvak, such as parts of Sugluk and Deception inlets, this method was preferred, and a number of men from one camp would hunt together. In other areas, where the ice had open water, the hunters would try to entice the seal to the edge and harpoon it there; this method required only two hunters, one to attract or frighten the animal and the other to kill it (Payne 1888:218; D'Anglure 1964:122–40). When the seals were killed on the tuvak, they could be dragged home or, more usually, carried by sled. Dogs were both a help and a nuisance. A good dog would smell the seal holes through the snow, but a team would often be restless and scare the seals away. Both these methods of hunting were practiced all along the coast, but at Ivujivik-Nuvuk, where the Hudson Strait meets the Hudson Bay, the currents are very strong and the tuvak is treacherous. The warmer current welled up underneath the ice and the unwary hunter may have found himself supported only by the superficial layer of snow which gave way; a number of Nuvugmiut died this way.

Winter fishing was very poor, because the lake ice got so thick.

In some places where the ice was thinner a hole might be kept open for some time with the ice chisel, which had a long wooden handle and an ivory or bone point. Jigging with the use of a bone or antler hook, often baited with fat, was one method of fishing. If the hole was wide enough, spear fishing with the leister was attempted. This implement had a wooden handle and tied to one end were two springy bone points with barbs pointed inwards. The fish would be caught without much damage to it. Regardless of method, fishing was an unrewarding occupation and was practiced only by those who could not hunt seals or when no seals were in the area.

When food supplies were very low, attempts were made to trap foxes and other small game in crude traps. However, these traps were little used until the Eskimos heard that the white men wanted to trade fox skins.

In the winter the Eskimo might get either owls and ptarmigan with bow and arrow or the latter just by throwing stones. Slings were also used. Occasionally, in both winter and summer, a hunter would try to catch hares in a noose, a wooden stick holding up the sealskin or sinew loop. All these methods could be used by an individual and did not require group participation.

Food stored after the good hunts of late summer and early fall was put in caches either near where it was caught or where it might be needed. Game was put in depressions in the ground and covered by many large stones. The game was always cut up, and the meat or strips of blubber put inside a container, which could be either a white whale's stomach sewn up or a whole seal or walrus skin sewn together at the ends. If polar bears and wolverines did not reach them first, these stores were reopened in the winter either for consumption at the cache or for transport to the igloo.

Spring and Summer. In spring the Eskimos moved out to good seal-hunting places, often near the floe edge. At this time the ringed seals emerged frequently from their blow holes to bask in the warm sun. Although wary, they could be approached closely enough to be harpooned by an Eskimo with a sealing or sliding harpoon. The Eskimo, lying on his side, partially hidden behind his white hat and polar bear skin portable blind, would slowly

47

approach the seal. Some Eskimos wore all sealskin clothing and imitated the seal during this approach. Seals sleep for about 30 seconds and are awake and alert for about 10. The Eskimo, therefore, had to crawl for a few seconds at a time until he was close enough to throw the harpoon, hanging on to the line. Bow and arrow were not good for this kind of hunting because the seals sleep so close to their holes that they can slip down into them when killed, wounded, or frightened. Dogs would scare the seal and were kept far from this type of hunting.

Soon after this early seal hunting the better hunters went inland for the spring caribou hunt. They might have to travel many sleeps and so went in groups by sled, building igloos or using small tents on the way. The men tried to surround a small herd by hiding behind natural cover such as rocks and approaching upwind. The dogs had to be kept far away because they went wild at the smell of caribou and would have stampeded the herd. Caribou were hunted by bow and arrow. Bows were made of one piece of wood backed by a strip of leather with a bowstring of caribou skin, when available, because it worked better than sealskin. The arrow, about 3 feet long, was a straight piece of wood with a pointed, not barbed, bone or ivory head.

Dead caribou would be cut up on the spot and loaded on the sleds. If there were too many to transport at once the remainder would be cached sometimes on a platform in the trees, a custom probably learned from observation of the Indians in southerly areas.

Fishing and hunting for eggs were other spring activities. Fishing was sometimes at the melting lakes but more often in small rivers that could be dammed with a weir made of rocks, where a group of Eskimos, including women and children, speared the fish with the leister. Quite often the leister was also used by one individual or a few in shallow places where there were no dams. Women and children gathered eggs, such as those of geese and ducks, on flat ground, although men would also gather them if they came across them. The eggs of the murre and sea pigeon were gathered from the cliffs by intrepid men who would climb up hundreds of feet to do so. The eggs were lowered down to those below in some kind of container and were taken home by boat, or on foot in a few places.

Birds were usually hunted with the bird dart and its thrower. The former was light like an arrow, but had three prongs like a leister, although more barbed. It was thrown either on land or from a kajak. The throwing board, about 2 feet long, was usually made of wood with a handgrip at one end and a socket for the dart at the other. This equipment was useful everywhere on the coast and was particularly useful in the Ivujivik area, where there are millions of murres.

As the tuvak was breaking up, the kajak came into use. This craft was about 20 to 25 feet long in this area, weighed perhaps 100 pounds, and was pointed at both ends. Although the kajak had only a single seat, its buoyancy would allow the transport of more than one person or small seals on the top or inside. Every able-bodied man had a kajak and a whole array of hunting implements which were stored on deck. In front of the paddler would usually be his spear and harpoon readily at hand. The spear or lance was simply a wooden handle firmly attached to an ivory forepart carved into a fine bladed point. It was used without a line for killing sea mammals or caribou. The *igimak*, the best known Eskimo harpoon, had a heavy wooden handle the front end of which had an ivory butt with a socket into which fitted the rear end of a tusk, pointed at the front. This point fitted into the ivory head, which had a socket for it and two angled barbs, and sometimes the head had a slate fore-edge sharpened and set into the ivory. All three pieces were tied firmly together with sealskin line, the head through its rear part, the tusk at its base, and the handle through two separate holes. In addition, the line was hooked onto a small peg set into the handle, the other end being held by the hunter. When the harpoon hit the animal, the angled barbs drove it through the flesh in a curved path so that it ended at right angles to the path of entry. When so lodged it could not come out and tension was released on the line holding it which in turn loosed the head from the tusk and the tusk from the handle. This prevented the implement from breaking but kept all the parts tied together. The handle would float, and the Eskimo would retain

49

the line to haul the animal in. Attached farther back along the line was another short line tied to the *avatak*, a small sealskin blown up and plugged with ivory to act as a float. This impeded the animal's efforts to flee and assured that it would float and be visible. For larger mammals, such as whale and walrus, an additional line was tied to a shallow drumlike *niutak* made of a wood frame covered with skin. This traveled at right angles to its line and further retarded the efforts of strong animals to get away. On the kajak behind the paddler was the *nitsik*, a piece of wood with a bone or horn hook at one end for hooking dead animals out of the water. One side was serrated to supply a better grip on the wet handle and the other end was cut in a V shape to push the dead game down into the interior of the kajak between the hunters' legs. Usually, however, game was carried on the back deck if the journey was not too far or too rough.

The kajak paddle was about 10 feet long, made of wood and very heavy. Its blades were small and curved so that wind and waves would not knock it out of the hunter's grasp. When harpooning was in progress the paddles rested alongside the cockpit edge on a small hook.

Hunting by kajak was tedious and difficult. To get close to the animal, the Eskimo had to judge where it was next coming up to breathe, paddle furiously to that point, and then wait silently, drifting, with the harpoon poised. The harpoon could not be thrown very far with any accuracy, maybe 50 feet at the most, and the loss of a harpoon was a disaster to be avoided at all costs. Waves did not bother a kajak, and if one overturned it could even be righted by the hunter if he was wearing his watertight seal-intestine clothing and thus could withstand the icy water. However, wind was a bane for the kajaker; the vessel was so light that steering required constant correction with the heavy paddles, especially as most of the boats, made "by eye," did not run straight.

To make a kajak, which had to be kept in constant repair, about six bearded seal skins without the hair were required (even more if smaller seals were used). Some kajaks were made of deerskins and were lighter but not much good in salt water. The frame was

50

generally made of driftwood and was held together by seal-line lashing. The construction of a kajak in this area is well described by Arima (1964). In winter and spring, the kajak had to be kept on a high platform of snow or rock to prevent the dogs from eating it. When the kajak was slightly damaged by rocks or ice the hunter would plug the hole with a wad of fat or skin kept for the purpose, but larger cuts, which were common, necessitated a quick landing. The instability of the kajak made getting in and out difficult unless someone was there to hold it. If the hunter was alone he had to hang on to the shore with one hand and quickly step out while balancing himself on one foot, or he crawled along the deck if there was nothing to hold on to.

In the late summer, the families who were better off traveled along the coast and up inlets and rivers using the large skin boat, the umiak. Arima says there were some twelve or more umiaks along the coast of the Takamiut area about 1900 (1963:76); however, I believe his data on umiak owners at the turn of the century includes all who had such craft at one time or another because it is unlikely there were so many at any one time. The construction and mode of operation of an Ivujivik umiak is described in some detail in Arima's work. In brief, the craft was made of some twenty to twenty-five bearded seal skins stretched over a wooden frame and open at the top. It was 20 to 25 feet long and could hold twenty people including all their dogs and equipment, and up to double that number in calm water. Although the umiak was generally a safe craft, sharp ice or overloading could lead to disaster. One umiak went down in Wakeham Bay in the 1890's and more than twenty people were drowned, most of them women and children. The boat was said to be carrying forty people, which was considered overloaded by my informants.

The umiak had two large oars, attached one at each side by thongs, and generally was rowed by women. At the rear was a steering oar, often worked by an older man. It was a slow and awkward craft but could take rough water and carry an enormous load because of its high ratio of volume to weight. In fair weather with a following wind the square sail of seal intestine (or occasionally of caribou skin) would be raised up the mast. Traveling was slow but sure, and camp was made on land every night. Under the best conditions the umiak probably made only 25 miles a day, and in this area it was not used for hunting. The ownership of an umiak, however, gave great prestige; the owner could sit back and watch the others who took a ride in his boat and whose kajaks were being towed behind. The collection of the necessary materials, the construction, and the sailing and use of an umiak required a number of adults in cooperation, usually a larger group than a single household.

The late summer inland caribou hunting was most often done on foot. Leaving the umiak on some river bank, the party moved off toward the herd. The dogs had packs on their backs and the women and girls were also heavily loaded. In the summer all the families lived in tents, although hunters might sleep outside in good weather. The tents were made of sealskins and were extremely heavy, especially when wet, and they took a long time to dry after rain. They were held up by one or more poles depending on the size of the tent, and the door was a flap of sealskin. There were no guy ropes, but the edges were held down on the ground by heavy stones to keep the dogs out. Thus, a traveling party of families, with their tents, poles, stone lamps, provisions, and weapons was very heavily loaded and moved slowly over the soggy summer ground. Generally, the caribou hunt was planned to take place after the bulk of the mosquitoes and blackflies of July and August, but the hunters were still very much bothered by insects and would light small fires of shrubs to keep them away. Both men and women went on the hunt, although men did most of the killing.

The technique might be like that described earlier for the spring hunt, but there were also other methods. If at all possible, the caribou were caught crossing a lake or river during their migration. Some men brought kajaks especially for this purpose, and the rest of the people drove the caribou into the water, where the hunters would spear them with their lances. Another method was for lines of people to herd the caribou down a valley with a corral at the bottom. Lines of piled up rocks looking like people were also used to frighten the herd. When the caribou reached the corral the man hiding behind it would emerge and shoot the caribou with arrows. Another method, used when a suitable place was available, was to drive the herd over a cliff or ravine and then to spear the survivors at the bottom. All these methods were mentioned by many informants in this area.

After a successful hunt, all haste was made back to the coast. There was much to carry, and sometimes the carcasses were cached to be fetched later by sled in the winter (see text of story above). The women began making the new caribou-skin winter clothes as fast as they could for it was getting colder, and taboo forbade the men to hunt walrus until they were finished.

During the middle and late summer, both whales and walrus were hunted. Whales were hunted by the same method as seals and were easy prey as they cruised in schools around the shallow bays and inlets. Some thirty miles east of Wakeham Bay is an inlet (Tinukjavik) which has a bar at the mouth, turning it into a lake at low tide. Many whales swam in there and were easily caught. When enough whales were caught they were towed to the shore and cut up by the men and women. As much meat as necessary was taken back to camp, but most of the fat was cached for use as dog food and for lamps in the winter. The black meat was carefully cut up into thin strips and dried in the sun to form a portable and storable food. Dried fish served a similar purpose but was more likely to get moldy.

Walrus were more formidable beasts and were rarely hunted from kajaks and umiaks. At times of migration walrus generally traveled in groups of small herds and were to be found close off-shore at certain islands or even on land. The Eskimos approached them stealthily along the shore, and the best hunter threw the heavy harpoon. The huge wounded animal would try to escape into the water, and as many men as possible would hang on to the line to prevent this and the loss of the harpoon. Often men were dragged into the water rather than lose beast and weapon. Once on land, the animal was killed with the lance, and there was great rejoicing. When walrus were hunted from kajaks, the method and equipment was as described earlier. Generally, a number of kajakers would attempt the task together, all trying to harpoon the animal and slow it down with a number of floats and niutaks. This was very dangerous because a wounded walrus would turn on the boats, and the tusks could easily rip the kajaks' skins.

In the late summer, gathering berries was a task for the women and children. This might be carried on during the inland caribou hunt or anywhere along the coast where there was fertile ground. Groups of women from the same camp roamed the hills picking the berries. They usually ate as many as they wanted during the day and returned to camp in the evening with their bags and containers full. There was no attempt to preserve any of the gathered plant life.

Food and Clothing. The first partition and distribution of game was carried out by men. After the parts had been taken back to the camp or household, the women took over with their many duties. They prepared skins for clothing and boots by scraping to remove the excess fat and mesentery and stretching them on large wooden frames to dry in the sun.

The edible parts, meat, intestines, liver, kidneys, and brain, were stored, eaten raw, dried, or cooked. Generally only meat and fish were stored or dried as we have described above. Food was eaten raw most of the time although a good proportion was also frozen. It was a great deal of trouble to cook things as the slow-burning lamp took a long time to boil water in the clumsy soapstone pots, which were hard to make, heavy to carry, and fragile. Lighting the lamp itself was quite a problem; this was commonly done by igniting the dry wick with sparks from stones. Occasionally the bow drill was used, but the Eskimos usually kept this tool for drilling holes in making harpoons, kajaks, and umiaks. The only method of cooking was boiling in water. The resultant gravy was relished as much as the meat and, together with pre-chewed food, was fed to babies when they were being weaned. In summer, small fires of brush were used outside the tent to cook things faster. Vegetable products and some meats eaten raw were usually dipped in rancid sea-mammal fat to improve their flavor. The Eskimo method of cooking left the meat in large chunks. Each person would take a chunk and holding one end between his teeth would cut off a bite-sized lump with his knife or her *ulu* (semi-

54

lunar knife). An ordinary knife was generally made of one piece of shin bone sharpened on both sides. The ulu, like the scraper, had a slate blade and a bone or wooden handle. Drinking water was fetched and stored in seal or caribou skin pails.

In this area skins for clothing were not usually "tanned" with urine but were prepared on the frames by sun and frost. Clothing for the different seasons required materials from both inland and sea mammals. Generally speaking, two layers of clothes were used in winter. These were made of skins from caribou killed in late summer, when their condition was best. In late spring caribou shed their hair and such skins were generally used only for bedding. The skins were sewn together with caribou or white whale sinews dried and split. The women sewed with the bone needle, which was a laborious job, especially under the late summer pressures described above. Generally, men's and children's clothing were all made along the same plan. The upper garment (parka, to use the Russian word) covered the arms, torso, and head. Some informants say that the fur ruff is a new invention. The inside upper garment was *attigi* and the outer *qulitak;* both reached down to the hips. The trousers, which went just below the knee, fitted under the attigi and under the tops of the boots. A woman of child-bearing age wore a parka with a large pouch in the back for carrying small children; both the front and rear of the parka hung down below the knees like "tails" and could be sat on.

Boots were the most critical part of Eskimo wear, both for keeping the feet warm in winter and for keeping them dry in summer. Winter boots had soles of bleached bearded seal hide, and the leggings were made either of ringed seal skin or of caribou skin, both with the hair on. In spring and summer such boots were not waterproof, and the Eskimos used another kind of boot, made of unbleached bearded seal skin soles and scraped ringed seal skin uppers. These required an intricate double stitch for waterproofing but were very effective; however, they would not stand the frost and became very hard when dry, requiring scraping and chewing to soften them before use. In the winter mitts were worn, often double. Damp clothes and boots were hung out to freeze in winter and then were beaten with a stick in the morning to knock the ice out. Clothes were dried on a frame above the lamp either held up by posts or stuck conveniently into the walls of the igloo. During rainy weather in the summer clothes were almost impossible to dry, and the untanned hide became heavy and sticky and sometimes moldy. No wonder rain was called *silaluktuk*, "it is bad weather"!

SOCIAL ORGANIZATION

In describing the social life of any group of people, we must be careful to distinguish between groups (and the relations between them) that actually exist "on the ground" and those that are categories in the minds of the people. Firth (1951) makes the useful distinction by calling the first *social organization* and the second *social structure*. An example from contemporary life might be the two meanings of the word "family": in the first sense it would include those people who actually live together in a household or get together at "family gatherings," whereas in the second sense it would include all those people you consider related. Everyone has such a category so any one person can be thought of as belonging to a large number of "families" at the same time — those of all his relatives. However, that one person can only be a member of one household grouping or at one family gathering at any instant in time. Naturally he may, over time, change his actual affiliations and join another household or a different family grouping. Organizational groupings, then, are discrete: an individual can belong to only one at any one time. Structural groupings may overlap at any time and exist only in the minds of people.

For the most part, we will be dealing with organizational groupings. The structural groupings of the Takamiut have been considered at length elsewhere (Graburn 1964). The following sections also consider some of the relationships between organization and structure, that is, how the ideas "of the mind" were actually carried out and translated into action "on the ground."

Residential and Territorial Groups. The Eskimo household, in an igloo or tent, was the basic unit of social and economic solidarity. The people considered themselves *illuqatigiit*, "sharers of the

56

house," and kept together for longer periods than any other grouping. A household might consist of a nuclear family (parents and their unmarried children) or of an extended family (parents and married children and their spouses and children). Sometimes a household might also include other dependent relatives, for example, unmarried brothers and sisters, widowed parents, or even nonrelatives who were dependent on the good will of others and had no close relatives.

A number of households close together constituted a camp or village, *katimajut*, "a coming together," such as we have seen was common during the winter and at the spring hunting camps. Generally, a few households stayed together during much of the year, migrating to the various places where game was likely to be found. This group was usually made up of close relatives, and the men of the households were probably brothers or father and sons. Such a group has been called a band (Graburn 1960, 1964; D'Anglure 1964) and was commonly found at Chimo during the last century by Turner (1894), although the latter called it a "gang." Such bands would generally share food and sometimes eat together. They might cooperate in inland caribou hunts or in owning and using an umiak, and they would certainly cooperate in such matters as constructing and sewing the skins of large equipment, for example, kajaks, umiaks, and tents. The composition of the band varied according to circumstances. Brothers did not always stay together, and some men would have no brothers, in which case they and their families might join the bands of their married sisters or of their wives' brothers or fathers. We have seen how flexible and divisive Eskimo life could be, especially in times of hardship. A band might even include a nonrelative and his family, if he were known to be successful at hunting and generous at sharing and providing. This would give added prestige to the leader of the group.

A number of bands might make up the winter village and the population might comprise a dozen households in the best winter hunting areas. There would be less solidarity within the total group if they were not somehow related, but if they met regularly year after year they might very well become related by (1) wife-exchange between the band heads ("exchange-spouses"), (2) betrothal of children, or (3) intermarriage. People who lived at the same camp, temporarily or permanently, were called *silaqatigiit*, "neighbors," or *nunakatigiit*, "together on the same land." The people of an area who met from time to time but did not live together, such as the people of the camps near Ivujivik, were *nunaqatigiit*, "sharers of the land."

Nunaqatigiit were the largest group of people exhibiting some solidarity and constant friendship. Larger groups such as the Takamiut or Itivimiut lived in the same very large area of land, but might not know each other personally or feel any solidarity. Takamiut and Itivimiut were, therefore, conceptual, structural categories, of little importance except as geographical labels.

There were times of the year, for example, during summer fishing or occasionally during spring sealing and winter fishing, when single households would locate in an area far from the others. Such a group of people, tent or household, was known as *nunalituak*, "there is nothing but land," because they had no neighbors, and a grouping of this kind was not considered the norm but always a part of a larger band and a temporary situation. If in winter one's family or band left one nunalituak, it was an omen of abandonment.

The Structure of Groups. The household was a social and economic unit maintained by an adult man and woman, usually husband and wife. Both were essential for successful existence in the Arctic and the numerous tasks of living were about evenly divided between men and women. Thus the main division of labor was by sex, although Eskimo adults never hesitated to cross roles when this was warranted. Older people and young children could not perform the essential tasks well and were the first to suffer in bad times; the former might be abandoned and the latter killed and even eaten. The active man and woman, then, ruled the household, each directing and performing the appropriate tasks.

In the band the oldest active male would usually be in charge, perhaps a father or an older brother, for age was the criterion for authority among able people. Younger sons and brothers, when adult, did not have to obey their elders — they could always leave and join another group — but if they remained they generally listened to the advice of the older men. The older men, on their part, never made arbitrary decisions but consulted all concerned and weighed the evidence carefully. In Eskimo there is no word for "obey," only *maliktuk*, "he follows," and *nalaktuk*, "he listens to," and the idea of command or discipline was absent. Adult married sons were usually quite willing to "follow" their fathers and older brothers. The decisions of the older man were often quite crucial for the group, determining when to move to another campsite, what particular game to seek out if there was a choice, the distribution of the products of the hunt, when to build a new umiak, kajak, or tent for which many skins and a cooperative effort were required. The older women, too, generally had the say over the younger ones in cooperative tasks. The "boss" of such a camp group was often known as *isumatak*, "the thinker" for the group, and he might even be an *umialik*, "boat owner," if it were a prosperous group. Both were positions of prestige and aspired to by the active hunters. Such heads of groups were de facto leaders of the residential group whether it consisted only of kin or included nonkin.

When a number of bands got together in one place there were often no clear-cut lines of authority within the group and no single leader. Accession to the position of isumatak was achieved by being a very good hunter and a likeable and fair person; these qualities were necessary if other families were to follow. A most outstanding hunter might be a de facto isumatak for a gathering of bands and might organize the largest cooperative hunts if he consulted the others.

Among each group of people in an area there was likely to be a shaman or angakuk; rarely there were two with complementary functions. The shaman was the Eskimo most directly in control of the world of the supernatural and therefore of health and good luck. As such, he was most often beneficial to the community (Balikci 1960b), although his powers were potentially harmful too. The shaman was able to control the free-floating spirits of good and evil, *turngak*, or those of the animals, *inua*, "its person," which determined the fate of the group. He could also *ilisirktuk*, "perform evil magic," by sending his spirits to do harm to others. Sometimes he did this of his own accord and sometimes at the behest of a friend or kinsman.

Shamans could be men or women and usually learned their art from an older one, after showing some outstanding ability on their own. The principal personal involvement most ordinary Eskimos had with a shaman was in curing diseases. Although in many ways the Eskimo felt at the mercy of the shaman, he had to go to him on occasion. Curing usually involved getting the sick person to confess in front of the group what taboos he had broken, and the release of guilt itself probably effected many cures. They were supposed to know many things that were going on, such as which women were pregnant or menstruating and who had broken what taboos. Many shamans also entertained the camp group by extraordinary performances such as disappearing, visiting the spirit world, changing into animal forms, speaking "in tongues," or wounding themselves without observable harm. Such performances maintained the prestige of the shaman and entertained the group during the long winter, often in the *qaggialuk*, meeting house. Although most shamans were feared and powerful, not all were treated with respect. One shaman, Piluktu, who lived in this area, used to fancy himself at these extraordinary performances, and the Eskimos constantly encouraged him to put on a show. However, when he was up on the platform doing his tricks, the other men used to play with the genitals of his wife Tiriganirk! This happened time and time again, but it is said Piluktu never knew about it. The men of the area thought it was so funny that they made up an obscene song about it, which is still remembered in Wakeham Bay.

There was generally only one shaman in each group of nunaqati-giit because of rivalries and jealousies over their powers and performances. There were about five active angakuk in the Takamiut area in the latter part of the last century, one of whom was a woman. Most shamans were treated just like other Eskimos when not actually performing. However, if they were such good hunters that they were also isumatak, they were in a very powerful position, having control over both the supernatural and material world. Such cases were rare but are well remembered. A group in which the shaman was also the isumatak was likely to be quite highly organized, in contrast to most winter camps and summer caribou hunts which had only a temporary solidarity based on mutual economic interest.

Social control of the family-household was generally divided between husband and wife, each being "boss" within his own sphere, but it was the husband who made the large decisions concerning territory and hunting. In the family-band, the isumatak, aided by the other men, was in charge; generally he would not interfere with domestic problems unless they concerned his own junior kin, but he and the other adults were always concerned with social problems involving the large group. Those who would not cooperate or hunt when able were ostracized to the point where they often left the group, or sometimes they were left isolated by a quick departure of the group during the night. Those who were continuously antisocial, who, for instance, persistently stole, committed adultery causing jealous fights, or were completely lazy were encouraged to leave; if they did not, the older men might decide among themselves to execute the offender, taking him by surprise. Shamans, if antisocial, were generally too feared to be executed, but families might leave the area one after another hoping to get away from such a shaman.

Kinship and the Life Cycle. Eskimo kinship has been the subject of many publications, (Damas 1964; Giffen 1930; Graburn 1964; Guemple 1962; Hughes 1958; Lantis 1946; Pospisil and Laughlin 1963; Valentine 1952), and we need describe it only briefly here. At birth the mother was attended by older women, generally relatives or friends from other households in the camp, who acted as midwives. Long before birth the child's name was decided on, generally that of a deceased ancestor or person of note, for it was believed that the name embodied the name-soul, *atirk,* of the person and the child would grow up to be like him. A child was breast fed for three or four years and was kept constantly on its mother's or another woman's back in the *amaut.* Walking and talking were not particularly forced, and the child took its own time to learn things. Very quickly, the roles of boys and girls diverged, the girls helping their mothers and the boys going out with their peers pretending to hunt. Often groups of neighbor girls would get together and "play house."

61

Children learned little else than their respective roles and by ten or twelve could be useful, although not fully self-supporting, members of the community. A young man, on the killing of his first game, "celebrated" by sharing it with the village and giving a gift to his mother's midwives. There were no great *rites de passage*, and adulthood was eagerly sought by both sexes. About the age of puberty there was a change in status of both boys and girls. For girls it was marked by the wearing of the woman's parka and by being tatooed on the face and body. Boys were invited by the older men to partake of the parts of the game usually reserved for men whereas prior to that they had shared with the women and other children.

Betrothals were often made by parents at or before puberty, and the young had little choice of partners. However, a father usually made himself aware of his son's wishes before agreeing with the girl's parents on the arrangement. The young man moved in with the girl's family with no further ceremony; they were "engaged" for a while and this was a sort of trial marriage. If all went well, that is, if the girl got pregnant within a year or so, they were considered "a married couple." Sooner or later, if they came from separate areas, they generally went back to the man's camp. However, the story was rarely as simple as this. Some young people got married against their parents' will or even against the girl's will. They might decide to stay with the girl's family or they might move off elsewhere. Furthermore, this was rarely the last sexual partnership that either might enter into. The mortality rate was high, especially for men through accident, homicide, and starvation, and for women through childbirth, and most couples lost a spouse at one time or another. Since the division of labor required adults of both sexes to operate a household unit, remarriage was encouraged and most usual, especially if the woman was still able to bear children. If she was a *ningiuk*, "beyond fertility," or he an *ituk*, "an old disabled man," their chances were slimmer, and, if single, they would have to depend on the good will of their friends and relatives for tasks performed by the opposite sex.

Polygyny was not uncommon, especially among the isumatak and angakuk classes, the "successful men." Those who could afford to support them took more wives, often from less successful men who only had one. Such co-spouses were called *aviliariik*, "the rivals," a name also applied to unmarried rivals. Some men had two or more wives because their first or second did not have children. I know of one man who had six childless trial marriages in succession, each ending with a separation, and all the women except one went on to have children by their later husbands. The children of co-wives were considered siblings, but step-siblings were not felt to be so closely related as full siblings. Polyandry was extremely rare in this area.

Eskimo marriage was not only fraught with probabilities of the loss of a spouse but was also notoriously fragile. Partners could leave each other if they did not get on well together or if they thought they would get on better with someone else. In these separations, the younger children usually stayed with the mother and the older boys with the father. The woman might return to her family or go to another man. Often, an outside party was involved. All men wanted to be married and many wanted more than one wife. When bereaved or separated, a man would make every effort to get a new wife, to the point of stealing another's. Adultery was rife and sexual jealousy the norm. Few men or women could trust one another in sexual matters, nor could they trust one another in times of hunger — in fact, in most cases of cannibalism in the area, the women ate their husbands after they had both eaten their children! To cement ties of friendship, men would exchange wives for a short or long period and the children of both women would be considered siblings. Gambling abounded (Turner 1888:178) and anything would be staked except children or harpoons. One man won two extra wives in a night, but soon returned them in exchange for small gifts.

Children, especially sons, were welcomed in times of plenty and were well treated. The child's household was, from time to time, situated among a number of other households made up of relatives and friends. It was a small world, and everyone had an intimate personal knowledge of everyone else, seeing them and gossiping every day. This integration was reinforced by the economic cooperation and solidarity for most of the year. The for-

tunes of one were the fortunes of all. This group was the prototype *ila* or "in-group" — the "we" of the child's life. Ila, in one
sense, designates any group that is solidary for a short or long
period, and it can even mean "my side" in a team game. It has
also been translated as "family" or "relatives" (Balikci 1964: 25–
36; Damas 1964:55; D'Anglure 1964:189) and the term may be
extended to all consanguinals who are addressed by kin terms, although Damas notes: "This designation by terms has vague
limits . . . but is sharply set off in the case of affines." These *ilagiit*,
"relatives" or "we-group," were more trustworthy than others
and, in addition, felt primary obligations to support each other
in times of need. The child soon learned that there were other
ilagiit in other camps whom he might visit or who might visit his
home, and these, too, he was assured, were trustworthy, friendly
people. The meeting of relatives from another area was great
cause for warmth and joy in the household. They might bring
gifts and were treated well. Old stories of childhood and past
companions were retold. News was exchanged, and there was
generally a common interest, especially in each others' children.

These were the positive aspects of group life, but we have seen
that there were many divisive forces too: loss of spouse, separation
of couples, splitting up to hunt or when food was scarce, marrying
into another area, and so on. It behoved Eskimos, therefore, to
extend their circle of ila as far as possible for these were the people
to be relied upon, although no one was to be trusted at the worst
times. The circle of ilagiit was extended by mechanisms of kinship
and pseudokinship:

1. Kinship was reckoned bilaterally through father and mother,
although the actual organization of the local kin group might be
patrifocal and patrilocal.

2. There was no set boundary to ila; it might extend to second
cousins if they were known. Distant, but known, relatives were included as *takujaksak*, meaning approximately "I've just seen
them."

3. Nonkin might be incorporated for their economic and social
qualities:

The function of spouse exchange is to provide for the inclusion of non-kin within the kinship circle . . . insuring . . . both the characteristics of kinship and non-kinship statuses. . . . Chosen for his competence, . . . he is also a kinsman, assured of continued cooperation and aid during difficult times. (Guemple 1962:54)

4. Betrothals were often arranged between nonkin, as we have seen, although the question of whom to marry was ambiguous:

Eskimos preferred to marry outside their area; they did not like to marry a kinsman. (D'Anglure 1964:225)

The *ilagiit* . . . was a category of people among whom mates were preferably sought. (Balikci 1964:28)

In other words, the extension of exogamy was a variable. Ideally one should marry as far out as possible (Graburn 1964:89), but if this ideal was carried too far there was the possibility of giving a daughter (or a son) to some unrelated group where one had no connections. In fact, some Takamiut have always married relatives, even first cousins, and claim that this is proper. Others say that such a marriage partner is too close a relative and that one should marry outside *ilamarik*, "real, close kinsmen." Marriage, then, was usually a compromise achieved by marrying distant kinsmen or close nonkin.

5. Adoption was common, usually from relatives who were unable to support (any more) children because they had lost a spouse or were poor. Nonkin orphans, too, might be added to the family circle of a good hunter. Sometimes exchange-adoption performed the same functions as exchange-marriage.

6. Illuriik were song-contest partners, who regularly competed with each other in the qaggialuk but became good friends.

Thus, there were two kinds of kinsmen or "we people," ila. Balikci (1964) has suggested the term "extended ilagiit" for the large circle known to each individual, those whom one occasionally met and who were one's hosts when visiting their area, and the term "restricted ilagiit" for the kin-based camp group that actually lived together or cooperated at various times of the year. The restricted ilagiit was a solidary group performing the daily and regular supportive functions, and the extended ilagiit was called upon for irregular and out of the ordinary acts such as being a host or participating in blood revenge. The larger group was a conceptual category and each person's group of *ilalimat*, "total relatives," differed from that of the next person, although there was much overlapping. The restricted ilagiit, usually katimajut, "living in the same place," was a real group "on the ground" that acted in concert but could split up or join another similar group as conditions warranted. Thus, we come back to the distinction drawn between structural and organizational groups that introduced this section.

ECONOMIC ORGANIZATION

The economic organization was an integral part of the necessary connections between the ecology of the area and the social organization discussed above. This organization had to balance factors, including the variability of the game, the seasons, various kinds of group life, and distribution, that insured the survival of the maximum number of people.

Obviously, the actual acquisition of game was a very unequally distributed factor because of differential skills, wisdom, and luck and the ever-present differences of age, sex, and health. This section describes the complex solutions to the problems of distribution and efficiency that the Eskimos had worked out and had to choose among.

Rules for Sharing. To insure distribution of large game there were fairly explicit rules governing who, other than the lucky hunter, was to benefit from the kill. Of course, no one man got a kill every time; therefore, each in turn provided the food and materials for the rest of the group. In theory there was complete reciprocity: each person took from the group and contributed to its welfare as much as the next. However, some men were better hunters than others and consistently contributed more to the "common pot." These men took less than they gave, but reciprocity was fulfilled in the form of the prestige and followers they gained. The balance was redressed in terms of nontangibles.

Generally speaking, the extent of the sharing of game depended on its size. It may roughly be stated:

1. Whale, walrus, bearded and harp seals, all of which weighed

over 250 pounds, were distributed in some manner to all those living at the camp, kinsmen or otherwise.

2. Caribou, ringed seals, young bearded and harp seals, weighing between 50 and 250 pounds, were distributed among the closer kindsmen, generally the restricted ilagiit.

3. All smaller game, birds, hares, owls, eggs, and the like, were retained by the household of the hunter or gatherer.

One further rule modified the rules set forth above:

4. When an abundance of smaller game was acquired, such that the total bulk approximated that listed under categories one or two, it was divided according to the rules of the larger category, for example, a man with fifteen hares would give parts to all of his restricted ilagiit, or a household that collected five hundred eggs would distribute the eggs to everyone in the camp.

A cross-cutting set of rules was brought into play according to the occasion of acquisition or the types of hunt. D'Anglure has outlined these in some detail (1964: 160–169), and I shall follow his classification of these rules, with modification.

On hunts that involved a large number of men in a limited area, either cooperating in or pursuing the same activity, there were strict rules of division in order to avoid quarrels and disorganization. When the men were not all members of the restricted ilagiit or family camp, one man was in charge of the distribution. D'Anglure calls this man *l'acquéreur* which is best translated as the "procurer" of the game. On a hunt for large game, one man would be the procurer for each kill, generally the man who was most responsible for that particular kill. If the game was a polar bear or stranded whale, the procurer was the man who discovered it; if it was a sea mammal, he was the first man to harpoon and therefore secure it; and if it was a caribou, he was the man who actually killed it. Sometimes the procurer was merely the one who supplied the major equipment, such as an umiak or a fish weir.

The procurer took the first and, in many respects, the best part of the kill and then oversaw the fair distribution of the rest, first to the other hunters who participated, then to other people who watched the hunt or saw the cutting up, and finally, if it was a very large animal, among the various families back at the camp.

Generally, the procurer's parts were those that had the most lasting value, such as walrus ivory or the best part of the bearded seal skin; he also took some edible parts. The rest was divided among the other categories of people. Hunts in which this kind of distribution was likely to occur would include the late summer caribou hunt, the fall walrus hunt, cooperative hunting on the ice, or even the egg-gathering excursions of a large group. We have seen that in a way the procurer was a temporary isumatak in a group where there were no pre-existing lines of authority.

The more common types of hunting were done by a family-camp group, members of those few households living together as a restricted ilagiit, and in this kind of regularly cooperative group there was already a pre-existing leader, the isumatak. If it was a rich family, he might also have been an umialik and so control the summer migrations of his whole group. In such hunting, the isumatak was the one who oversaw the distribution of game. No matter who killed the game, it was nevertheless brought to the isumatak, who usually made the first cuts and gifts himself. In any case, he watched the whole performance, making suggestions as to which parts should go to whom. His household would often get the best parts, or those parts he particularly wanted or needed. And, if the game was very large or plentiful, he might later invite all the men to his household for a feast. Here we see the prototype for redistribution as an economic mode: "Appropriational towards a centre and out again." (Polanyi 1957:250) However, it can be said that for each kill the economic mode was redistribution integrating the group present through the center, but that taken over all the system was one of reciprocity in that small groups in turn were obligated to give to each other in similar ways.

Consumption. We have seen how the products of the hunt were initially distributed and hence how they arrived at each household. But this is not the end of the story. Each household presumably got an adequate supply of those various essential raw materials through the system described above. Figure 2 illustrates the rules of consumption of the most important sea mammals; note that certain parts were designated for men, others for women

FIGURE 2 DISTRIBUTION OF GAME

Parts of the animal: 1. Eyes, 2. Head, 3. Thoracic vertebrae and ribs, 4. *Maktak* and blubber on lower ⅔ of thoracic section, 5. Viscera, 6. Forelimbs, 7. Maktak and blubber of upper ⅓ of thoracic section, 8. Lumbar, sacral and caudal vertebrae, 9. Maktak and blubber of rear section, 10. Flukes, 11. Cloaca, 12. Heart.

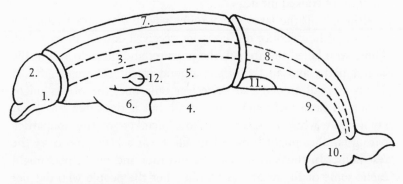

A. *Qilalugak* (White whale)

1. Dogs, 2. Men, 3. Everyone in the settlem'ent, 4. Women, 5. Dogs of the hunter(s) who killed it, 6. Everyone, 7. Hunter's household, 8. Women, 9. Hunter who killed it, 10. Everyone, 11. Dogs, 12. Men.

B. *Aivirk* (Walrus)

The walrus was cut up and distributed in the same manner as was the white whale, except for the skin. The skin of the walrus was not highly valued and was distributed for dog food among all those in the camp.

C. *Natsiq, Qairulik, Ujjuk* (Seals)[a]

Head, eyes, forelimbs, thoracic vertebrae, and heart	Women
Cervical and lumbar vertebrae	Men
Ribs, sternum, and attached meat	Hunter who killed it
Lumbar meat	Men in the hunting party
Sacral and caudal vertebrae, hind flippers	Cooked in broth and eaten by all

The skin goes to the successful hunter and his party.

---

[a] Slight differences among the three seals have been ignored.

and children. A boy was asked to eat of the men's part "in his own right" when the other men felt that he was a competent enough hunter. This was by no means at the time of the first kill but occurred some years later. Cooked parts, however, might be eaten by anyone and broth was an essential and relished part of the meal of cooked meat.

Although all the large game animals were distributed among a number of households, not everyone received equally of each kill. Those who killed the animal, the procurer and his helpers, got the largest parts, and all the others around might get small gifts. If it was a small animal and there was only one, the others might come and eat a piece and that was all; but if the catch was large, say a white whale or several caribou, members of the nonparticipating families might bring a bag, fill it, eat a little, and carry the rest home. In times of plenty, the procurer and his helpers might cache some of the meat and blubber, but the people who did not participate rarely had enough for more than immediate consumption.

After the kill and the distribution, sharing did not stop. Anyone who happened to be visiting when the household members were eating was asked to join in, and visiting was the major social recreation of the Eskimos. Small gifts were given to family members especially when they were in need, either in the same camp or even when visiting other camps. These might include not only food but also essentials such as ivory or sinew and sometimes caribou skins. When people were in need, they were taken care of after the household members themselves. However, those nonrelatives who had experienced either temporary or long-term hardships would also be provided for and no one was ever refused when he asked for something when it was available, although those who constantly begged were looked upon as burdens and would be the first to suffer in times of real hardship.

Economic Ideas. The Eskimos held in the highest esteem a generous man who was always ready to give of what he had. Such men were thought of as rich because, presumably, they always had plenty to give, whereas those who did not share but hoarded for themselves were seen as poor and of low prestige. To be distinguished from the latter, one had to keep parts of the kill for one's whole family rather than for oneself; this was a "worthy cause" so long as it was not carried to extremes. The same ideals applied to help given or withheld as well as to material objects.

Particularly reprehensible was any kind of dishonest act that involved lying or withholding the truth. Stealing was differentiated from taking, which was quite all right as long as one told the person from whom one had taken about it as soon as possible afterward. A constant thief was often run out of the community or even killed. If he was very old or infirm, however, and could not possibly provide for himself, he was tolerated as long as there was reasonable plenty. Similarly, envy of material items or of sexual partners was frowned upon, although it was basic to much of the gossip. Those who acted as hosts as often as they visited had prestige as opposed to those who were always to be found at someone else's when they knew food was available. The ideal in most matters was to share or exchange so that no one was left without. This carried through to the most highly valued items, such as spouses and children in marriage or adoption.

However, not all items could be exchanged for each other. Generally, food was shared all around. Help was exchanged between those who were undertaking tasks greater than one person could carry out, such as a caribou hunt or the building of an umiak. Help and food were often in the same sphere of exchange. When a man helped a widow to erect a snow house, he would get a meal, or when a widower did a favor for a woman, she might soften his boots. Women, however, were only exchanged for women; there was no idea of "buying" a man's daughter or wife for sex or marriage with a gift of a kajak or plenty of food, unless the match was suitable on other grounds. Similarly, children were exchanged for children, but only in the most extreme hardship. These were some of the most deeply held values of the society, and anyone who crossed them was looked upon either as a scoundrel or a fool. There was one exception: a shaman would always ask something for his personal services, although not for his public exhibitions. He might ask a man for his wife for a few days in return for bringing him better hunting, or he might take someone's daughter for a second or third wife in return for curing him of some affliction. Thus the shaman broke the rules but he was, after all, in charge of many of the rules, the taboos, himself. Indeed, it appears from the accounts of many of my informants that he made up many of the minor taboos as he went along to suit his own purposes (Turner 1888:179–180).

The shaman, then, was the only one who could regularly and without fear of supernatural or human punishment "cross-up" the spheres of exchange. Even so, these "conversions" between different spheres of exchange (Bohannan and Dalton 1965:8) were made up on the spur of the moment. Both within the spheres of exchange and between them, there were no set equivalents, except perhaps women for women and children for children. There was no measure of value, nothing like two tusks for a bearded seal skin or a cooked meal for building a kajak. In other words, there was nothing resembling in any way our commercial ideas of "money" or "value."

Abnormal Circumstances. Under this heading are considered (1) annual and life-cycle events, (2) periods of great food shortage, and (3) economic relations between Eskimos of different areas.

When there was an abundance of game of one sort or another, the procurer (or procurers) of this game would invite everyone in the camp to a feast in or near his tent or igloo. If a large sea mammal was caught, these feasts would be separate for the two sexes. The women were invited by the hunter's wife to eat the raw meat and cartilage of the thoracic vertebrae. Each would arrive bringing her ulu knife and the children who were too small to be left alone, and the feast might go on for two or three hours. If the kill was really large, the invitees might bring small bags to take home what they could not eat. For men, a similar feast was held for the consumption of the cervical and lumbar meat. The male host basked in the prestige of being able to provide for so many *tujurngminat*, "guests, invited strangers." Men did not usually take excess meat home. As mentioned above, when the kill was a land animal, such as caribou, the affair included both sexes and it was most usual for the women of other households to turn up to carry off the gifts, even though both the host and his wife were present to entertain. Sometimes such feasts were held after the first successful spring hunts of caribou or seal, for this was an exciting time of year when game began to appear and visiting and sociability lost their late-winter overtones of self-interest.

One of the very few special nonkin relationships was that between a boy and his mother's midwife; the latter called him *angusiak*, meaning "beautiful male." A month or so after birth, if the child was still living, the parents of a child gave the midwife (or midwives) a small gift. Later on, when the young boy got his first game, he sent or gave a good and useful part of it to the midwife and gave the rest to the whole community, even though each might only get a small part. A similar custom was usually observed by all men at the end of their first successful hunt of the season. Thus, the older women who acted as midwives were provided for at this time of year as long as they lived, relieving the burdens of old age and, probably, widowhood.

Times of great shortage of food usually came at the end of the winter, although if the fall hunting had been too poor to cache a good stock of provisions, they occurred at the beginning of winter. At these times, the essential sharing patterns often broke down. Generally, those who were of least "use" to the group, such as very old people, cripples, and young children, might be abandoned, not necessarily without hope of being returned to if hunting became good. Often the old people would ask to be left behind or even killed if they felt they were useless, for those who died a violent death were thought to go to the highest of the Eskimos' "three heavens" (Balikci 1960b). The first to suffer were those who had no ilagiit to help them for people usually tried to help their own families, but if things got worse even members of one's family might be abandoned.

There came a point at which each man or couple was out to save his own skin, although it went against the grain to let kin suffer. The ambivalence of these dire situations is well seen in the words of my old informant quoted earlier in this chapter. When there simply was no food and the people were hungry for days on end, they would eat their dogs, bedding, and clothing, roughly

73

in that order. After that, they resorted to cannibalism. Generally, the children were eaten first; they might be killed or they might have died already of starvation, but they would keep their parents — the mainstay of the society — alive for some time. At length the point was sometimes reached when there were only adult men and women alive. Those who died first were eaten by the survivors, but sometimes the latter did not wait for the weakest to die. In this area, it was far more frequently the women who killed or outlasted the men and who in the end ate their husbands. Perhaps it was because their slower metabolism allowed them to survive the rigors of starvation for longer. At Deception Bay, four women were found one spring, having eaten all their husbands and children, more than ten people.

The aftermath of cannibalism was never happy. Although they might be accepted into the group that found them, people who had participated in cannibalism were always looked upon with suspicion and suffered from guilt. For instance, the Sugluk Eskimos said that, although all four of the women mentioned above remarried and had more children, one after the other they all went mad, probably from guilt. Another woman, the last to survive of her group, could not bring herself to eat her kinsmen but managed to survive by eating the lice on their bodies. One further result, although rare, was that the successful cannibals would come to prefer human flesh and after rescue would neglect the meat brought them by their rescuers and instead would kill and eat the rescuers themselves. Two men were said to have done this on Akpatuk Island in the last century and the island was abandoned for many years.

Economic relations with Eskimos of other areas were not of vital importance to the Takamiut: their area had most of the essentials of life, although large supplies of wood were only to be found in the southern parts. There seems to have been no organized enmity against Eskimos of any adjacent regions. One of my informants stated that when the Takamiut were coming south to Chimo to trade, they might meet a camp of the Ungavamiut just south of Payne Bay and would have wrestling matches and other competitions, but such activities were customary men's entertainment. Generally speaking, travelers visiting distant areas would try to meet or at least mention to strangers their ila, takujaksak, or *ilangnak* (friends). In time of plenty there was little to fear, but in bad times strangers were looked upon with even more suspicion than were local people. Of course, one of the yearly meetings was among people from all the coasts of Ungava who went inland for the summer caribou hunts. Favorite meeting places were lakes on the Povungnituk River, the headwaters of the North Payne River near Klotz Lake, Payne Lake, the headwaters of Kogaluk River beyond Tasiat Lake, Lac Bacqueville off the Leaf River, and even at Lake Minto at the head of the Leaf River. At these places camps would be made together after a successful hunt, and stories and news would be exchanged and small gifts given back and forth, especially if each group had a different selection of goods. Not all Eskimos made these migrations to the interior, but many might even marry or change their residence as a result of these meetings. Generally, a stranger or nonrelative would be expected to give a gift to his hosts if he was a good hunter, or he was expected at least to "listen to" and "follow" the isumatak of the strange camp. Shamans, however, were likely to be able to "get away with murder" on such visits (Turner 1894:179–180).

Low (1898:131A) thought that the northern Itivimiut Eskimos traded or obtained whalebone, which was rare in their area, from those on the north side of the Hudson Strait, and there are many references in literature to the crossing of the Strait. Hawkes (1916:142) reports an Eskimo legend that all those in the Hudson Strait originally came from Cumberland Sound and that many crossed the Strait between Cape Dorset and Wolstenholme via the three large islands, although it was considered a very dangerous crossing according to Boas (1888:462–463). Other Eskimos are thought to have crossed the Strait at the eastern end via Resolution Island and Killiniq. However, a Chimo version of the story stated that a man came walking on the water and was a great shaman making war on all he met!

There was and is a great affinity between the Takamiut and the Akianimiut (of southern Baffin Island). Most older informants remember repeated crossings by umiak (see Arima 1963:76) and meetings between the two groups when hunting walrus on the islands in the fall. Whether they traded is not really known but they were very friendly. Another factor, mentioned by early writers, was the need for Baffin Islanders to cross to Ungava for economic reasons. Chappell thought that:

Eskimo inhabiting the Northern Shores of the Hudson's Straits, migrate in the fall of the year, towards the South; for the double purpose of taking up their winter quarters, and of procuring fuel and game amongst the pine-tree forests of Labrador. (Chappell 1817:97–98)

Although such large-scale annual migrations probably never occurred, several other writers mention the latter reason for the long journey (e.g., McLean 1849). Payne (1888–89:217) mentions a man at Wakeham Bay who had lived many years on the north shore and my own records are full of people being related across the Straits.

Relations with the Indians were in great contrast. All my many informants, both Eskimo and Indian, stated that the Eskimos and Indians of the area had as little to do with each other as possible before the white man arrived, except when an opportunity presented for one group to surprise and kill the other. The Eskimos thought the Indians were aggressive, militant poachers. The Indians thought the Eskimos, whom they called *aijatsimijuuts* (the original word for Eskimo, meaning "eat-their-food-raw-people"), were crude people who behaved like animals and did not even know they had souls! My informants advanced no economic motive for this warfare; the Indians said they used to enjoy it and the Eskimos said they only attacked the Indians in revenge. Quite often, however, both groups were out hunting the same group of caribou and each would gladly raid the other's caches.

Only Kohlmeister and Kmoch (1814) state that the Indians and Eskimos of Ungava traded with each other, but even they admit that this was the calm between storms and that trading often broke up into fights and killing. Even these early attempts at trading were probably the results of the influence of the white man in the south of the area.

The bad relations Eskimos had experienced with non-Inuit were probably reflected in the behavior they first exhibited towards the white man, as we shall see in the following section.

We do not know if the Norsemen from Greenland ever visited the Hudson Strait as there are no records to indicate that they did so. There are no traditions of such a visit among the Eskimos nor are there any remains that could be interpreted as Norse. The first significant contacts in the area were probably made by the ill-fated voyage of Hudson in 1610.

The New World was discovered in the latter part of the fifteenth century and within a few decades many ships were crossing the Atlantic, partly for the good fishing to be found off the coasts of Newfoundland and Labrador. Some of these fishermen, most of whom were Portuguese, probably entered the Hudson Strait, but there are no exact records or remains of this. The English were more interested in exploring and in finding the trade routes to China and India, just as was Columbus. They generally sailed farther to the north than did the fishermen and so made most of the major discoveries of the eastern Arctic. Frobisher in 1576 discovered Baffin Island and, he thought, gold. Four of his crew on this voyage were killed by the Eskimos. In 1577, he returned to start a mine and again fought with the Eskimos. The following year, Frobisher came back to Frobisher Bay, but en route he entered the east end of Hudson Strait by mistake. In 1586 John Davis visited Frobisher's Bay, and then sailing southward he crossed the entrance of the Hudson Strait, remarking on the strong currents and tides there and naming the southern shore Cape Chidley. George Weymouth in 1602 sailed some way up the Hudson Strait, possibly as far as Cape Hopes Advance, but he does not mention the Eskimos. A few years later, while exploring the same area, Captain John Knight and three of his crew were killed by the Eskimos.

Henry Hudson, looking for a route to Asia, set out on his fourth voyage in 1610. After entering Frobisher Bay by mistake, he sailed into Ungava Bay, was trapped in the ice, freed the ship, and sailed on up the Hudson Strait. He sailed along the south shore, naming it Magna Britannia, and then struck northward because of the ice and sailed directly from Charles Island, passing (but not naming) Deception Bay, to Nottingham Island and Cape Wolstenholme. I mention this because this route became the accepted one for some 300 years and explains why Sugluk and the area around it were neglected so long. Hudson discovered the enormous rookeries of murres — some 7,000,000 nesting birds — at Digges Islands and near Ivujivik. His crew also discovered a cache of strangled birds there but made no contact with the natives. Wintering south in James Bay, they met an Indian the next spring and exchanged gifts with him. When food began to run short, some of his crew mutinied and cast Hudson and his loyal followers adrift in a small boat, never to be seen again. The rest of the crew returned northward trying to get home to England. They were nearly starving and were glad to reach the rookeries at Digges Islands, where they raided the nests and killed the birds.

In this area they met and befriended a group of Eskimos camped there. Prickett's description (in Asher 1860) of their intercourse is the first good account of the natives of this area, who form part of the same "tribe" as the peoples of Sugluk and Wakeham Bay. While entertaining the natives, the sailors dropped their guard and were set upon treacherously, four of them being killed by knives or arrows. The rest fled to England where they told their story in considerable detail (Asher 1860).

In 1612 Sir Thomas Button sailed up the Hudson Strait and into Hudson Bay, naming the Button Islands, Coats Island (Cary's Swans Nest), Mansel Island, and many other places. However, there is no record of contact with the Eskimos. An interesting part of his voyage was Button's explicit instructions from Prince Henry showing how to navigate up the Hudson Strait:

being in . . . keep the northern side, as moste free of the pester of ice . . . till past Cape Henry [Big Island?] . . . following the leading ice between King James [Cape Weggs] and Queen Anne's Foreland [Charles Island] . . . make all the haste ye may to Salisbury Island . . . (Low 1906)

In other words, the currents and ice of the Hudson Strait were well enough known by then for ships to be directed away from the area of Sugluk and Deception Bay. Following these pioneering expeditions, many others, including Baffin (1615), Jens Munck (ca. 1615), Fox (1631), and James (1631), made their way through the Hudson Strait either to trade with the Indians of Hudson Bay or to continue looking for the Northwest Passage.

Meanwhile, the French discovered and colonized the St. Lawrence River valley. They heard about the possible riches to be gained by trading furs with the Indians of Hudson Bay and sent two parties overland — Bourdon (1656) and Dablon (1661) — to claim the country for the king and to sign trading treaties, as well as to convert the natives to the true faith. The French authorities, however, were not shrewd enough to see the trading possibilities, so two Frenchmen, Radisson and Groseilliers, obtained financing in England for a "Company of Merchant Adventurers into Hudson Bay" (1667). This was to become the famous and still thriving Hudson's Bay Company of which we will hear much more. These two sailed for the Hudson Bay (1668) with a New England captain and established a trading fort at Ruperts River. Later, forts were opened all along the southern coast of the bay by Bayly (1670) and others. From this time on ships regularly sailed through the Hudson Strait carrying furs and trade goods for the trading forts or "factories."

The rivalries between the French and English grew, and from 1685 to 1713 the French sent many overland expeditions that methodically destroyed every fort and post of the English in Hudson Bay. The French, however, were defeated in Europe, and the Treaty of Utrecht forced them to give up all the lands and posts they had captured.

In the next fifty years, many traders and explorers passed through the Straits without making significant contact with the natives. In 1749 the Hudson's Bay Company opened a post at Richmond Gulf, probably the first post to cater regularly to the Eskimos and almost certainly the first to serve the Eskimos of Ungava. It is not known whether the Takamiut traded into this post or even if they traded with the intervening tribes to get European goods, but it is doubtful. The post was closed in 1756 because of unsatisfactory relations between the Indians and the Eskimos, and because a clerk was killed, most probably by the Eskimos. The store was removed to Great Whale River and this location was abandoned in turn in 1790. A new post was reestablished at Richmond Gulf in 1923 but this has been closed in the last decade.

The Hudsons' Bay Company was loath to abandon the area of Northern Quebec. In 1793 it reopened Great Whale for a time and the location of the post alternated between there and Fort George to the south until 1837, when a small new post was erected at Great Whale which has been in operation ever since. Little Whale River also has had a post intermittently from 1820 or so to the present. Both these posts were situated to benefit from the trade with the Cree Indians, and it is doubtful if the Eskimos were as frequent visitors there (until later in the century) as they had been at Richmond Gulf.

On the other side of the land mass other acculturative agents were also making inroads into the relatively unknown land. In 1770 the first Moravian missionaries established outposts on the Atlantic coasts of Labrador. These settlements, often quite substantial, ministered to the acquisitive desires of the Eskimo as well as the spiritual. Small stores selling only essential goods were opened along with each mission. Some of the Eskimos of Ungava Bay heard about them and occasionally traveled across the Torngat Mountains or round Cape Chidley to Okkak. The missionaries were bothered by the presence of more "heathen savages," and in 1811 Kohlmeister and Kmoch set out by boat and explored parts of Ungava Bay. They found the huge Koksuak River and a spot some miles from the sea that seemed a likely place to open a new mission for the further extension of Christian knowledge.

The publication of their report (1814) brought a further series of changes to the area. The Hudson's Bay Company, fearful of losing some potentially rich profits to the Christian traders, sent Clouston, and later Hendry, inland to explore the interior of the Ungava Peninsula (1819–20). Finally, the Hudson's Bay Company employed Finlayson and Erlandson, who crossed the Ungava Peninsula and built a new trading fort at Chimo in 1830. This was on the exact spot the Moravians had noted as being suitable for a mission building. Fort Chimo catered to both the Eskimos and the Naskapi Indians of the area, but the game proved poor and the problems of supply even more difficult, so it was abandoned in 1842. During this period from 1830 to 1842 a number of overland crossings were made between Chimo and Hamilton Inlet, far to the south on the Atlantic Coast. Also a number of smaller outposts were opened at South River, now called Fort McKenzie (1832), False River (1833), George River (1838), and Indian House Lake (1838), as well as many farther south. All these northern posts were abandoned when Chimo was shut down in 1842. An interesting and vivid account of the whole saga of the first Fort Chimo was written by the novelist R. M. Ballantyne in his book *Ungava* (1857). Although many Eskimos from both sides of Ungava Bay traded into Chimo and the other posts, there are no records of extensive trade with the northern Takamiut at that time.

In 1845 Sir John Franklin, with his two ships the *Erebus* and the *Terror*, was lost in the Arctic islands area while trying to find the Northwest Passage. This event aroused the curiosity and interest of much of the world, and parties, publicly and privately supported, set out to find him. Low reports (1906) that from 1847 to 1859 more than thirty separate expeditions set out to find the lost British Navy party. Most of these people passed through the Hudson Strait and, although they did not add to our knowledge of the Takamiut, they probably added more knowledge about Arctic geography and the Eskimos, in general, than in any other period of history. A number of good publications concerning the Eskimos and the area resulted (e.g., Hall 1862).

From about 1860 on, the American whaling fleet moved its operations from the northern Atlantic and Davis Strait to dominate the hunt in the Hudson Bay. The Americans hardly touched the south coast of the Hudson Strait except for the crew of a rowing boat escaping from a shipwreck which put into Wakeham Bay, and they were murdered by Eskimos who could not resist trying to steal their equipment (Payne 1888–89:223). The Eskimos of the northern coast of the Strait, however, became quite familiar with the white man: they were employed in the summer for hunting and mining and traded well-made implements and carvings. Though there has always been some intercourse between the Eskimos on both sides of the Strait, it is probable that the activities of those in the north had relatively little influence in the south compared with the reopening of the store at Fort Chimo. American whaling continued in force until about the turn of the century, by which time many other new developments had taken place, and then its decline was rapid.

The most important influence in the second half of the nineteenth century was the reopening of the post at Fort Chimo in 1866. This was soon followed by the reopening of the smaller outposts at Whale River and George River. Within the next two decades, the fame of Fort Chimo spread and the Takamiut some 300 to 400 miles or more to the northwest began to take an interest in trade. At first, they probably passed on their excess skins to their neighbors to the east in exchange for the white man's products. Very soon they began sending representatives to Chimo by sled each spring with loads of furs from all the families, thus familiarizing themselves with the white man face to face. At first, trade was intermittent at Chimo because of the mutual fear between the Eskimos and Indians who both used the post. However, the Hudson's Bay Company cracked down on any open hostilities in the area, and later missionary efforts also did much to allay overt expressions of interethnic violence. A Roman Catholic mission was established at Chimo in 1873.

In 1867 Canada ceased to be a British colony and became a dominion. As we have seen, the Canadian government had displayed little interest in its Northland until this period, but this neglect was replaced by enlightened self-interest. At that time, also, Canada bought from the Hudson's Bay Company the whole of Ruperts Land, some 1.5 million square miles surrounding the Hudson Bay and including much of the Northwest Territories that had until that time been the private preserve of this enterprising company. Arctic Quebec, that area north of civilization, was also deemed to be under control of the federal government of Canada and was ceded to become part of the province of Quebec only in 1917.

In the late nineteenth century the Canadian government started to send official expeditions to explore the regions of the Hudson Bay and the North. One of the more famous authorities was Bell of the Canadian Geological Survey, who explored both the east and west coasts of the Hudson Bay — mainly for geological reasons. In addition to having an official interest in the geological resources of the area, the Canadian Parliament raised the possibility of opening a sea route to England from Fort Churchill via the Hudson Strait. This route, tied in with building a railway from Winnipeg to Churchill, cut the distance from central Canada to Europe by nearly 1,000 miles because it followed the great-circle route. The two main motivations were the export of the agricultural riches of Manitoba and Saskatchewan to England and, it was hoped, the importation of hundreds of thousands of immigrants from Europe at very cheap rates.

Although the distances were known to be shorter, there were questions about the feasibility of the navigation of the Hudson Straits because of the well-recognized difficulties of ice, currents, and weather. The Canadian Government Expedition of 1884–86 was mounted to solve some of these problems. A ship was chartered and sent north to make observations of the conditions. In addition, a number of observation posts were set up on land at various points on the Hudson Strait, the most important object being the reporting of ice and weather conditions. These observation stations were at Port Burwell (near Cape Chidley), where Mr. Burwell was in charge; Ashe Inlet (Big Island), where Mr. Ashe was left; Stupart Bay just east of Wakeham Bay, where Mr. Stupart was in charge and Mr. Payne stayed; Nottingham Island; and Point Laperrière, Digges Islands. These measures not only made great contributions to the Canadian economy and meteorology, but also resulted in a number of publications describing the Eskimos and resources of the area around Wakeham Bay, then known as Prince of Wales Sound (Stupart 1886; Payne 1888–89). These are the earliest reports of the Takamiut written by residents in the area. The Eskimos there, who had been accustomed to trading more than 300 miles away at Fort Chimo, were most pleased to see civilization "brought to their doorstep." The post, however, was not there for trading and the Eskimos' many attempts to steal from the stores in times of starvation led to some unpleasant disruptions and suspicions. In addition to the many reports from those stationed at Stupart Bay, the captain of the ship and a government observer both wrote lengthy reports, much of which related to the Eskimos (Gordon 1886; Tuttle 1885).

Further information about our particular group of Eskimos was gathered and published by Lucien Turner (1888, 1894) who lived for a year at Fort Chimo collecting natural history specimens for the Smithsonian Institution. He noted that the Takamiut arrived every spring or so to trade their furs and that they were considerably wilder and more aboriginal than the Eskimos around Chimo itself, who had been in direct contact with the white man for some twenty years or more. The writings of Turner, Payne, and Stupart provide a large fund of information on the traditional life of the Eskimos and the effects of the early contacts.

During the 1880's the Church of England in Canada, now known as the Anglican Church of Canada, started to move north in its missionary efforts. A mission had been established at Little Whale River and had been visited intermittently since a few decades earlier. The Reverend Peck, who had worked with the Cree Indians, visited there in 1876 and then attempted an unsuccessful journey across the Ungava Peninsula to Fort Chimo. In 1885, taking the route previously taken by Hendry of the Hudson's Bay Company, he successfully crossed from Richmond Gulf to Chimo, where, seeing the need, he had an Anglican mission opened in the 1890's. Another mission was also set up for the Indians of Fort George in 1885 and for both Indians and Eskimos at Great Whale River in 1890. A method of writing Cree in syllabic symbols had been worked out earlier. Reverend Peck translated the Bible, the Prayer Book, and some hymns into Eskimo, using a modified version of the same syllabary which the Eskimos found extremely easy to learn, even teaching themselves. In 1894, Reverend Peck felt the call to go to Baffin Island and set up a mission at the site of an old Scottish whaling station at Blacklead Island in Cumberland Sound. His place at Great Whale was taken by the Reverend Watson and the incumbency at Chimo by the Reverend Stewart. Both these men extended their teaching north in the following decade: Reverend Watson went as far as Povungnituk and Reverend Stewart traveled throughout Ungava Bay and perhaps farther west along the Hudson Strait. The church now at Sugluk claims to have converted the Eskimos as early as 1902, but there are no other records of this. Low (1906) said that the Eskimos there in 1904 had never seen white men. It is probable that a great many of the conversions and acquisition of holy texts took place during the spring trading excursions to Chimo and Great Whale River.

After the observations in the Hudson Strait from 1884 to 1886, the government continued to support exploration in the area. Most of the explorations were under the charge of Low of the Geological Survey. Low wrote voluminous reports on James Bay and the country east of Hudson Bay explored in 1887; the interior of the Labrador Peninsula (1892–95); the south shore of Hudson Strait (Douglas Harbour to George River, 1897); and the east coast of the Hudson Bay from Cape Wolstenholme to James Bay (1898–99). This left only the Takamiut area unexplored. In 1903, in his last expedition aboard the *Neptune*, Low explored the area from Douglas Harbour to Wolstenholme as well as other parts of the Hudson Bay. He noted then that this was the last coast in the area to be officially explored and mapped, and he passed by Deception Bay where he said the whaler *Arctic* had twice anchored.

About thirty miles west of Deception Bay the mouth of another long inlet, known as Sugluk Bay [to the Eskimos] was entered . . . the water was very deep and an anchorage could only be obtained . . . close under the rocky cliffs of both shores. . . .
    At the head of the bay three families of natives were found, living in a state of destitution. This was their first direct contact with white men; they were somewhat shy and frightened, but a present of tobacco and biscuit soon made all good friends. These people do not visit any of the far away trading posts [Chimo and Great Whale], but trade their furs with their neighbors on the east or west for guns and other articles of civilization. (Low 1906:66)

This is the first published report on the Sugluk area and confirms that it was one of the most out-of-the-way places even until this century. Although Low mentions only three families, it is quite possible that others were inland caribou hunting and that some of them may very well have visited Chimo. Low later visited Eric Cove, near Cape Wolstenholme, noting:

> . . . the fine convenient stream of fresh water. . . . Eric Cove is an excellent harbour . . . and a good anchorage is found within a quarter of a mile of its head. . . . An excellent site for houses might be found on the plain near the mouth of the river. (*Ibid.*:15)

He does not mention the population of the area, and it is quite likely that there were no Eskimos there at that particular time.

Social Relations with the Early White Men. Before either the mainland or the islands of North America were "discovered," contact had been lost with the Greenland colonies. When contact was later re-established by Davis and others, there were no "Norsemen" left — only Eskimos who had not been in the area of Greenland when it was originally settled by Europeans. It is most probable that the white settlers were all killed by the Eskimos, and Eskimo mythology confirms this. Hypotheses that the Norse interbred with the Eskimos leading to a race of "blond Eskimos" or that they migrated south and west have been effectively disproved. It is probable that the Norsemen were wiped out by the modern Thule Eskimos who had spread eastward throughout the area since 1200 A.D. Perhaps this is what happened to the Tunit as well, although interbreeding was more likely in that case.

In the sixteenth century the first explorers had trouble with the Eskimos. Earlier in this chapter we mentioned the difficulties of Frobisher, some of whose men were killed, and of Captain Knight, who with three of his crew was killed in 1602. Since we have no accounts of these encounters we do not know why the trouble started. However, Abacuk Prickett (in Asher 1860) gave a very full first-hand account of Hudson's fateful voyage. The first encounter in the Hudson Bay was with a single native, and there was a generous exchange of gifts. The crew of Hudson's ships, especially Hudson himself, seemed extremely well-disposed towards these "savages" and generally lavished gifts upon them and liked to entertain and befriend them. Unless Prickett is lying, they acted in a most "Christian" manner. The second encounter, after the mutiny, was made with Eskimos in an umiak and six kajaks at Digges Islands while the crew were hunting murres and their eggs. The Eskimos gave every appearance of being friendly; so, as a gesture of confidence, an Eskimo came aboard the ship while one of the Englishmen went into the umiak and back to the Eskimo camp. At the camp this man showed the Eskimos that his gun could kill more murres than their snares. The Eskimos greeted the small boat that carried more men to their camp:

They made great joy with dancing, and leaping, and stroking of their breasts: they offered diverse things to our men, but they only took morses teeth [ivory tusks] which they gave them for a knife and two glass buttons: and so receiving our men they came on board, much rejoicing at this chance, as if they had met the most simple and kind people of the world. (Prickett in Asher 1860:128)

The crew was so enamored of the natives that no one stood on his guard; Prickett says, "God blinding him so!" The next day, seven of the crew members, including Prickett, went back to the camps. The Eskimos came bearing more gifts "to barter" but Henry Greene held out until the Eskimos had brought venison (caribou meat) as they had promised by signs. While the whites were entertaining them, the Eskimos signaled as if to walk somewhere:

Not one of [our crew] had any weapon about him, not so much as a sticke, save Henry Greene only who had a piece of pike in his hand: nor saw I any thing that they had wherewith to hurt us. [Two men] had looking glasses and Jews trumps, and bells, which they were shewing the people. The savages standing round about them, one of them came into the boats head to shew me a bottle. . . . (Ibid.:129)

This was an idyllic scene, and an example of good interracial relationships, each group being friendly with and confident of the other. However, while Prickett was talking to the man at the front of the boat:

. . . another stole behind me at the sterne of the boat . . . but suddenly I saw the legge and foot of a man by me. Wherefore I cast up my head and saw the savage with a knife in his hand, who strooke at my breast over my head: I cast up my right arm to save my breast, he wounded my arm and stroke my body under my pappe. (Idem.)

Although struck again and badly wounded, Prickett managed to fight off the savage.

Whiles I was thus assaulted in the boat, our men were set upon on shore. [Two men] had their bowels cut out and [two others] being mortally wounded came tumbling into the boat together . . . [another] manfully made good the head of the boat against the savages, that pressed sore upon us. . . . The savages betook them to their bowes and arrowes, which they sent amongst us, wherewith Henry Greene was slaine out right and Pichael Perse received many wounds. . . . I received a cruelle wound in my back with an arrowe . . . [the savages] ranne to their boats [but did not follow]. (*Ibid.*:130–31)

Thus, four men died, and for reasons that Prickett could not explain. I mention this story at length not only because it is the first account, but also because it is so detailed and sets forth so clearly that the attack was initiated by the Eskimos, and, as such, is typical of many other occurrences.

Presumably by the late seventeenth century, the Eskimos — themselves relative newcomers to the area — were fairly familiar with tales of these new strangers in the area. The Eskimos called them *qallunak* which some have claimed as originally Greenlandic, but in all accounts this was the only word for white men. This leads us to hypothesize an early diffusion of the word for them and the idea across the whole of the eastern Arctic. Qallunak is probably a derivative of the word *qalluk*, meaning "eyebrow," a feature in which the white man is better endowed than the Eskimo. Early relations with these strangers were ambiguous and often ended in disaster for one or both groups.

In the eighteenth century, events similar to that described by Prickett occurred all along the Labrador coast. The first ambitious settler, Courtmanche, had his large fishing station destroyed by the Eskimos:

During the winter [of 1704], they tore down his stages, destroyed his nets and stole his boats. He tried to make peace with them but was unsuccessful. . . .

Their system of attack was to creep up upon the unsuspecting fishermen in the dense fog and so terrify them with their unearthly yells that they would abandon their property and flee. . . . At other times, the Eskimo would advance and engage in trade, when they had thrown their adversaries off their guard for the moment, they would attack and kill the whole crew. (Hawkes 1916:4–5)

This is familiar! Some opinions are raised, from time to time, that the Eskimo only became warlike after having been badly treated by the white man or set upon by the Indians for the white man's purposes, but these and many other stories effectively dispel such notions. After all, Hudson was the first white man in the area when his crew was attacked!

After the first tragic attempt of the Moravians at converting the Eskimo [1752, when a party, including the interpreter, were murdered] a successful station was established at Nain in 1771. (*Ibid.*:19)

Because of these, and many other encounters, the Eskimos became known as warlike and treacherous savages. Chappell, who was in the Hudson Strait during the second decade of the nineteenth century, warned:

But the master of a vessel, during such an expedition, should be particularly cautious in not trusting a boat on shore, unless well armed; and by no means ought he to admit more than two or three Eskimo at the same time into his vessel, however friendly they might appear to be. (Chappell 1817:69–70)

He relates the story of an unfortunate Mr. Darby who tried to establish a whale fishery on the Labrador coast civilizing the "Esquimeaux Indians" (as he called them) only to have them burn his settlement, murder many of his people, and turn the product of their toil adrift on the merciless ocean (*ibid.*:161). More serious, perhaps, in the long run, was the encounter with the Hudson's Bay Company which opened a whale fishery and post at Richmond Gulf in 1749. The white men there were constantly harassed and when a clerk disappeared the white men took an Eskimo for hostage and later shot him in cold blood to "make an example." Trade became impossible, and the post was abandoned in 1756 and transferred to East Main and later to Great Whale River. Later reports told of seven more white settlers killed by the Eskimos in this area. The Eskimos of the area related to me that the young clerk had been killed in a game and then the post ransacked while the adults were away. There are other explanations for these events that put the original blame on the white man (Honigmann 1962:7–8).

Chappell and, slightly later, Captain Lyon (1824) had no trouble in dealing with the Eskimos of the Hudson Strait, although they were aware of the dangers. There were, of course, many peaceable and pleasant encounters with the Eskimos, such as that described by Prickett before the slaughter. These usually resulted from trade or a promise of trade that pleased both groups. Not all trade, however, led to peaceful good-byes. Chappell relates that when the ships came into view, the Eskimos' exultation knew no bounds. He also relates that the way to establish successful relations with the Eskimos, as with all "barbarous nations," was to bestow gifts upon their chiefs and priests but not on all, for that would lead to more demands and begging (Chappell 1817:71–72). Lyon notes that after trading:

The strangers were so well pleased with our society that they showed no wish to leave us, and, when the market had quite ceased, they began dancing and playing with our people on the ice alongside. (Lyon 1824:24)

Lyon reports that in addition to showing their satisfaction with what they had received from the whites, the Eskimos often seemed just plain sociable:

The exertion of dancing so exhilarated the Eskimaux that they had the appearance of being drunk, and played many extraordinary pranks. Amongst others, it was a favorite joke to run slyly behind the seaman, and, shouting loudly in one ear, to give him at the same time a very smart slap on the other. . . . Among other sports, some of the Eskimaux, rather roughly, but with great good Humour, challenged our people to wrestle . . . (and one officer taught the Eskimo ladies how to bow, curtsy, shake hands, and turn their toes out!). (*Ibid.*:26–27)

Later, near Cape Dorset, Lyon sighted a party of eight kajaks and one umiak, but they would not come near the ship. Although the white men caught up with them and they exchanged a few commodities, these Eskimos seemed very shy and different from most others (*ibid.*:34–35). When the Hudson's Bay Company post was first opened at Fort Chimo in 1830 the Eskimos were at first shy and, although they were afraid of the Indians, they seemed to have a fear of the white man, too. The details of the problems in getting the Eskimos to trade were related by Erlandson (1834) and Ballantyne (1857).

Payne, who was at Wakeham Bay in 1884–85, relates:

Among those living at Cape Prince of Wales were three desperate characters who, some years ago, attacked part of the shipwrecked crew of the whaler named "Kitty" while they slept in a tent on the shore not far from the observatory. (Payne 1888–89:223)

One of my older Sugluk informants told me that two of the men were Pakvik and Qiatsuk, the former being the leader. They killed the white men because they thought they were "taking away the food." As a result, these two were tatooed across the bridges of their noses, as was the custom in those days for people who killed white men. This suggests that such killings were quite common and that the killers were held in high regard. My informant admitted that such things were common before the coming of the missionaries (in the first decade of this century).

As described above, Low, who was the first white man to arrive at Sugluk, in 1904, found Eskimos who had not seen white men before. The Eskimos were very shy and frightened, but after being given gifts and food they became more friendly. Jimmy Ford, who opened a store in the Payne Bay region for the Hudson's Bay Company in 1923, gave a similar description of the isolated inland Eskimos there.

My Eskimo informants, when asked what their forefathers had passed on about the first encounters with whites, recall similar ambiguities. They told me that some of them had fled for the hills, leaving everything behind at the sight of the huge ships and the sound of the thunderous guns. Others, however, became friendly, but were always suspicious and killed the intruders whenever they had the opportunity. In later years, after stories about the whites had diffused through the area, the Eskimos often blamed the white men for poor hunting years, claiming that the white men were getting too much game. We do know, in fact, that by the use of large nets and guns the whites were able to get far more seals, whales, and walrus than the Eskimos ever had. The informants said that this was an additional reason the Eskimos wanted to kill the white men in the area.

The early social relations between the native and the visiting peoples were, as we have seen, extremely unpredictable. They ranged from extremes of joy and companionship to extremes of slaughter and treachery. Some hypotheses may be considered in the light of the evidence. Among the common hypotheses are the following:

1. That the nature of the Eskimos was always treacherous — and still is!
2. That the Eskimos were unable to overcome their desire for European goods, and, when thwarted in any way or when they could see the possibility of getting more than by mere trade, they would turn on the visiting whites. This is the commonest explanation in the literature.
3. That the Europeans were seen as, and were in fact, allies of the Indians who were the Eskimos' long-time mortal enemies. (Balikci 1960b:66)

All these are partially true but do not explain the particular *occasions* when one or another type of behavior was exhibited. The Eskimos, themselves, in addition to their reasons I have already mentioned, explain that the natural reaction of anyone when he first sees a strange being is to flee or to kill it. They point out that today when someone strange walks into a tent the children all cry. But this explanation does not account for the variety and occasions of behavior reported, for much of it does not apply to situations of "first contact."

In their relations with their long-time enemies, the Indians, the Eskimos were slaughtered more often than vice versa. They would only attack the Indians when they were sure they were in larger numbers (although the Indians are known to have been beaten, rarely, even when they were the aggressors). Similarly, when one man wanted to murder another, either to get a wife or in revenge or execution, he would attack him from behind, or even when he was asleep, or when he was distracted by conversation or hunting. Thus, in all cases of premeditated violence, the Eskimos chose the most opportune moment, giving them the greatest chance of success and the least danger to themselves. They were realistic opportunists and did not seek out danger: there was enough in their everyday lives. They always used methods of stealth, surprise, or treachery in killing the whites. Where the whites were obviously overwhelmingly more numerous or powerful, such as when Lyon met the umiak and seven kajaks or when Low's party met the poor people of Sugluk, the Eskimos acted shy, meek, and frightened, with consequently little danger to themselves. This technique, however, did not work for the Indians who would kill Eskimos in whatever state they found them. There must have been many, many occasions when the Eskimos fled at the approach of white ships, and these went unreported because they were unobserved. I think this principle of realistic opportunism fully explains the type of behavior the Eskimos exhibited in these early contacts.

Why they attacked the whites at all is another matter. Obviously, Balikci's explanation that it was because of the whites' Indian allies is not the whole story, for whites were killed long before they associated with Indians and in Arctic regions far from the Indians' lands. This may have been an additional and important factor in the south Hudson Bay and along the Labrador coast after whites had established settlements, but not all over the eastern Arctic. The second hypothesis is probably the most basic. There are many descriptions of the Eskimos' ecstacies over the acquisition of white men's products and their great eagerness to trade, as we shall see in the next section. Metals, above all iron, made such an improvement over their previous bone, stone, and ivory implements that they would go to any length *within the limits of personal safety* to obtain them. As Payne says concerning the behavior of Pakvik and Qiatsuk towards the shipwrecked crew of the *Kitty*:

At first they treated them well, often bringing them food, but their guns and blankets were too great a temptation, and with knives they dispatched them all, excepting one poor fellow whose feet had been badly frozen. (Payne 1888–89:223)

Presumably, this last man was no great threat, and the Eskimo's other nature, their great humanity and sociability, saved him, although he died the next spring.

Economic Relations. The very first recorded encounter between the natives of this region and visiting white men is again that of Hudson in 1611 (Prickett in Asher 1860). Prickett is quite explicit about the savage's idea of "trading" — more so than most later authors. Unfortunately, however, the "savage" seems to have been an Indian; although Prickett does not distinguish the various races, the mention of beaver skins, a sled being dragged behind, and the natives' setting the woods on fire, all in the south Hudson Bay, leads me to believe it could not have been an Eskimo (*ibid.*: 114–15).

The next encounter, which we have described above as ending in treachery near Digges Islands, also involved "trading." The description states quite explicitly that the Eskimos offered many gifts to the whites although the latter only took a few of them and gave a knife and two glass buttons in return. It seems the Eskimos gave gifts to ensure friendliness rather than to initiate some trade for "profit," for they were willing to give more than they received, and there had been no other white man in the area from whom they could have become familiar with trade. The next day again the Eskimos offered more gifts, but the white men held back and demanded venison. The Eskimos had obviously admired the first gifts of the whites, especially the knife, and wanted to enter into another series of gift exchanges, much as they probably did with strangers of their own kind (see the section on "Economic Organization" in this chapter). However, the reluctance of the whites and the intense desire for more white goods led the Eskimos to take the opportunity offered by their superior numbers and they slaughtered the whites. Although most of the whites managed to get away in the boat, they probably left some items and clothes behind so the Eskimos may have profited from the encounter, even though one was seriously wounded or killed (*ibid.*:130).

Frobisher too, as we described above, was harassed by the Eskimos during his three voyages after they had discovered the value of his possessions, and some of his men were killed when the opportunity was presented to the Eskimos (Hall 1865).

There is no doubt that the Eskimos soon acquired a great desire for the white man's goods, both out of curiosity and for their very practical use. At the top of the list was metal and we can quite imagine how much better metal parts of implements were compared with ivory harpoons, stone knives, and bone needles.

The early raids made upon white settlements on both the Labrador coast and the east coast of the Hudson Bay have been noted above, and in each raid the Eskimos sacked the posts and stole everything that seemed useful to them.

The Eskimos would seemingly go to any lengths to acquire what they wanted. Mr. Davison, exploring the Cape Smith area in 1786, stated: "Here we found Esquimeaux, who bartered away their dresses &c. with great avidity, for any sort of metal" (quoted in Chappell *op. cit.*:170–71). Captain Lyon mentions similar behavior in the Lake Harbour region (Lyon *op. cit.*:23). By the beginning of the eighteenth century, the Eskimos of the north coast of the Hudson Strait were most familiar with the annual arrival of the ships:

It should be observed that the arrival of the ships is considered by the Esquimeaux as a sort of annual fair; their little manufactures of dresses, spears &c are reserved for the expected jubilee. (Chappell *op. cit.*:57–58)

But this was not so common among the Takamiut, even late in the century:

[On the north shore] the men of the whalers [who] are constantly bartering with them [the Eskimos]; while those to the southward never have a chance of doing so. . . . (Payne 1888–89:216)

However, Chappell writes, when passing Charles Island which is on the southern side of the Strait:

[We were] visited by three canoes of Esquimeaux, bringing their usual commodities for traffic. (Chappell *op. cit.*:134)

Payne also hypothesizes that the Takamiut had:

. . . their furs . . . sent by one or two trusted traders to Captain Spicer's post on the north side of the Hudson Strait [near Lake Harbour]. (Payne 1888–89:221)

This must have been rare in view of the distance involved and the relatively few opportunities for making the dangerous crossing of the Straits.

It is obvious that in many places the Eskimos became quite familiar with these visiting ships, and Gordon observes:

Each of these ships [was] an unlicensed trader, competing with the Hudson's Bay Company for the trade of the natives. (Gordon 1886:62)

Tuttle remarks:

Every man on board ship, as soon as we got into Hudson Strait, became a trader, from the cook's-devil to the skipper, and for a few weeks it was unsafe to leave powder, shot, tobacco or any other article of commerce lying round loose, as they were liable to be converted into peltries. . . . (Tuttle 1885:80)

The nature of the trade carried on with the Eskimos is confusing when one reads the many accounts.

[It] should be called barter, for it consists of the direct exchange of commodities; in considering the value of this trade, the temper and character of the natives is a most important element. (*Ibid.*:65)

We know, then, that money or other common measures of value were not introduced by the itinerant ships. A system of standardized prices was used only by the Hudson's Bay Company at their permanent settlements, but their ships, also, were still engaged in such "barter" at this time.

Although the Eskimos were obviously familiar with trading activities, it is certain that they did not look upon them in the same light as did their white partners. Their behavior was most irregular, and different individuals or groups had different ideas about how to go about trading. The only thing they had in common was the intense desire for European goods.

In their dealings they manifested a strange mixture of honesty and fraud. At one moment I observed an Esquimeaux striving, with all his might, to convey into a sailor's hands the article for which he had already received equivalent; and, in ten minutes afterwards, I detected the same man in an endeavor to cut the hinder buttons off my own coat. (Chappell *op. cit.*:63–64)

Although there were no over-all means of comparing values, the accounts give us a fair idea of what the Eskimos received in trade:

A nail was considered a fair equivalent for a spear with ivory head, and with line and bladder attached to it. Small pieces of iron hoop were equally valuable and a knife might purchase any article. (Lyon *op. cit.*:23)

96

A more detailed list for the same period states:

> They value metals more than any other article of barter, and iron most of all. . . . I shall insert the prices . . . for some little curiosities, viz.
>
> A seal's-skin hooded frock, quite new, for a knife
> A seal's-skin pair of breeches . . . needle
> Seal's-skin boots . . . saw
> A pair of wooden spectacles . . . one bullet
> A pair of white feather gloves . . . two buttons
> A fishing lance or spear . . . file.
> (Chappell *op. cit.*:63–64)

In this instance, and we may suppose others, the Eskimos exchanged their manufactured objects for the European manufactured objects, although the latter, presumably, would last much longer than the former. Such exchanges with the Europeans were known as "Chi bo," according to Lyon (*op. cit.*:22), or "Chymo," according to Chappell (*op. cit.*:77–78), or at least were initiated by the calling out of the word. Most of the Eskimos seemed satisfied to exchange almost anything for metals or iron, although a few were more sophisticated:

> One Eskimo, finding no competitors, and that he was likely to have the market to himself, with great shrewdness exhibited only one article at a time, and kept at such a distance from the ship as to preclude all possibility of our overlooking his cargo. (Lyon *op. cit.*:30)

> . . . One man afforded much amusement by lying at a short distance and holding up a raw and bloody piece of blubber, for which he demanded a nail in exchange; showing at the same time his high sense of value of this equivalent by uttering loud cries, and licking the inviting morsel with as many smacks of the lips, and expressions of satisfaction. . . .

> There was another man, who possessed a far more enticing piece of goods, a fine unicorn's [narwhal] horn; but when he had received a piece of iron in exchange for it, he, with a shout of triumph, shoved off without giving up the horn. He seemed perfectly insensible to all our stratagems to allure him alongside, and in vain were glittering knives and other treasures displayed for this purpose. (*Ibid.*:36)

Others had nothing at all to offer to the whites:

> . . . one child . . . ran about holding up the red legs of a dovekie [bird] in hopes that their color might attract a customer; but meeting no success . . . a button I gave him. . . . (*Ibid.*:23)

97

A fine lively boy, in a most elegant white canoe, came paddling to us and keeping way with the ship, endeavoured to insinuate himself into our good graces by talking and laughing incessantly. He succeeded in his wish, and was enriched by presents of buttons, nails, beads, and pieces of old iron . . . cramming them into his mouth. (*Ibid.*:31)

This custom seems to have been very common:

No sooner had they received an article in exchange for their goods, than it was instantly applied to their tongue, and licked several times . . . (*Ibid.*:21)

Gifts, however, were not so licked. (*Idem.*)

The Eskimos, it seems, would go to any lengths to gain European goods:

Several . . . brought their wives on board the ship, and, in return for a tin spoon or a pot, compelled them, nothing loath, to receive our salutations. Nay, one man plainly intimated, that if I wished to hold a private conversation with his lady, he would have no objection to her visiting this cabin, provided I rewarded him with an axe. (Chappell *op. cit.*:65–66)

Some of our visitors . . . were very importunate in offering their wives in exchange for a knife, and the women were anxiously pressing the bargain. (Lyon *op. cit.*:26)

The men [of Chimo] would prostitute their women for gain very gladly with us, yet they are highly offended if their women commit a fault without their knowledge. (Finlayson 1830 in Davies 1963: Nov. 12, 1830)

None of these white men noted whether the bargains were struck, but some seem to have been, for Chappell notes that:

. . . women carefully remove [their hair] from every part of their body. (Chappell *op. cit.*:60). [Of course, in fact, they do not grow any!]

Both sexes sold their clothes, and some went away nearly naked, notwithstanding the severity of the weather. I must say, however, in justice to the softer sex, that they were more correct in the choice of what parts of their clothing they would dispose of, than the men even; for I do not remember to have seen a single lady part with her breeches, while the gentlemen were by no means so scrupulous, and evinced no shame at appearing nearly naked. (Lyon *op. cit.*:23)

Payne states, however:

On the north side of the Hudson Strait where vessels often call on their way to and from the Hudson Bay exchange of wives is sometimes practised, while on the south side, where there is little or no intercourse with these vessels, such a thing was never heard of, and it is well known that sailors who were allowed to act much as they liked on the north side were met with virtuous scorn by those living on the south side. (Payne 1888–89:224)

This does not mean, as we know, that the Takamiut did not exchange wives among themselves.

Surprising as it may seem in view of the Eskimos' great love of their children, some even tried to trade them off to the sailors when they had nothing else (Lyon *op. cit.*:24, 35), although the author admits that he might possibly have been mistaken. Perhaps, however, he was not, if the small child was a girl (not nearly so valued as boys among the Eskimos).

When all their goods had been exchanged, the Eskimos would resort to other methods. One of these involved various forms of begging:

One woman in particular attracted general notice by her unwearied application for presents, and by feigning to be hurt and by crying to excite compassion; in which she no sooner succeeded . . . (Lyon *op. cit.*:25)

They continued to pester us with the continual whine of this people, repeating incessantly the word "Pillitay! Pillitay!" signifying "Give us something!" . . . (Chappell *op. cit.*:71–72)

During the year that the observation station was at Stupart Bay (1884–1885), Payne notes many occasions of begging when the Eskimos were poorly off, and Tuttle generalizes about them:

. . . over sixty inhabitants . . . are in the habit of visiting the station building daily. They are peaceful and quiet but quite persistent beggars. (Tuttle *op. cit.*:175)

It seems, then, that the Takamiut were not much different from those on the north coast. The Stupart Bay observers, as well as those at Ashe Inlet, also noted that the Eskimos brought them presents of meat, venison, and fish whenever it was plentiful, thus preserving the essential reciprocity.

If all this failed, and when circumstances looked opportune, the Eskimos would steal whenever they could. John Davis notes as far back as 1586:

They are marvellously given to stealing, especially of iron . . . (quoted in Lyon *op. cit.*:30)

99

However, Lyon says that this is to be expected:

A few instances of dishonesty occurred where iron lay neglected in their view; but it is scarcely to be wondered that such a temptation should prove irresistable: had small gold bars been thrown in the streets of London, how would they have fared. (Lyon *op. cit.*:29)

John Finlayson remarks of the Chimo natives:

Everything belonging to us is sacred in their eyes; and considering their poverty and the temptation of a number of useful articles would naturally create, they are the most honest people in the world. (Finlayson 1830 in Davies 1963)

And among themselves, Chappell notes:

[When absent] the only security for their property . . . consists of a few loose stones piled against the flap of seal-skin which covers the entrance of the tent: and although they be not rigidly honest towards strangers, yet the Eskimo appear to have great respect for each other's property. (Chappell *op. cit.*:76)

As late as 1885 the Eskimos broke into the storehouse of the station at Stupart Bay five times during the winter and spring. It may be said, however, that some of them were starving at these times, and their own generous return is noted above.

What, then, are we to make of these varieties of forms of exchange that the Eskimos of both sides of the Hudson Strait used in dealing with the white man, both at first contacts and after they had become used to "trading"? There are three themes here.

First, there is the essential theme of reciprocity, which guides the normal transactions between ordinary Eskimos and which they applied to the white man. We have noted above the gifts that were given back and forth from time to time between une Eskimos and the observers at Stupart Bay, in spite of the fact that they also begged or tried to steal. Chappell states that the only result of giving gifts to the Eskimos was to encourage further begging — but this is to be expected when the whites had so much and the Eskimos so little. In any case, the "beggars" to whom he was referring (*ibid.*:71–72) were young girls who had been pointedly attentive and were offering, perhaps, something that Chappell did not wish. Tuttle describes in some detail some "bartering" at Stupart Bay which appears to be a series of gift exchanges (Tuttle *op. cit.*:79).

Everyone seems to have been happy with these exchanges, though, and the white men thought they were doing pretty well:

. . . All [those trading] obtained something [from the Eskimos] and got that something cheaply. (*Ibid.*:80)

In all exchanges the natives showed as much joy as if they had acquired great riches, although in many instances they were the losers by the bargain. (Lyon *op. cit.*:23)

In addition to the actual transaction of "fair" exchanges, a second principle from everyday Eskimo life was expressed in these affairs. As described above ("Economic Organization") and by D'Anglure (1964), the Eskimos believed that those who had more should give to those who had less. And it was quite obvious that the white man had more by far of nearly everything than the Eskimos. In Eskimo life, the man with a good kill invites all to partake of it and basks in the prestige. Presumably, the Eskimos thought that the white man would derive as much prestige from sharing his numerous goods and, as in their own camps, those with less asked or "begged" of those who had more. If the whites did not respond to their overtures, something they could not understand of such rich people, the Eskimo would believe them to be stingy and hold them in very low respect. This would, of course, lead to stealing, even when the Eskimos were not in very dire straits. Such stealing would be done in their own land to anyone who continually refused to give when he had so much.

Third, the white men, although often treated as the Eskimos would treat themselves, were not Eskimos: they were strangers. Nevertheless, they were not treated so badly as other strangers such as the Indians. The Eskimos gave the white man the benefit of the doubt. They did not treat them as Indians at first. If they had done so, there would have been nothing but constant slaughter. The Eskimos soon learned the value of white goods and that the white man, unlike the Indian, was not always out for blood. The Eskimos did not form long-lasting attachments to these visiting whites and saw them as pleasant people on some occasions and as another migratory resource on others. When they were able, they got as much as possible from the whites by stealing, murder, and plunder, in a way corresponding to what they did, for instance, with the walrus herd when it came through twice a year.

To summarize, we may say that economic transactions with the whites were governed by three rules: (1) reciprocity, (2) generosity, and (3) exploitation.

So far we have only considered the visiting traders on the ships. The posts of the Hudson's Bay Company, however, were permanent, and trading with them was slightly different. The Eskimos knew that the traders were there to stay and that they could undertake dishonest dealings only once. If they wished to benefit from the trade, they would have to obey the rules set up by the white man. When they did not, as at Richmond Gulf, the source of goods might disappear, and, as happened there, the store might be removed.

Good accounts of the actual processes of trading conducted by the early Hudson's Bay Company posts are not so abundant as those for the visiting ships:

I cannot enter into all the particulars of the fur trade, the secrets of which nothing short of a railroad will lay open; my experience with Hudson's Bay officials being [that they will not talk shop]. (Gordon 1887:65)

We do have some accounts, however, of the events that occurred at the opening of the trading post at Fort Chimo. Although the Eskimos had sometimes gone over to the Labrador coast to trade at the Moravian missions at Okkak, they were reluctant at first with the new white men. Again gifts and inducements had to be brought into play to establish good relations with the Eskimo traders.

But previous to our leaving the foot of the river [at Pilgrim's Rest, we] hung up some knives, awls, needles, etc. on a pole for the Esquimaux with a mark signifying that the donors were at hand. (Finlayson 1830 in Davies 1963:109)

Later, Finlayson remarks:

Every useful article in the store was displayed to their view and every encouragement was held out to induce them to hunt for fur animals, seals and whales. (*Ibid.*:123)

The women and children remained in the boats, but when I showed them some beads, the temptation these raised overcame their fears. . . . (*Ibid.*:115)

The Honorable Company was not a charity institution, and although "instructed to supply poor Indians with ammunition and fishing tackle, gratis" (McLean 1849 [1932]:326), nevertheless:

. . . [commercial] rule, wherever established or by whomsoever exercized, is gain. In our intercourse with the natives of America no other object is discernable, no other object thought of, and no other object is allowed. (*Idem.*)

The same underlying motive, McLean says, did not allow Hudson's Bay Company traders to be generous, to teach the children, or to minister to sickness as the company claimed to instruct them to do. Unfortunately, these Chimo Eskimos had nothing much to offer:

But they had nothing to trade, having bartered any article they had to dispose of with other Esquimeaux who are in the habit of visiting Okkak . . . annually in the course of the summer. . . . On their return out to the coast I supplied each man with a beaver trap and some ammunition. Our system of trading was explained to them, the value of each article of trade, and of the different species of furs. (Finlayson 1831 in Davies 1963:183)

It appears that the Hudson's Bay Company were the first people in the area to have standardized prices for commodities and hence a common means of reckoning value. At first this common standard was, I believe, a mink skin, but at a later date and among the Eskimos it became either a ringed seal skin or a white fox pelt. Money was not used for many years, and the company did not "barter" or bargain for its skins. Although it does not refer to our area, the Hudson's Bay Company tariff for Northwest River (Hamilton Inlet) may be compared with the approximate equivalents already given:

Eskimo produce	*Mink skins*
Fox, silver	10
red	4
white	2
Mink	1
Buck deerskin (caribou)	6
Doe	4

White man's goods	Mink skins
1 yard common cloth	30
1 blanket, plain	15
1 gun	30
1 pocket knife	1
1 skein of twine	1
½ lb. tobacco	1

(Erlandson 1834 in Davies *op. cit.*:259)

Thus did regular trading first get a start in this area. The Eskimos were grubstaked for a new hunt after they had traded their furs:

. . . a few flints, awls and hooks, and a trifle of ammunition is given them, in proportion to their hunts, and then — "Va-t-en." (McLean *op. cit.*:326)

Apparently, some of the Eskimos thought of the idea of credit themselves, although it is possible the custom was also used by the Moravians at Okkak:

The poor creatures' wants were so many that they did not know what they would have till we displayed several useful articles to their view. A gun they wanted very much to trade in part, promising to pay for the rest in the summer. (Finlayson 1830 in Davies 1963:157)

The idea of being given something at one time, and then returning something else to the same person was familiar to the Eskimo. It is inherent in the principle of reciprocity that one does not require immediate repayment but only the "obligation to return the gift" at sometime or another when one is able. Thus, the Eskimos were willingly "hooked" onto the company's credit system; they thought the white man was being very generous in giving the first gift and felt quite bad if they were not able to bring something of value to give him later after the hunt. Not only was there an exchange, which in itself gave pleasure and cemented social ties, but also each man was given gifts in proportion to his ability as a hunter. It pleased the more skilled men immensely that they, who were already leaders in their own society, should be recognized as such by the white men, too.

The Hudson's Bay Company post at Fort Chimo was kept open only from 1830 to 1842, during which time it was a losing proposition; in fact, some people thought it should never have been opened at all. It was not opened again until 1866. The

Takamiut, if they traded at all, probably made the very long journey to Great Whale River or to the north side of the Strait, or even traded through intermediary Eskimos. We do not have any good accounts of the reopening of Chimo in 1866. Presumably by then the Eskimos were quite familiar with Hudson's Bay Company trading procedures, if they had not changed in the meantime.

From Turner's account (1894), we know that the Hudson's Bay Company trading post was well established at Chimo by 1885, even to the point where some of the clerks had "married" Eskimo women. The Takamiut were visiting regularly, but we do not know exactly from where on the Hudson Strait they came. During the earlier operation of the post, some men had gone as far north as Hopes Advance Bay to encourage the natives to trade; later they may have gone farther north for these purposes or the news just may have spread. During the latter part of the nineteenth century, the Hudson's Bay Company personnel regularly sailed to Leaf Bay to kill white whales and they had a similar operation at Whale River. At both places the whales were taken in large nets. At George River and at Whale River, and possibly at other places, Eskimos were employed in the commercial fishing of salmon (or char) by net. These fish were shipped out by the Hudson's Bay Company ship *Diana* in her freezer (Low 1898:25L, 27L). Similarly, the whaler *Arctic* also employed many Eskimos around Big Island every summer for both whaling and mica mining.

By the end of the century, then, a number of Eskimos were regularly employed in the summers at the behest of the white man. Among the Takamiut, however, we do not know of any natives employed, even at the observation station at Stupart Bay.

Effects of Early Contacts. In the Hudson Strait area there were no metals until the white man arrived. This is shown by the Eskimo words; north of the Strait iron is called *saviksak*, meaning "material for knife," and on the south side metal is called *kikiaksak*, meaning "material for nails." These two objects were doubtless among the commonest forms in which the Eskimo first met metals. Metal in any form was cold-beaten into the tips of harpoons and spears and the blades of knives and ulus. These would remain much sharper than their native equivalents, thereby increasing their efficiency and decreasing the amount of work for the Eskimos. Needles and saws had to be acquired already manufactured. The former must have been a great boon to the Eskimo women not only because they were less fragile than the bone ones, but also because they were finer and much sharper. They probably both improved and speeded up the work of making clothes and boots. Saws were used for two purposes: first, as a substitute for the snow knife in making igloos; and second, as material for blanks for all metal knives and ulus. Presumably, some metals were used as tips for bow drills, again increasing speed and quality of workmanship.

Other European objects were purely decorative. Reports of the appearance of Eskimos in the nineteenth century (e.g., Hall 1865) describe the Eskimo women wearing parkas decorated with the bowls of spoons, English coins, and buttons. On some they were so thick that they jangled, and others were believed to have been used as supernatural charms or fetishes. Men, except perhaps shamans, do not seem to have decorated themselves until European clothing began to be worn.

Along the north of the Hudson Strait, the Eskimos soon learned to expect the arrival of ships in early summer, and this had two effects. First, they gathered at those places where the ships were likely to anchor and this may have had some minor effects on the path of their seasonal migrations (Chappell *op. cit.*:57). This did not occur along the south coast, however, until this century. Second, they regularly manufactured models and objects that were reserved for trade with the white man. Although this may have taken some additional work and time, it was probably well worth it, compared with the economic value of the goods they received. It is also probable that the quality of their manufactures improved as they found that the better-made items would bring more goods. This may have applied not only to the objects especially made for the whites but also to their everyday clothes and implements, because these, too, were bartered away, and they had better tools, through trade, for fine handiwork. Payne notes:

. . . a marked difference in quality of mechanical work done by the Eskimos of the north and south shores of the Strait, especially in clothes by the women, and hunting implements and carved work made by the men, those on the north shore doing far the neatest and best work. (Payne 1888–89:217)

During this earlier period, even before the acquisition of guns, there was probably a slight increase in the number of game animals killed because of the better quality of implements and the large numbers of skins needed to barter for them. I doubt very much, however, if there were any drastic changes in the annual cycle.

One of the earliest important innovations from the white man was the use of nets for fishing. There has been considerable argument about the aboriginal use of nets among the Eskimos. Davis said that, in 1586, the Greenlanders made fishnets out of the fin of the whale (Hakluyt's Voyages: 782), and others have claimed that these must have diffused to Labrador. Hawkes discusses this matter in detail and summarizes his opinion:

It seems probable, then, that the Labrador Eskimo may have made nets in older times, but given up their manufacture when they could procure the civilized article so much more easily in their summer raids to the south. The Moravians mention that when they went among them, they found the Labrador Eskimo well supplied with fishing gear and nets, the results of their plundering trips to the Gulf of St. Lawrence. (Hawkes 1916:3)

The Eskimos themselves call claim that they never used nets before the traders came. In any event, the Moravians and the early Hudson's Bay posts all fished with nets and presumably traded them to the Eskimos so that the knowledge of the use of nets must have been common by the nineteenth century. Some Eskimos had even been employed using both sea-mammal and fish nets and so must have known all about their manufacture, maintenance, and use. Whether the Eskimos had previously had their own nets or not, the European twine nets would have been far more durable and efficient as well as cheaper to make. The adoption of sealing and whaling nets would have meant even greater changes and larger kills to the Eskimos, but these were more expensive and only a few Eskimos ever used them on their own account, even in this century.

Balikci, referring to the Povungnituk area, states:

[Nets] assured the Eskimos of a more regular supply of Arctic char and enabled them to catch the whitefish which abound in the lakes. The adoption of individually-owned nets resulted in the abandonment of the collectively-operated stone weirs. The leister, however, continued to be used in early winter for fishing through the lake-ice and in autumn in shallow waters along the streams. The introduction of special steel hooks greatly eased fishing through the sea-ice for cod. (Balikci 1964:90)

Hooks, of course, were always used by the Eskimos, but the metal variety must have been a great improvement. In 1885, nets were very rare in the Takamiut area:

. . . the most common mode of trapping is by building walls of stones shaped like a bag about six inches above the surface, and then with sticks and stones splashing the water higher up the stream and driving the fish into the trap. (Payne 1888–89:218)

The leister was gradually being replaced:

. . . the most common implement employed being a long handle with an ordinary knife firmly tied near one end making a fork, one prong of which is the end of the rod, the other the blade of the knife, its sharpened edge turned inward. With this ugly weapon the salmon are speared or, more properly speaking, are slashed and are often found nearly cut in halves. (*Idem.*)

By far the most important introduction to the whole area was that of powder and shot. We do not know exactly when the Eskimos first obtained guns. Probably a few were obtained from raids on the southern Labrador settlements and the massacres of ships' crews. However, without a supply of powder and shot, they would have been useless except as mere metal for the manufacture of other objects. Finlayson (1830) and Erlandson (1834) mention that when they first arrived in Fort Chimo, many of the Eskimo men had guns but little powder and shot. These guns had been obtained either from trading at Okkak or in raids farther south. The Hudson's Bay Company grubstaked the Eskimos with ammunition, and ammunition was one of the major trade items. The Eskimos bought many guns, often on credit, and this was encouraged by the company so that the Eskimos might be able to defend themselves against the ever-aggressive Indians. The whites were liberal with their credit for guns because they reckoned that if the Indians knew that the Eskimos could shoot back, for a change, they might hesitate in their attacks. Thus, the company hoped to bring, and in fact did bring, peace to the area and thereby was able to trade more freely with both races.

Obviously, the Takamiut acquired guns during their trading trips to Chimo and by 1885:

The gun, with which many are supplied, has almost taken the place of the bow and arrow, nevertheless they are still used by a few in deer hunting. . . . (Payne 1888–89:218)

Low, at the turn of the century, mentions that the Eskimos of the Ivujivik area traded into Great Whale River for "powder, shot and other necessaries." (Low 1902:5D) Some of my oldest informants, including those in the story earlier in this chapter, used guns for hunting inland and on the coast. They certainly remembered the older muzzle-loading guns, but their use of bows and arrows was probably occasional and due to their having run out of powder and shot. In some areas I have visited, the adolescent boys still make very effective bows and arrows with which they shoot birds and small mammals; their older kinsmen advise them and tell tales of their youth.

The use of guns, and more recently of repeating rifles, had an enormous effect on the Eskimo way of life. It allowed for far easier hunting of all kinds of animals and has been singled out as the major cause for the great decline in caribou since the last few decades of the last century in the Ungava area. It must be remembered, of course, that the Indians may have been as responsible for the caribou decline as the Eskimos: some Indians are even said to have slaughtered the caribou for their tongues and skins, much as did the Plains Indians with the buffalo. Balikci, in his incisive analysis, points out the enormous social implications of the use of guns:

. . . breathing-hole sealing was gradually abandoned for the easier technique of ice-edge hunting. . . . The sliding harpoon which fell into disuse was replaced by the rifle behind a white screen. . . . The use of guns and later of repeating rifles produced individualizing effects in winter sealing. . . .

With the introduction of guns, caribou hunting became greatly simplified. Very quickly the collective caribou drives were abandoned. . . .
The acquisition of shotguns and .22 rifles by the Eskimos stimulated waterfowl hunting. The bird dart disappeared. . . .
For a time, as long as caribou were plentiful, the use of guns resulted in greatly increased game returns. Groups of Eskimos were not afraid of spending prolonged periods inland in search of caribou. Soon after the turn of the century the herds rapidly diminished, and new sources of subsistence had to be found. (Balikci 1964:89–90)

As Balikci suggests, inland caribou hunting may have become a larger part of the annual cycle and may have been pursued in seasons other than the summer. It is quite possible that the Eskimos which lived far inland all the year round (D'Anglure 1964), or for a large part of the year (Payne 1888–89), had not done so until guns were available. Turner (1894) writes of the Itivimiut who traveled overland to Chimo and spent much of their time in the interior of the Ungava. These, too, probably depended on rifles for their caribou hunting and nets for their fishing. But the possession of guns probably does not account for the inland Eskimos mentioned by Finlayson (1830).

Balikci summarizes the effects of both guns and nets on the social and economic life of the Eskimos as simplifying and individualizing. As well as changing the annual cycle, the actual method of hunting demanded less cooperation. Probably the solidarity of winter hunting camps and summer caribou-hunting parties was diminished. Individual men and their families were far better able to exist on their own, and this may have had some modification on the relatively strong authority that older men had had over their married sons. In addition, I suspect, and my genealogies bear me out, that there was more intercamp and interterritory movement during this period; the increased kills are said to have provided more dog food, allowing for larger teams and faster trips. A concomitant effect was the widening of the area of hunting, of the circle of kin, and of the diversity of friendships in the area. A similar effect has been thoroughly documented for Pelly Bay (Balikci 1964:6–78).

The most valuable fur in the tundra regions was, and still is, fox pelts, although these have probably not averaged so high a price as the beaver and otter pelts that are the mainstay of Indian trapping in the area immediately south:

[The Eskimos] were repeatedly exhorted to exert themselves in bringing us plenty of oil etc. during the summer. . . . They all promised to exert themselves in the fox hunt for they saw with admiration the stock of useful articles a few of them who brought foxes traded. . . . Those whom I persuaded to go to the eastward to kill whales were entirely unsuccessful, not having killed one fish. . . ." (Finlayson, July, August 1830 *op. cit.*)

Finlayson also mentions that the Eskimos had no proper fox traps, save those I have described earlier in this chapter. The Eskimos were given metal traps on credit, and these spread throughout the area.

By the 1880's the Takamiut were very familiar and expert in the setting of steel fox traps. Payne describes in some detail how the Eskimo put the trap into a small hollow in the snow and covered it with a very thin layer of hard snow with bait all around (1888–89:219). Thus, in collecting the scattered bait, the fox was sure to put one or another of its legs through the snow into the metal jaws. This did not usually kill the fox, and the trap had to be anchored or the fox might carry it off. Traps had to be visited fairly often or the catch might be eaten by wolverines, wolves, or other foxes. Fox fur, particularly that of white fox, was not prime except in the winter, and the traders refused to take pelts of poor quality. Thus, the Eskimos were forced to trap during the winter, a time they had normally spent seal hunting on the tuvak. When the foxes were near the coast, this did not upset the annual cycle too drastically, for the Eskimo could sled inland every week or so. If the foxes were far inland and the men were moved to trap them, they would have to abandon their families and take extra provisions for the journey, remaining away some weeks. This extended inland winter activity would probably not have been possible before the acquisition of guns, which was another reason for the Company to extend general credit for them. During the period between the acquisition of guns and the disappearance of the caribou, these extra activities probably did not put too great a strain on the food supply. For the Takamiut, however, trapping did not become the major activity until there were trading posts established in their area, in this century. Along with the individualizing effects of the abandonment of the communal breathing-hole tuvak hunting, trapping was an individual or very small-group activity. Once more the solidarity of the winter katimajut was lessened at the expense of nuclear or extended family cooperation, emphasizing perhaps the restricted ilagiit. The Eskimos did not like a man's leaving his family behind for some weeks unless there were other members of the larger family present to look after them. Some men took their whole families with them when trapping, but this required a far greater supply of provisions and slowed down the frequent visits to the trap line, decreasing the output of tradable skins.

In addition to the actual technological effects of trade, the very travel involved required new forms of social interaction and organization. Sugluk was about at the dividing line between those who normally traded into Great Whale River on the west and those who journeyed to Chimo in the east:

[The Nuvugmiut — of the Ivujivik area] are the most distant of those trading at the Hudson Bay post of Great Whale River, which is situated nearly 600 miles from Digges islands; their next neighbors to the east send their hunts to Fort Chimo in Ungava bay. They start on their journey to the post in January, and do not reach home again until June, as they travel with their entire families and hunt their living along the way. (Low 1902:19–20D)

The Eskimos leave the coasts in early August, going inland to kill deer for food and winter clothing, and remain in the interior till December when they slowly make their way Southward to Great Whale River, trapping foxes as they move along. (Low 1898B:125A)

We can see that for five months of the year these people pursued activities entirely different from their traditional annual cycle: not only were they hunting different game in different areas, but they must also have been making far more regular contacts with the Itivimiut to the south. This probably resulted in interterritorial marriages and even in some minor cultural and linguistic changes.

The people of Wakeham Bay and the Takamiut to the east traveled overland to Payne Bay, Leaf River, and Fort Chimo to trade. Observers of the period disagree concerning the difficulty and length of the journey and hence the extent of the disruption of the annual cycle. Turner, who was at Chimo in 1883 and 1884 and met the Takamiut, gives a long and detailed account of the effort. He wrote (1888:177) that the distance was so great that a few experienced men, maybe three, four, or five sleds, were sent off annually to trade for the whole group. These men were commissioned to trade for each separate family and so carried each bundle of furs separately. The furs were kept from the previous winter. In November or December, sled teams would travel from west to east along the Hudson Strait, passing on their furs to other teams until the ones selected for the whole journey finally set off for Chimo. They would arrive at Chimo at the end of April or beginning of May, quickly barter their furs, and set off back again before they could be caught by the melting snows. They would follow the coastline on their return, presumably via Diana Bay, for the snow lasted longest there. Often, however, they would be caught by the melting snows and streams and not arrive home again until mid-summer or even the beginning of the next winter. This whole journey, therefore, took some five to eight months, which seems an extremely long time, although quite comparable to that taken by the Nuvugmiut previously described. Perhaps the length of the journey is explained by the fact that the men took their families along and hunted or even trapped along the way, as did the Nuvugmiut, but these, of course, were only a few selected families.

Payne, who was at Stupart Bay in the same period that Turner was at Chimo, does not mention the great length of the journey or the long time that the party was away. Low, when visiting Douglas Harbour in July 1897, found a few Eskimos who rarely ever saw white men:

. . . they send their winter hunt furs by some picked men in the Spring to Fort Chimo, the journey being made overland by dog teams and occupying nearly three months. (Low 1898b:11L)

And Tuttle, who was present at the founding of the Stupart Bay observation station in 1884, describes the feelings of the Eskimos, who had:

Hitherto travelled 300 miles to Fort Chimo to exchange their peltries . . . the establishment of the station (they thought) was bringing civilization and commerce to their very doors, and they welcomed the movement enthusiastically. (Tuttle op. cit.:78)

In spite of this, Payne records the fact that he sent off some letters to Fort Chimo on May 1st and got back the replies by the same Eskimo on May 21st (Payne in Gordon 1887:48). In another place he states:

. . . it does not seem to be generally known what communication there is between the Eskimo at one place and those at a distant part of the coast. [One man at Wakeham Bay] . . . had lived far up the Fox Channel and had crossed the Strait with a number of others in an *umiak*. . . . Another man who lived nearly 200 miles to the West [probably at Sugluk] made the journey four times in the spring of 1886 travelling nearly 800 miles with his wife and child. It is a common thing to run down to Fort Chimo a distance, there and return, of six hundred miles. . . . (Payne 1888–89:229–230)

I made the same journey in the early spring via all the coastal settlements and in some very bad weather. The journey from Chimo to Wakeham Bay took only ten days and to Sugluk another four. It is difficult to reconcile the varying interpretations of this journey except that one should emphasize the difference between traveling alone with a lightly loaded sled and traveling with a heavy sled and one's whole family. Even so, those who went to Chimo annually spent a good deal of their time hunting on the way and socializing with other Eskimos on the way back. Most likely they went caribou hunting on the way down as the caribou were very plentiful inland of Leaf Bay at that time of the year. They may also have stopped for spring hunting of seals basking on the tuvak as, in fact, I did.

It is also possible that the long journey to trade was sometimes made by umiak. It is known that Eskimos at Payne Bay and the Quartak regions did so:

Dogs were used to track the boat along level, even shores. It was even possible to go from Sugluk or Wakeham Bay to Fort Chimo and return in the same summer. (Arima 1963:76)

Let us now consider the nature of the economic activities during this period from 1870 to 1909. The trading was called "barter" but it was, in fact, not a direct exchange of commodity for commodity with haggling (which is how I define barter). It was fixed-price trading and the Hudson's Bay Company had a well-known tariff of prices; the only "bargaining" was over the quality of the skins brought in, and in this matter, the company staff always had the last word. After all, there was no competing store, and the Eskimo could not take his skins all the way back to Takamiut land if he was unsatisfied with the price. The common measure of value that the Hudson's Bay Company used in reckoning was the white-fox skin which was worth about fifty cents at that time. In these transactions, one or two men were acting as agents for many:

. . . it is remarkable that, although these traders carry as many as 30 or 40 parcels of furs owned by different families, they seemed quite able to remember on their return, to whom the goods they obtained in exchange belong, apparently the only note being made by a few marks with their teeth upon some of the articles. (Payne 1888–89:221)

I also suspect that mistakes were made, but the families were well pleased with what they received and probably had great difficulty in remembering exactly what they ordered more than five months back!

From these descriptions it appears that there was individual ownership (by the head man of a household) of the fox skins that formed the bulk of the traded items. The pelts of such small animals as foxes would have fallen into the class in which sharing was not expected (see the section on "Economic Organization" in this chapter). Even when a man had a large number of these skins they were not shared, because they represented a valuable trade item. The economics of fox trapping and trading probably, then, did not really break the long-established rules. We have already seen that extensive time taken out for these activities would have meant changes in the annual cycle and in the winter cooperation and food supply. The long journey made to Chimo, of course, seriously disrupted the annual migrations of those few families who made it. We can only wonder about the effects this had on the rest of the group. It seems that the most competent Eskimos were chosen for the journey, depriving those behind of their services. This was probably mitigated by two factors. First, with the advent of guns the general efficiency of all hunters improved, allowing the second-rate hunters to provide for those still on the coast. Second, the hunts requiring the greatest measure of cooperation, those of late summer caribou and fall walrus, probably did not take place until after the trading men returned.

By the end of the last century, the major material changes of the Takamiut consisted of the increasing use of guns, nets, and tobacco. There were few others at that time. Low remarks of the Douglas Harbour Eskimos in 1897:

No articles of European manufacture were noticed, beyond guns, rifles, some iron in the spears and a few knives. . . . The skins of Arctic foxes, bears and wolves are exchanged for guns, ammunition, needles and knives, while any credit remaining is used to purchase tobacco. (Low 1898:11L)

Of the Nuvugmiut he saw in 1901, he says:

. . . only a few could boast of fragments of European clothing, such as shirts, skirts and hats. Their fur hunt consists chiefly of white foxes together with few skins of red, cross and black foxes, wolves and white bears, which with walrus tusks constitute their articles of trade for powder, shot and tobacco. (Low 1902:19–20D)

By the turn of the century, the Takamiut were profoundly influenced by the permanent settlements far to the south. For those who made the long trading journeys, the whole pattern of their lives was changed. For those who stayed in the area, their material equipment changed in a few fundamentals, but their way of life was still governed by the seasons and the game. Living had become easier with the advent of needles, guns, and nets, but the Takamiut were beginning to face a serious shortage of caribou early in this century. The solidarities of winter camps and summer caribou hunts were declining, but as long as the game held out, this did not matter. Mobility was increased, and the circle of friends and relatives widened.

In the last part of the last century, it is possible that there was a gradual population drift towards the south in order to be nearer the trading posts. My genealogies show that a few families moved close to the Chimo area, and some others migrated as far as Payne Bay and Hopes Advance Bay, Cape Smith, Povungnituk, and Port Harrison.

Two other influences that seriously affected the life of those living near the southern trading posts were not yet felt. These were the diseases of civilization, to which the Eskimos had no immunity, and the works of the Anglican missions. These new phenomena are discussed in the next two chapters.

CHAPTER FOUR

White Residents
in the Ungava Area

TRADERS IN THE AREA

During the latter part of the last century the Hudson's Bay Company was finding its operations in Ungava quite profitable, and after the turn of the century it operated fisheries on the Koksoak River and at Leaf Bay. Later it netted much salmon at other points in Ungava Bay, and also caught white whales (beluga) very successfully in Whale River near Chimo. These products were sent out on the ship *Diana*, which had a refrigerated hold. In 1905 the company opened a permanent post at Leaf River, one of the richest locations in the eastern Arctic.

Apparently the price for Arctic fox pelts rose on the world markets soon after the turn of the century for in 1909 the company opened a permanent post at Eric Cove, near Cape Wolstenholme. Histories of the company do not tell us why, but this was the first all-Eskimo Arctic post in the more than two centuries of the history of the company. I assume that Eric Cove was chosen be-

cause of its suitability as a harbor, as judged by Low (1906:15).
Very soon after this, more posts were opened in the eastern
Arctic (Lake Harbour, 1911; Chesterfield, 1912; Cape Dorset, 1913;
Frobisher Bay and Stupart Bay close to Wakeham Bay, 1914;
Fort McKenzie, 1917; Port Burwell, 1916; Coats Island and Re-
pulse Bay, 1918; and Port Harrison, 1920).

The trade must have been very profitable, for Révillon Frères
and some independent traders followed the lead of the Hudson's
Bay Company and set up more posts, matching the company
post for post (Jenness 1964:23). Unfortunately, history does not
record the exact date, but I was told that an independent trader
came to Sugluk in 1916 and that this post was maintained on and
off until 1946.

Other white agencies were still active in the north. The government regularly patrolled the eastern Arctic with its ship *Arctic*
from 1905 on. This ship was replaced in 1918 by the *Nascopie*,
which foundered off Cape Dorset in 1947 — to be replaced by the
C. D. Howe, which still makes its annual round. Private explorers
penetrated the interior as well as explored the coasts: the Hub-
bards, along the George River (1903 and 1905); Tasker, from
Nastapoka to Ungava Bay (1906); and Flaherty, the Belchers and
the coast to Port Harrison, crossing Ungava to Chimo and making
his famous movies (1910 to 1916 and 1920). In addition, Todd
explored the wildlife of Ungava Bay (1916), and the famous
Fifth Thule Expedition crossed from Greenland to Alaska via
the Canadian Arctic under Knud Rasmussen (1921 and 1925 to
1926).

The main activities, however, were in fur trading. The Hudson's
Bay Company by 1921 had posts in the area at Great Whale River,
Port Harrison, Povungnituk, Wolstenholme, Wakeham Bay, Diana
Bay, Payne Bay, Leaf River, and Chimo. The Stupart Bay post
had been moved to the better anchorage of Wakeham Bay in
about 1918. Payne Bay was opened from Fort Chimo by Jimmy
Ford of the famous northern family. His father had been a trader
at Nachvak and interpreter on the Hudson's Bay Company ship,
Diana. One of his brothers, Harry, had been an early trader at
Wolstenholme in 1913, and another Ford, Isaac, was an indepen-

118

dent trader at Sugluk until 1946. Jimmy Ford told me in 1964 that when he first went to Payne Bay many of the Eskimos there had never seen a white man, although obviously the fitter ones had traded into Chimo. He had great difficulty enticing the Eskimos of Payne Bay into the store to trade.

Until this period government representatives had sailed only around the coasts, but the Royal Canadian Mounted Police established some posts for reasons of Canadian sovereignty and took over nominal control of criminal and legal matters in the region. None of their posts was in our area, although one was established at Lake Harbour in 1927 and another at Port Burwell in 1920. These posts also kept vital statistics, and these have been helpful to anthropologists in establishing dates and ages of Eskimos. The post at Port Harrison was established in the next decade and that at Fort Chimo in the 1940's.

By the later twenties, the demand for white (Arctic) fox furs was sky high. Prices were enormous, and small settlements could support traders as never before. The Hudson's Bay Company opened more posts, including one at Fisher Bay and at Amadjuak across the Strait by 1929, and these were matched by the competition. Later posts were also opened at Cape Smith and Deception Bay. In 1927 the Hudson's Bay Company tore down their store at Wolstenholme and moved it to Sugluk, an area where there were more Eskimos and easier access to the inland trapping lines. They maintained a camp store at Wolstenholme, run by an Eskimo trader, and opened another on Mansel Island. In 1928 they re-erected the large store at Sugluk, where it still stands today.

This situation of having two or more stores available to trade into was heaven for the Eskimos, who were able to bargain one against the other, raise the prices, and buy large motorized boats. It is still the Golden Age in their memories. However, with the Depression this situation ended: prices dropped and competition grew. By 1936, Révillon Frères were forced to sell out to the Hudson's Bay Company, and most of the independent traders folded, although some were able to linger on for another decade. The Eskimos found it harder to maintain and run their expensive boats, and there were many hardships.

In 1927 a Canadian government aerial expedition made its base at Wakeham Bay. It also established a meterological station there and flew all over the eastern Arctic. This was one of the first uses of the airplane in the Arctic and was a portent of things to come. The next year the meteorological station was moved to Cape Hopes Advance near Quartak and it has been operating there ever since.

By the beginning of World War II a large number of trading stations had been closed down, including Deception Bay, Fisher Bay, Wakeham Bay (1940), Diana Bay, and, I believe, Leaf River. At the few remaining posts prices of furs were low, supplies were low, and the company could no longer afford to grubstake the Eskimo trappers. Even in the Fort Chimo area, so long a center of civilization, more than 100 Eskimos and Indians starved to death in the winter of 1941–42.

World War II kept conditions at the level of destitution. Even the best hunters were only marginally well off, often because the supply ships either did not arrive or brought too little ammunition to go around. By this time the Eskimos could no longer go back completely to their old hunting methods with bows and arrows. U.S. Army Air Bases were opened at Frobisher Bay, Coral Harbour, and Fort Chimo, and for the Eskimos of these areas the Americans are heroes who saved them from certain starvation. There were considerable migrations from other places to the environs of these generous newcomers who offered gifts and employment. In the outlying areas, such as that of the Takamiut, the War was a near disaster, following as it did on the Depression. Although the game supply was such that few starved, things appeared very bad.

During the 1930's some prospecting in the area confirmed that there were relatively rich mineral deposits worth mining. The Depression put a stop to this project, and actual mining and the accompanying employment had to wait another three decades.

MISSIONARY ACTIVITIES

Late in the last century, the Anglican missionaries had started their work among the southern Itivimiut. Most of these had been nominally converted to Christianity long before the Takamiut or the Sirqinirmiut had.

Although the missionaries have devoted considerable energy to the work of converting these people, and though many of them profess Christianity, these professionals proved on examination to be merely minimal. As soon as the converts are beyond the teacher's influence, they revert to the shaman for guidance. (Turner 1894:179)

The effects of these conversions may not have been deep, but Turner probably underestimated their influence, for these people have clung to the same faith until today in spite of powerful efforts by other sects to change them. In the same summer that Turner made his observations, the Reverend Peck visited Chimo after an overland journey from Little Whale River, where a mission had been started two years previously. He decided that the Eskimos of Ungava Bay were ripe for his teachings for some of them had already been considerably influenced by the Moravians at Okkak. Although Peck himself did not return to Chimo, he sent the young and dynamic Reverend Stewart, who arrived in 1899 (Malaurie 1964:433). Reverend Stewart, with the assistance of Henry Ford and later of the Reverend Hester, set about converting the Eskimos of the area:

The constant travel of Mr. Stewart was not confined to visiting the Eskimos of Ungava Bay, for he travelled almost as far west as the western end of Hudson Strait. (*idem.*)

The nominal conversions were followed by the training of Eskimos to become catechists who further spread the Gospel and maintained the body of the Church between the infrequent visits of ordained ministers. These men were usually Eskimo leaders in their own right, although not shamans. The actual mechanisms of conversion were not recorded, but we know that considerable resistance was offered by some of the shamans who were about to lose their hold on the people. Balikci (1962) offers explanations for the relative ease of conversion of the Eskimos, although they refer to another area. Among the major factors seem to have been (1) that the missionaries were agents of white society, which had already overwhelmed the Eskimos in other areas of life and promised more advantages if cooperation were forthcoming; and

(2) that in many ways the minister resembled and took the place of the shaman: he seemed to have a good control over the supernatural, his "taboos" were relatively easy to follow and promised a more peaceful life, and his efforts at curing were probably more successful than those of the shaman.

The old saying that "H.B.C. means here before Christ" (i.e., the missions) did not apply among the Takamiut. The missionaries visited the area before the resident traders and when Low was in Wakeham Bay in 1904:

Several books, given for distribution by the Rev. Mr. Peck, were handed out to them [the Eskimos], and they immediately held on deck a service of song and prayer. These natives had never seen a missionary [in 1904] but had learned to read from others at Fort Chimo who had come in contact with the missionaries on the east coast of Hudson Bay. (Low 1906:65)

Low was probably wrong about the missionaries' never having visited and certainly wrong in stating that the only missionaries at that time were among the Itivimiut. However, as we mentioned above, the syllabic script first adapted for the Cree and later for the southern Itivimiut was in use by the Reverends Walton and Stewart and was easily learned by the Eskimos. The very fact of literacy itself was probably a powerful incentive for conversion. Hawkes notes:

. . . Eskimos as a rule do not like civilized music. They say there are too many notes, that the time is confusing, and that they prefer the simple rhythm of their native songs. Of the "white man's songs," they like best the old style hymns. (Hawkes 1916:124)

These hymns, translated into Eskimo, were exactly what they got from the Anglican missionaries. After learning to read and becoming familiar with the tunes, they were quite happy to spend many hours amusing themselves in their homes singing the new songs.

Of the same 1904 expedition, Low says that the people he met at Sugluk had never seen a white man and that they did not even trade directly into Chimo but exchanged their furs with those to the east in exchange for trade goods. Although the latter may be true, the Anglican mission at Sugluk claims that the Reverend

Stewart visited the area in 1902, and he is still something of a hero along the coast.

In the 1930's the Roman Catholic Church, which had long been active west of the Hudson Bay, moved into the Ungava area in force. In 1936 it opened missions with resident priests in Wakeham Bay and Cape Dorset. These were followed by further missions at Ivujivik' (1939), Quartak (1947), Chimo (1952), and Povungnituk (1956). In 1946 the Catholic Church bought the buildings of the former independent trader at Sugluk, and an incumbent was sent north to run the mission in 1947. There has been continuous occupancy ever since. As we have seen previously, all the Eskimos of this area were nominally converted to Anglicanism in the first decade of this century and learned to read and write in the syllabic script invented by the Anglicans. The Eskimos, with their intense loyalty to the first comers, presented a difficult task to these capable new missionaries. Although the Anglican representatives only visited this area every other year or so, the native catechists kept the Church going. The only significant successes of the Roman Catholic Church were made at Ivujivik and Wakeham Bay.

ECONOMIC AND DEMOGRAPHIC CHANGES

Thus, after decades of trading and some years of mission activity, the Eskimos were not at all unfamiliar with the white man and his strange but useful ways. In 1909 the Hudson's Bay Company set up a permanent trading post at Eric Cove, not far from Cape Wolstenholme and Ivujivik. The first trader, a Mr. Shepard, was accompanied by his wife. He died by drowning off the Cape in 1914 and is still remembered in the area. For a year before his death he had been assisted by Mr. Harry Ford, also accompanied by his wife, perhaps the same Mr. Ford who had assisted the Reverend Stewart. Mr. Ford was drowned at the same time. Their wives were picked up by the supply ship the following summer.

Just before the opening of the store in this area there had been an unusual number of murders and attempted murders by Eskimos. The men involved were Sakiatsiak, Pakvik, Natsingaijak, and the famous Augautialuk. Most of these attacks seemed to be for personal reasons involving wives, although some Eskimos claim that two of the men were "crazy." Nearly all these incidents involved the use of guns, presumably traded from far away, and some ended in cannibalism.

This store at Eric Cove and the others that followed within the next decade had both immediate and far-reaching effects on the Eskimos. Among others, they brought an influx of people into the area. My charts show that between 1910 and 1920 at least seven families, comprising more than thirty people, came from the Ungava Bay area to live permanently at Wakeham Bay, Sugluk, and Ivujivik. Nearly all these people had relatives in the area already and may very well have been descendants of those who had previously left and gone to live farther south when the only stores were at Chimo. There was also some movement across the Hudson Strait from the Cape Dorset region, although we are not so sure that these latter moves were motivated purely by the presence of stores.

Another immediate effect was to end the necessity for the long journeys to the south to trade. This affected those people who had done all the trading at Fort Chimo for the eastern Takamiut. It had an even greater effect on the entire Nuvugmiut population around Ivujivik who, as we have seen, had been spending many months well outside their area. The store in Eric Cove was centrally placed for those very Eskimos previously most neglected by the traders. For the majority of the Takamiut, it was no more than a three weeks' journey by sled or ten days by umiak, and for the Nuvugmiut it was right on their doorstep! Some of my informants who had been living in the Cape Smith and Kovik regions said that they regularly used to walk overland to Eric Cove in summers and that the sled journey was only a few days.

There were other effects of these local stores, too, during the second decade of this century. Some Eskimos regularly made the trip to Eric Cove in the summer to be at hand for the annual arrival of the supply ship. Later they made similar journeys to the other stores as they were opened (Wakeham Bay area in 1914, Diana Bay circa 1920). They were employed to help unload the ship and got credit, which was paid in kind. In general, the annual migration patterns of many Eskimos were thrown off their previous cycles. The stores, being so close, could be visited at any time of the year and families were generally independent of the services of the best sledmen, who had previously traded for them. At the same time the more intensive hunting perhaps accelerated the decline of the caribou herds and after 1920 caribou became a less important source of food and raw materials, resulting in some shortage of clothing.

Some people began to cluster around the posts, never going far away to hunt and working at odd jobs or as store assistants for the Company. The life of these few is described by Tuttle a few decades previously in another area:

The Eskimos stand in the same relation to the Moravians as they do to the Hudson's Bay Co., that of well-used slaves. They are wholly subject to the dictates of the whites, but the obedience is one greatly founded on respect. (Tuttle 1885:50)

Every Hudson's Bay Company post employed a few servants (*ibid.*:53), both male and female. In many areas those post managers who were not married took young Eskimo women to live with them. In the Takamiut area, many individuals were born between 1915 and 1935 whose fathers were traders or Royal Canadian Mounted Police. After the men left or tired of these women, the latter, if they had had children, were usually able to find Eskimo husbands. However, there were two women in this area who never married (a very unusual phenomenon for the Eskimos), but had many children by various white men.

During the first few decades of trading in this area the Company never used cash. Apparently they very soon introduced the idea of tokens, small metal discs, as a measure of value. These were called *tatauti*, "that which causes (something) to be filled up or completed." The method of trading, which lasted in Sugluk until after my first visit in 1959, was thus. The Eskimo, either an individual or the leader of a restricted ilagiit, came in bearing a bundle of skins that he wished to trade. The trader or his assistant took the skins one by one and appraised each for quality and value. Each was then laid aside behind the counter and the number of tokens equivalent to its value was put on the counter in front of the Eskimo. This continued until all the skins were behind the counter and a pile of tokens was in front of the Eskimo. Of course, if the Eskimo had been in debt when he came in no tokens were put in front of him until he had paid off the debt in skins. Then the Eskimo, consulting with his wife or whomever else had come with him, pointed to the various objects on the shelves that he wanted, or, if the trader spoke Eskimo, the Eskimo could ask him directly. As each item was taken off the shelf and put on the counter, the equivalent value in tokens was taken away and put back in a small box kept for the purpose. Gradually, the tokens disappeared, and the pile of goods in front of the Eskimo grew larger. When there were only a few minor tokens left, the trader usually took them and threw a few matches down on the counter. The Eskimo took his goods and walked out.

If the Eskimo wished to go hunting or trapping, but brought little or nothing to trade, the trader would look up (or would know) his "credit rating," determined by how good a trapper he was, and he would select what he thought the Eskimo needed for the hunt and what he would be likely to be able to pay off.

This process of trading is called *niuvirktuk* which means both buying and selling, the whole process. It differs from the normal words of gift exchange and the swapping of equals, *tauksijuk*. The word for value or price is *aki*, meaning "opposite or across (something level)." This very well describes the action of exchanging across the counter. It does not have the connotations of equal but opposite pairs, *aipariik*, nor of identical equivalents, *ajjigiik*. Aki signifies a trading of unequals, not a swap or exchange of equals. The idea of debt is conveyed as *akiliksak*, meaning "potentially there is a price or value," a negative concept of something to be filled up by tatauti, "fillers-up" or tokens. As I have said, the acquisition of debt was something the Eskimos were proud of, as it was a measure of their hunting ability.

During and after World War I, the demand for white fox skins began to rise, and by 1920, the average market price was nearly $40. The fur trading companies, taking advantage of this boom, opened up settlements all along the coast in the early 1920's.

126

There was intense competition between the established Hudson's Bay Company and the newcomers (Jenness 1964:23). The competition as well as the demand forced the prices to remain at a high level until the Great Depression first began to have its effects in 1929–1931. In some communities the competition gained additional benefits for the Eskimos:

In the period of competition between Révillon Frères and the Hudson's Bay Company at Port Harrison, each company tried to ensure the trappers' loyalty by offering inducement gifts. Most of these were rifles, traps, cloth etc.; but several large boats, including Peterheads, were given to leading men in different camps to ensure the whole camp's trading at one store as well as to improve the efficiency of the trapping. . . . It is certain that the ownership of a Peterhead enhanced the authority of the leader and it continues to do so today. (Willmott 1961:49)

The Eskimos put greater efforts into fox trapping than ever before and found credit easy to obtain. The decade of the 1920's saw great changes in their way of life. Trap lines were extended far inland and these were usually worked by single men or two or three men who were close relatives. The Eskimos had never previously recognized any territoriality or exclusive ownership of game in an area. However, some such notions came about implicitly during this period of intensive trapping. It was useless for men to set trap lines close together for each man would be lowering his chances for success. There were no quarrels in these matters and the plateaulike hinterland back of the Hudson Strait became regularly frequented by trappers radiating out from such centers as Ivujivik, Sugluk, Deception Bay, Wakeham Bay, and Diana Bay. These trap lines often extended as far as Lac Nantais and Lac Allemand, more than a hundred miles inland. Sometimes the trappers went farther, and at these inland places they often met Itivimiut from Cape Smith and Povungnituk, and Uqumiut from the Payne Bay area. They had been used to meeting at these very places during the traditional late summer caribou hunts, but such intensive occupation of the hinterland during the winter was unprecedented. Under these new conditions, the parties were most often made up only of men, whereas the previous caribou hunting and trapping was engaged in by whole families.

127

This new activity brought further long-term changes. The caribou were disappearing or had disappeared, so the trappers had to carry their considerable provisions of food for themselves and their dogs from the coast. Although they had nets they did not have time to set them in the inland lakes, but with their small rifles they were often able to hunt hare. Dog food was the most critical problem and need for it led to an intensification of the late summer and fall hunts of white whale and walrus which was made possible, as we shall see later, by new boats and guns.

As the trapping intensified, men left their families at coastal camps and around the trading posts increasingly frequently. Along with those men who could not or did not wish to trap, these women and children lived a rather static life. The men did not abandon their families for whole winters at a time; they might only be away for an average of two or three weeks. During some of the winter and certainly in the early spring, they hunted seals on and at the ice edge with their repeating rifles. These hunts, however, were no longer the cooperative affairs of traditional times. Probably there was an increase in the kill of sea mammals, large and small, most of this kill being cached and used as winter dog food on trapping expeditions. The late summer caribou hunt was abandoned both because of the decline of the caribou and because of the new concentration on sea mammal hunting. Furthermore, the summer was a time when the supply ships arrived, a period of enjoyment and employment for the most of the Eskimos.

With the decline of caribou hunting, the traditional clothing became scarce. Some clothing needs were met by the issuance of caribou skins by the eastern Arctic patrol ship in the 1930's (Jenness 1964:52). These animals were still abundant for a while in the central Arctic. However, these skins, often in poor condition, did not altogether fill the need, and the Eskimos were forced to rely on store-bought clothing. Their parkas were made along the same lines but the inner layer became woolen duffle cloth imported from Scotland and the outer garment twill or Grenfell cloth, made of cotton and fairly windproof. Woolen winter underwear became standard although the trousers of hunters were still often made of polar bear or other skins. Thus, another kind of commodity had to be stocked at the stores. The Eskimos often went further into debt in order to buy their clothing before going trapping.

In order for the Eskimos to trap more efficiently, their dog teams became larger and often numbered more than ten. Also, sleds became longer and the timbers for the runners were bought from the stores and were often shod with imported iron runners. Dogs and dog food were more critical than ever before, and much of the kills of sea mammals, if not most, was reserved for them. Thus, the Eskimo diet began to change. The major items of store-bought diet were flour, baking powder, and some fats which were made into a pan-baked bread, or bannock, a food introduced by the Scotsmen among the traders, who had long eaten it in their homeland. The fat used was more often sea mammal fat than store-bought varieties and the calorific value of such a food is very high. Bannock was made by mixing large quantities of these ingredients with water in a basin and allowing it to sit. Portions were then taken and pressed flat to cover the bottoms of large iron frying pans, which were then hung by a wire over the lamp and rotated slowly to insure even cooking for about ten minutes. The bannocks were then turned and the other sides cooked, after which they could be eaten immediately or stored. A large number of bannocks were made at one sitting. The wives of the trappers would cook a supply of bannocks for their inland trips, thus providing a portable and calorific diet which did not suffer by freezing. On longer trips, the men would take the ingredients for bannock themselves and make it in their igloos. Thus, one more important item was added to the grubstake. Not only trappers, but many of the general population began to rely on bannock. During the time the men were away the women and children and old people often had enough native foods, but the trappers' wives could go to the store and buy foodstuffs on credit against their husbands' accounts.

The large amounts of money earned by most of the trappers were converted into equipment at the stores. Until very recently this equipment consisted of items of white men's manufacture that replaced almost exactly the traditional Eskimo equivalents. Tents came to be made of duck, which was a great improvement over the old, heavy, soggy, and smelly sealskins. Of course, rifles and ammunition were among the first items of purchase, often replacing old muzzle loaders and supplementing or completely replacing bows and arrows, bird darts, and harpoons. Twine for fish nets was bought, but the Eskimos made the nets themselves and used them during their spring and summer fishing. Metal fishhooks had long been favored, replacing the old bone kind, and they continued to be used in quantity, as they still are, for jigging through lake ice and summer fishing along the seashore.

The biggest changes were in boating equipment. The last real skin umiak disappeared from Wakeham Bay some time between 1914 and 1920. Functionally, umiaks were replaced by large Peterhead fishing boats. These were powered by one- and two-cylinder engines but they also had sails. They weighed about ten tons and their holds could carry up to ten tons of cargo. They cost only about $2,000 during the 1920's, although they are far more expensive today. Their purchase, maintenance, and operation required a group of men somewhat similar to that demanded by an umiak and its attendant kajaks. Thus, the social form of the restricted ilagiit was preserved and strengthened and the office of umialik retained its prestige and importance. Some of the previous umialiks who had been talented men and successful hunters were among the first to get these new boats. Thus they were able to maintain an identical social position, although they may have had to spend more time trapping than previously.

Some of the less prosperous Eskimos bought smaller whale boats, runabouts, and wood and canvas canoes that tended to replace the kajak. Until these were powered by outboard motors, they were not very good for hunting, and kajaks have not yet completely disappeared from the region. The operation of motorboats required large purchases of gasoline and oil, for they do only 3 to 5 miles to the gallon. Thus, the men of a restricted ilagiit or an umialik found their income constantly spent in operating their Peterheads. However, these were the very people who were usually best able to trap intensively. The Peterhead allowed them to travel farther afield for whale and go to Nottingham Island for walrus in the fall. Their boat could carry their large kills back to the settlements fairly quickly. There the meat would be cached and used for trapping expeditions, which usually started in November.

One major effect of the new summer hunting patterns with the rifle was the sinking of seals. Earlier, a seal was either harpooned, secured, and killed or it was missed or slightly wounded and lived to be hunted another day. In the new hunting method, small rifles were used from the Peterhead or kajak when the seal was first seen at a distance. The shots would make the seal dive before it could get a good breath and hence it could not swim so far under water and get away. The hunter or hunters would then make for the spot where they had last seen the seal and shoot when they saw it again, continuing this process until the seal was panting with exhaustion or even wounded. Thus, the hunters were able to get close enough to kill the animal. Because seals lose their fat during the spring,

. . . the proportion of sinking seals shows a slow, steady increase in the early spring, a sharp increase with the commencement of the basking season, a peak in early summer just before the ice departs, and then a fairly rapid decrease from the commencement of feeding in the early summer to a minimum in autumn and winter. (McLaren 1958:68)

In the fresh waters at the mouths of large rivers, seals sank more easily. During the summer about fifty percent of the seals killed were lost by sinking. When the seal was killed, a kajak or motor boat made all speed towards the spot and the hunter tried to harpoon the seal in the traditional fashion. If they did not get there quickly enough the seal was lost unless the water was shallow, in which case the Eskimos grappled for the body with a large metal hook. The Peterhead was large and often clumsy, and perhaps of the seals shot the largest proportion was lost when hunted from this craft.

Both ringed and bearded seal skins fetched only a small price from the traders until the 1960's. Some ringed seal skins were still used for clothing, but most bearded seal skins were never traded but were used for traces for the dog sleds and as materials for both winter and summer boots. White man's footgear never really replaced Eskimo boots, which are far lighter, warmer, and more efficient. During this period of resident traders the only really valuable sealskin was that of the ringed seal in its first year, called silver jars. In this area these seals were hunted most often in the spring on the tuvak, although some were shot from boats in the summer (MacLaren *ibid.*:67). The hunt for silver jars usually took place in the spring after the hunters had returned from their inland trapping. Families would go off to spring camp just as in the traditional migration cycle. Thus, there were three main trading periods during a year: first, during and after the winter fox trapping; second, after the spring seal hunting; and third, after the summer and early fall seal hunting. Either of the latter two might be combined with a visit to the annual supply ships.

SUGLUK

Both the whites and Eskimos of Sugluk said that an independent trader first set up a post there between 1914 and 1916. It is estimated that by 1919 to 1920 approximately 120 Eskimos traded into this post, although very few stayed there the year round. There were other posts at both Wakeham Bay and Cape Wolstenholme (near Ivujivik) which received similar visits. Apparently, the Hudson's Bay Company was not satisfied with either the trade or the location and anchorage at Eric Cove. In 1927, the Wolstenholme store was taken down as we have mentioned, and transported by ship to Sugluk inlet, where the timbers were laid for the winter on the northwest shore. Trade continued to be conducted at Eric Cove, in one of the small outbuildings that had surrounded the post, by an Eskimo camp trader who had previously been an assistant in the store. Such camp stores were small and carried only what the Company considered bare essentials — rifles and ammunition, tent and clothing material, fuel, and foodstuffs.

Apparently there was temporarily no independent trader at Sugluk in 1927; my informants told me that no one at all, white or Eskimo, was living there. The first people to arrive and settle at Sugluk were members of a large extended family (see below), and

132

FIGURE 3 ORIGINAL SUGLUK CAMP GROUP (1927)

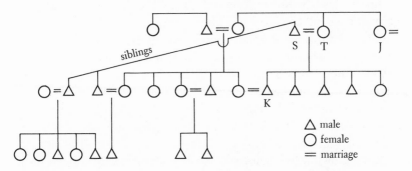

descendants of a group which had lived in the area some thirty to fifty years previously.

These twenty-seven people, of whom nine were children, had close relatives at both Deception Bay and Ivujivik, some of whom have since joined them. The group was perhaps not a really typical restricted ilagiit in that among them there were two in-marriages; there had been more such marriages in the past and there have been still more between the descendants since then. In size and functions, however, they were fairly typical of the hunting bands found in this area. The leader, S, was an isumatak, but not, as far as I know, an umialik. His son, K, is now the isumatak and, since the group acquired a Peterhead within the decade, K is now also an umialik. This group was joined about two years later by another similar group, one about the same size and consisting of a restricted ilagiit made up of a sibling group and their descendants. The leader of the group was the oldest brother and was accompanied by his younger brothers and sister and their spouses and children. This man was an isumatak and an umialik — as his father had been. He was a capable hunter and trapper and he and his family had amassed enough money or credit to get a Peterhead. The group came from Wakeham Bay via Deception Bay after two stores had been established at Sugluk. Wakeham Bay had become a little "crowded," owing to its being a better hunting area and having a Hudson's Bay Company store before Sugluk. Having a Peterhead, these people were able to move greater distances along the coast and exploit all the best hunting areas. They regularly visited Nottingham Island in the fall for walrus and brought the kill back to Sugluk for caching.

The relations between the groups were not too friendly in some ways, partly because the first group felt that they were the original people to trade at Sugluk and that the other group, which enjoyed more prestige and better hunting, had come "to take over." They were jealous of the Peterhead and saved diligently to acquire one. In the meantime, the Peterhead of the second group was wrecked when it ran aground in a storm on the way to Ivujivik, without, I believe, loss of life. They too then set about saving enough for a new one and finally achieved this in the fifties, by which time the price had risen considerably.

For a while things were very prosperous along the coast. The Hudson's Bay Company opened another camp store at Mansel Island and one of the Nuvugmiut went out there to be an Eskimo trader. In doing so, he acquired two extra wives and kept them while out of the reach of the white authorities until the R.C.M.P. took them away when he came to Sugluk in 1956. Other Nuvugmiut went to Mansel Island and some of them stayed for three years; they said that things were not bad in the summer and fall, but that the winters were terrible and that they nearly starved. Although Mansel Island is some 50 miles offshore, it is possible to go back and forth by sled in the winter, but the ice is constantly moving. This is done by judiciously moving the sled from floe to floe as the tide carries them back and forth. It takes about a week and is rarely done, whereas power boat takes only one day in the summer.

During the Depression, the prices for white fox fell continuously. The Hudson's Bay Company bought out Révillon Frères in 1936 and most of the independent traders "went under"; at Sugluk there was one trader who stayed there intermittently until the 1940's. During this period of the middle and late thirties, a few more people came to the Sugluk area for both personal and economic reasons. The two major groups continued to move around separately and there was little community spirit in Sugluk. At times when both groups were living in Sugluk, their groups of tents or igloos were set apart from each other. Although there was visiting between the two, it was not so frequent as within the groups. Even marriage was not a bond between them. The first group married within itself, or to relatives in other places. The second group continued to get most of its wives outside the area. There were, of course, two isumatak and no one over-all leader. When there was a particular abundance of game, there might well be invitations extended across the band lines and a generous social interchange. When food was short or a particular family was badly off, it was up to each group to look after its own. Store-bought products, either equipment or foodstuffs, were certainly not shared.

Catholic missions were opened in 1936 at Wakeham Bay and in 1938 at Ivujivik, about fifteen miles from the camp store there. These were the first permanent missions of any kind in the land of the Takamiut, and they brought the first Roman Catholic priests that the Takamiut population had seen. The first mission was opened by a man who had had experience with the Eskimos along the west coast of the Hudson Bay at Tavani. The previous Anglican missionaries, who were still visiting regularly by sled, had been called *ajukirtuijii*, "those whose job it is to remove inability." Up to this time all the Eskimos had faithfully followed the line of their original teachings. Each camp group had its own catechist, also called ajukirtuijii, who would hold two services every Sunday in the largest tent or igloo available. These catechists helped everyone to learn to read and write in syllables and supervised "Sunday schools." They could baptize, but confirmations were performed only during the rare visits of the bishop to the area. All the shamans had died out and none learned the trade to replace them. The powers had in fact become the isumataks and the catechists. Occasionally, the two roles were combined, as in the case of Paulasi Oqituk, and this made for a particularly powerful combined office, as it had earlier when a man was both a shaman and an isumatak.

The Catholic missionaries, who built themselves large establishments of combined houses and chapels, were looked upon with awe. They often had more material equipment than the local Hudson's

Bay Company and all of them soon learned to speak very excellent Eskimo. Few conversions resulted, however, except in Ivujivik. The Eskimos set great store by their original doctrines and the fact that they ran the Anglican Church themselves made them virtually invulnerable to other influences.

Fox pelt prices continued to be low during the latter part of the thirties and this had a corresponding effect on the Eskimo's abilities to trade:

Years	Prices (average)
1920–1923	$38.00
1924–1927	38.00
1928–1931	27.00
1932–1935	17.00
1936–1939	12.00
1940–1943	26.00
1944–1947	17.00
1948–1949	9.00

(Cantley 1950:39, quoted in Jenness 1964:74)

In 1939–1940, the Hudson's Bay Company at Wakeham Bay closed because of the low returns and the difficulty of getting supplies during the war. As had happened at Eric Cove, a camp store with an Eskimo trader was left to carry on with the barest essentials. Another migration was the result, and the local Catholic mission lost considerable importance after its favorable start (Gardner and Wilmot 1943:346). Some five families came straight to Sugluk to be near the store there. Another group, a fairly well-organized band under an able leader, remained at Deception Bay but traded into Sugluk. The area around Deception Bay was said to be better both for sea mammal hunting and for trapping than the area around Sugluk, so they decided to stay there even though there were no longer any white men there. The number of people who now traded into Sugluk was probably more than a hundred, almost as many as around the better hunting areas at Ivujivik, Wakeham Bay, and Diana Bay.

During the war, conditions were poor for the Eskimos. Although the prices of fox pelts had risen slightly, equipment was hard to come by and the store was very loath to give credit. In the Takamiut area there were no air bases or meteorological stations where large numbers of people were employed, as there were at Chimo. A number of families from the eastern Takamiut moved down to the Chimo area, where they thought conditions would be better after the American Army moved in. The Eskimos in the smaller settlements with only camp traders were very poorly off: the little stores often ran out of almost everything including essentials. That they managed to survive must be credited in part to the Catholic missionaries in these places, who used their knowledge and technical equipment to the benefit of the whole population.

Another four large families moved into the Sugluk area from the west and east during the war. Conditions were poor over the entire Arctic, but probably worse in this area than in most. In the census of 1941, conducted by interviewing post managers and missionaries, the government tried a new idea to keep track of the nomadic populations. Each Eskimo was given a small fiber disc with a number to wear around his or her neck, and the Eskimos were recorded on census sheets according to the areas where they lived and, at first, according to their family groupings. The Eskimos called these discs *ujamik*, necklace, but they did not wear them around their necks long. Sooner or later the discs were stored in safe dry places, such as where Bibles and prayer books were kept, and some were lost. But from this time on there were more accurate counts of the Eskimo population.

The Takamiut Eskimos still attempted to hunt according to the recently established cycle, including going trapping in the winter. Although people were badly off, only one person starved in the whole area. The post managers began to issue relief in foodstuffs and ammunition to those who needed it:

In the former Ungava District — the Arctic section of Northern Quebec north of the tree-line — it is known that the relief costs are relatively high, and the welfare of the Eskimos is not as good as in some other sections of the Eastern Arctic. One of the reasons is [the high population density for land area and coastline]. . . .
This region appears to be definitely overpopulated in comparison. . . . Caribou have disappeared in some areas and are scarce in others, while the resources of the sea and the limited fur catch have not been sufficient to supply food to these numbers. (Robinson 1944:133)

In this period two important families went to Cape Dorset where they thought the hunting would be better and their dependence on the white man less. The Quebec government persuaded the federal government to take over relief costs in the Sugluk area, so it was the federal government that subsidized the extra food and ammunition during the war.

At the end of the war supplies became easier to get, but the prices for furs fell even lower. In 1947 two Catholic missionaries were sent to Sugluk. They started to build a large house and chapel, which were finished some years later. No converts were made at Sugluk. This was one more agency that increased the importance and drawing power of Sugluk compared with other places along the coast. The Catholic mission supplied many gifts for the community and the missionaries helped the Eskimos with much of their equipment. During and after the war, it was impossible to run motorized boats for there was no fuel for them. When there was fuel again, after the war, incomes were so small that the Eskimos could not buy it. Peterheads fell into near disuse and kajaks made a comeback.

CHAPTER FIVE

Economic
Diversification
and Community Change

THE POST-WAR YEARS

The Arctic areas of Ungava were ceded to Quebec Province in 1917. However, the Department of Indian Affairs issued relief materials and medicine through the police to the Eskimos at the trading posts for a decade or so more, charging the costs to the Quebec government. The latter, not wishing to be burdened with the cost, claimed that in fact all Eskimos were technically Indians and, therefore, under the jurisdiction of the federal government (Jenness 1964:40). The matter was eventually referred to the Supreme Court of Canada in 1935, and the judgment issued in 1939 declared that Eskimos are Indians, and therefore the wards of the federal government. This did not at first change the behavior of the federal government, but the aftermath of World War II did.

In 1945, the Canadian government passed a bill ordering the

issuance of a family allowance to the parents of all children under sixteen. The rate, which has been raised since then, averaged about $6 per month for each child up to eight years of age and $8 per month for each child between eight and sixteen years of age. Soon after this measure was initiated, the federal government, presumably reversing its former stand, declared that Eskimos were citizens like everyone else and so should get these benefits, too. For Eskimos with large families and few means of support, these benefits were often a major portion of their total income. For some years, the system was administered by the Hudson's Bay Company post managers, and the Eskimos were allowed their payment in "essential goods." During the same period, fox pelt prices dropped lower, at one point to about $3 each (Jenness 1964:79). The Eskimos were no longer able to survive on their own without periods of starvation. Many of their older cooperative activities were no longer undertaken and reliance on guns was total, thereby ensuring a complete dependence on store-bought goods in the form of ammunition and, in this area, of clothing since the caribou were almost all gone.

In 1950 an official investigator estimated that from their own earnings the Hudson Bay Eskimos were defraying only about 40% of their purchases at the trading stores, and that the Federal Government was contributing up to 60% through various handouts. (Cantley 1950:38–39, quoted in Jenness 1964:80.)

In 1949 the Eskimos at Deception Bay finally gave up and joined those basing themselves at Sugluk, making a third major family ilagiit band in the settlement. There were also other families in Sugluk who were not strictly members of any of the three major family groupings. Either they tried through marriage or association to attach themselves to one of the major groups or they tried to make it on their own by hunting, trapping, and doing odd jobs. Between 1945 and 1949 three nuclear families left Sugluk to take employment as janitors and the like at the radio-meteorological stations operated since the war by the Department of Transport at Coral Harbour on Southampton Island and at Nottingham Island. One of these men worked for seven years without returning, sending back his money to Sugluk. This was put in a credit

140

account at the store where the rest of his family were also depositing money toward buying a new Peterhead to replace one that had been wrecked. The others also sent money back to their respective families. There was one man from each of the three major bands among these employees.

A pattern began to develop in Sugluk that affected the summer movements: during the spring the whole population would move out to the island at the entrance of Sugluk Inlet for spring and early summer hunting of seal and an occasional walrus. This island had always been a summer camp area, but before this the Eskimos had been far more scattered along the coast during their spring ice-edge hunting and the following search for birds and their nests. This camp, therefore, was much larger than it had ever been before. Some settlements had had more than a hundred Eskimos gathered together, but that was only when there was employment or at ship time. The numbers on the island were far too large for the available game, and hunting was very poor. Those bands with Peterheads were able to make longer trips, for instance to Charles Island where the ujjuk (seal) hunting was good, but they had to be back in time for the arrival of the *C. D. Howe* and the medical inspection.

After 1949, for a few years, the population of Sugluk remained fairly stable except for the natural increase, which was beginning to be significant. Until this period, the increase in population of the Sugluk area had been due almost entirely to immigration.

ESKIMO HEALTH IN THE UNGAVA AREA

Sickness had long been a problem in this area because both the Eskimo and Indian populations had little or no immunity to the diseases of civilization. Even colds turned into pneumonia and influenza was fatal to many infants and small children. As early as the eighteenth century, epidemics had wiped out large numbers of the populations around the Moravian missions in Labrador (Hawkes 1916:20). When Turner found the same phenomena at Chimo, he blamed it on igloo-living:

The principal diseases from which these people suffer are pulmonary troubles, chiefly arising from their filthy manner of living in crowded huts too ill-ventilated to allow the escape of odors emanating from their own bodies and from accumulations of slowly decomposing animal food. (Turner 1894:187)

Little did he know that the very germs that he had carried with him when he arrived may have killed a number of these "filthy people." An epidemic in the Fort Chimo area in the 1890's wiped out nearly half the Naskapi living in the area, as well as a number of Eskimos. Another epidemic of measles after the Americans arrived killed more than fifty Chimo Eskimos in 1943. This disease spread farther north to the Takamiut with serious consequences. During World War II the Takamiut area was not visited by many outsiders, and the rate of incoming diseases was reduced. However, by the late 1940's, Eskimos all over the eastern Arctic were likely to be stricken with tuberculosis, which had become endemic.

The airplane made white-Eskimo contacts even more frequent, and this brought to light the past, and continuing, terrible toll of death from the white man's diseases. In their previously isolated lives, the Eskimos had never developed resistance to most of the diseases of civilization such as colds, pneumonia, tuberculosis, mumps, whooping cough, and measles. With every new contact, hundreds became ill, and tens of people died within hours of each other. This situation was either unrecognized or kept fairly well under control before the war, when the white man and his germs arrived only once a year by ship each summer. Over the decades before the war the natural game of the Arctic had declined in numbers and increasingly the Eskimos were living off the white man's food, thereby lowering even more their resistance to disease. The Eskimos say that before the coming of the white man there were *no* diseases, and although this is a little extreme, it is quite true that most deaths were from causes other than illness. After 1947 the Catholic missionaries cared for the health of the Sallumiut with better results than those of the Hudson's Bay personnel who had preceded them. The mission was supplied annually with medical supplies from the eastern Arctic patrol ship, and the missionaries became very expert at treating all sorts of ailments. Until the present decade, the remaining missionary was the sole medical practitioner in the settlement. Reports of these sad conditions got to Ottawa and the federal government revised its procedures and budgets for dealing with health problems of the north (Jenness 1964:84–85). The eastern Arctic patrol ship C.G.S. *Nascopie* had a medical staff added to its crew and X-ray equipment was installed. After the X-rays were developed in the south, those Eskimos who showed lung diseases were shipped or flown out to hospitals in Quebec. Unfortunately, the next year the *Nascopie* went aground and was lost off Cape Dorset, and the Health Survey was not able to carry on until the building of the new C.G.S. *C. D. Howe*, which was completed in 1950. This ship was designed for hospital work and its X-rays could be developed in a matter of minutes, thereby ensuring that all diseased Eskimos would go out to the hospital immediately. Now, because the Eskimos had to be present for health check-ups, they did not leave the settlement for part of the summer. The whole population was supposed to be involved, and when the resident whites heard the ship was coming, via the radio, they made sure that a call went out for all Eskimos to be on hand.

When Eskimos were told they had to go out to the hospital, they were usually very sad and often frightened. It meant that at a moment's notice they had to pack up and leave their families and environment for a year or more. Many who had gone before them had never returned. In the few weeks before the ships arrived, the Eskimos began to get understandably tense; some would even try to hide or go off camping somewhere where they could not be found. But since the institution of the disc list the whole population had to be accounted for, and heads of families were made responsible for their members. If someone was missing, the other Eskimos would be sent out to fetch him or her. If someone had left camp, presumably by boat or sled, he might be followed by the motorboats of the *C. D. Howe* and picked up. Later in the decade, the *C. D. Howe* and other government ships were equipped with helicopters. These could roam large areas of land and coast and pick up any Eskimos who were still in hunting camps.

There was some criticism of the government for taking the Eskimos out of their environment, but medical opinion held that

143

they recovered more quickly from tuberculosis in the south than they did in hospitals built in their own area, as tried at Pangnirtung (Cumberland Sound), Chesterfield Inlet (West Hudson Bay), and Aklavik on the MacKenzie Delta. The program has been fairly successful although tuberculosis is still endemic to the Arctic. "In 1956, 1,600 Eskimos [out of a total of some 12,000] were in hospitals in southern Canada. In [1962] there were only about 350." (Jenness 1964:89, Note 3) So the program worked, and fewer each year were carried to the strange and faraway land where they could not speak the language and the weather was too hot. In addition to X-rays, the C. D. Howe staff also performed minor medical work and simple dental work. Since the Eskimos had begun eating quantities of bannock, their teeth, which had been superbly healthy, had become subject to extensive caries and, until the C. D. Howe, there had been no opportunities for dental work at all.

After each person had been through his medical examination and passed as fit, the visit of the ship became a time for rejoicing. There was a small store where candies could be bought and movies were sometimes shown. Above all, the men liked to look down into the bowels of the ship and see the enormous engines. Ships were always fascinating to them and most of them were thoroughly familiar with the workings of engines by that time. The ship's visit not only provided entertainment, but also there was work to be done unloading the year's supplies. All able-bodied men were employed for this and all got paid a small amount. If the ship had not left by the time it was unloaded, the men would rush back on board and spend most of the money at the canteen on goods that they could not get at the Hudson's Bay Company store.

For those whose relatives were being sent south, it was a very sad occasion. They watched the sick ones being taken up to the forward part of the ship where the Eskimos had their quarters in the hold and joined Eskimos from other settlements also going out to the hospital. When the ship arrived it brought another group, those who were returning from having gone out the year before. They were in an entirely different frame of mind and

144

chatted eagerly with all about them for news of the past twelve or twenty-four months. During the time they were in the hospital, the Eskimos were encouraged to write letters (in syllabics, of course) to their friends and family back home, and vice versa. These letters brought great joy and maintained hope that probably speeded recovery. Later in the 1950's, the Canadian Broadcasting Corporation started a daily service every evening in Eskimo. On this broadcast, an Eskimo girl read letters and notes from those in the hospital to their relatives all over the Arctic. These were listened to with great attention every evening, not only for news of one's own family, but for news of others in distant settlements. During the fifties, there were very few radios in Sugluk and people clustered around those. But for the people with spouses and children in the hospital, it was mainly a matter of waiting. During the period a member of a family was away, the government guaranteed them relief if they needed it, and on their return from the hospital Eskimos were automatically given rations and relief until they could get back to their normal occupations.

THE GROWING COMMUNITY AND ITS
DEMOGRAPHIC CHARACTERISTICS

We have already seen some aspects of the growing importance of Sugluk among the Eskimos of the south Hudson Strait. Not only the government, but also other agencies flocked to the settlement. The numbers of Eskimos based at Sugluk grew through immigration and natural increase and in these ways Sugluk resembles a number of other contemporary Eskimo communities. Comparative examination of demographic characteristics in these growing settlements will be left to the reader, but some general remarks on the most outstanding aspects will be presented.

In 1955 Sugluk again welcomed another agency from white man's land. The Anglican Church, having generally left the Eskimos to run their own versions of the Church in their tents and igloos, became worried about the influx of resident Catholic missions to the area, some of whom were making conversions, although at no great rate. Sugluk was seen as a central point from which an Anglican could also keep an eye on his flock at Ivujivik and Wakeham Bay. Thus arrived a new ajukirtuijii named Tivi. He built himself a house with the help of the faithful and was soon joined by his wife. Later he built a large church which, unlike the Catholic buildings, was separate from his house and big enough to accommodate the total population of Sugluk at that time. The minister soon set out to learn Eskimo and how the Church was run. He still retained the catechists who assisted him with the services and, although he was able to visit the two settlements on each side about twice a year, the main functions of the ajukirtuijii were still carried out by Eskimos in those places.

The increasing importance of Sugluk brought three more families to Sugluk, this time from Ivujivik: one man came to get work, another to get married, and the third to join relatives who had previously made the change in residence.

The population increased even faster during the 1950's. Between 1957 and 1960 five more large families came to Sugluk. Three of these were from Ivujivik, where economic conditions were very poor. These people tended to ally themselves with the previous arrivals from Ivujivik, forming another large family-band with various kinds of kinship connections between them. The other two were those who had been working at the government radio stations at Nottingham Island and Coral Harbour and were rejoining their families. Other agencies continued to arrive and Sugluk became the largest and most important settlement along the south coast of the Hudson Strait. The most recent population increase has been due almost entirely to natural increase with very little further immigration.

Of those who came to Sugluk during this period (approximately 125 people), many (50 percent) actually came to join relatives already there, but, of course, these people were the followers of trends. The most important reason — the one responsible for most of the initial moves — was the presence of the store and other white agencies. Other reasons, such as getting a wife or for better hunting or employment, accounted for only about 10 percent of the total immigrations.

During this same period, 1920 to 1964, about thirty-five people left Sugluk for various reasons and did not return. Thirteen of those who left went to Cape Dorset, where economic conditions have usually been better than at Sugluk and where the Takamiut have long had many kinship connections. The actual reasons for leaving were about equally divided between economic reasons, such as better hunting and employment, and personal reasons, such as the search for a wife or "divorce."

In addition to the continuing influx of Eskimos, the white population of Sugluk increased about fivefold during the decade from 1954 to 1964. The Anglican missionary came in 1955 and the first nurse in 1960. The first school at Sugluk was opened by Miss Marjorie Hinds and she was followed by a series of teachers. In 1959 two teachers were needed and by 1964 the school had been enlarged and there were four teachers, including a principal. After 1960 a new community generator was installed, necessitating a white mechanic and his family, who later also had to maintain the new Snowmobile tracked vehicle. As a consequence of the growing business, the Hudson's Bay Company added more white clerks to service Sugluk, Wakeham Bay, and Ivujivik. In 1958 the first Northern Service officer, Mr. Archie Fluke, was transferred to Sugluk from Frobisher Bay. He and his wife occupied a large three-bedroom house built that summer. The Northern Service officer, now called Area administrator, was responsible for all the employment and equipment of the Department of Northern Affairs in the area and the work load grew, necessitating the hiring of more Eskimo assistants.

Sugluk has been growing fast, not only in population, but also in the number of buildings and the amount of the paraphernalia of civilization. From an isolated village, Sugluk has grown to resemble a frontier town and is the metropolis of the south shore of the Hudson Strait. For some reason or other, it even has street lighting! The relations between the members of the white community, who used to be simply a missionary and a trader, are now between many members of a complex of occupational groups. Part of the time the social lines are drawn between the members of the various agencies, but for other occasions "class distinctions" are made in terms of rank, age, and sex. These whites, of course, remain altogether separate from the Eskimo population on the social level with few exceptions (see Chapter Seven).

The recent and present Eskimo population of Sugluk is typical of underdeveloped areas all over the world. Between 1955 and 1960, the period for which I have the most complete figures, the rate of natural increase passed two percent per annum and is now over 2.5 percent. The population climbed from 260 in 1960 to a total of 307 in 1964 and should reach over 350 by 1970, assuming no migrations of any kind.

The present population histogram has the typical wide-based pyramid indicating a larger proportion of children under five, making up nineteen percent of the total population. The birth and fertility rates remain very high, probably owing to three factors: the lack of knowledge of or desire for contraception, the great desire for children as a mark of prestige and security, and the lack of control (e.g., taboos) on intercourse at any period of marriage and to a great extent outside marriage. The birth rate in Sugluk for the past ten years has been approximately 35 per 1,000, much higher than in "civilized" populations but somewhat lower than in some other underdeveloped areas. One reason it is lower is that a large proportion of the population is in age categories that are not fertile and there has also been a rise in the proportion of unmarried persons (see next chapter). A more accurate indicator is always the fertility rate, that is, the number of live births per 1,000 women of reproductive age (from 15 to 45 years). In Sugluk this was 261 per 1,000 which is extremely high compared with, for instance, the rest of Canada (109 per 1,000 in 1957). With few or no controls on fertility, Eskimo women tend to bear large numbers of children. In a sample of women over 50, who have presumably finished bearing children, the average is 6.75 live births during their fertile years, and this may be an underestimate. The women of younger age groups seem to be keeping up the rate, too. One surprising aspect of fertility at Sugluk is the high proportion of women who do not bear children: twelve percent of all married women. The main factor here is that until recently there have been no possibilities of medical treatment to relieve barrenness.

The outstanding mortality figure is the death rate for children under five years of age. Twenty-two percent of the children fail to reach this age, and unfortunately this ratio does not seem to

148

have decreased even during the recent period of intense medical treatment. There are two opposing factors: on the one hand, the availability of medical care and the Eskimos' understanding of disease have been improving; and on the other hand, the number of white people in the area has greatly increased, especially the number of "arrivals," each bringing in more germs to which the children are particularly susceptible.

A typical example of such infection occurred during the winter of 1958. A party of mining prospectors came to Sugluk and hired twelve Eskimo men to work for them at Deception Bay. Soon after the party left, eight Sallumiut, including six babies, died in one week. All twelve men at Deception Bay became seriously ill and had to be flown out by charter airplane to the nearest hospital, which was at Frobisher Bay, Baffin Island. There one of them died, but the others recovered. Meantime two sled parties, not knowing of the sickness (probably flu), visited the mining camp and one went on to Wakeham Bay. There they soon discovered they were carriers of the disease because the members of the camp where they stayed became ill. They were put in quarantine and not allowed to travel to other Eskimo camps. However, the disease had already spread and four more people died within ten days.

Since that time, regular airline flights, once a month, have begun operating and the influx of white man's germs has been almost constant. I do not know how long it takes a population group to build up immunity to such disease but it is probable that there will be quick natural selection in favor of those who do withstand them for the death rate is very high among those who do not.

In 1960 a nursing station was opened at Sugluk under the auspices of the Indian and Northern Health Service. The station is a small building, equipped with a consulting room and a small two-bed hospital for emergency cases. The first nurse sent to Sugluk was an Eskimo from Labrador who had received full training down south. Unfortunately, the Eskimos were very unwilling to use her services because (1) they could not be persuaded that an Eskimo could be a real nurse or doctor after having been treated by whites for so many years, (2) they had considerable faith in the Catholic missionary who had been treating them with some success for more than ten years, and (3) the nurse had only one eye, and any kind of physical impairment is looked upon with suspicion and disrespect by the Eskimos. A year later she was replaced by a white nurse, who has a thriving practice among the ever-growing population. At first she had an Eskimo interpreter-assistant and later her efforts were supplemented by those of her husband, the Anglican missionary.

Figures on death rates are probably not too accurate as past records exist only in memories and deaths often occurred, until the nursing station was established, without the presence of a diagnostician. Apart from the high infant mortality, the death rate is not outstandingly high. In the past decade, it has probably averaged between 15 and 20 per 1,000. Although about double that of civilized countries, it is not nearly as high as in many tropical underdeveloped areas. Recent local and governmental medical measures probably have accounted for the lower death rate and the difference between this figure and that for the birth rate (ca. 30 per 1,000) accounts for the high over-all rate of population increase. In these respects, Sugluk is typical of most Eskimo settlements in the past decade or so.

The following table shows the major causes of death.

CAUSES OF DEATH AT SUGLUK 1945–1960

Cause	Percentage of total deaths (rounded to nearest 0.5%)
Pneumonia (from flu or colds)	36.5
In childbirth or at birth	15.5
Accidents	11.5
Tuberculosis	6.0
Other, and unknown	30.0

The low tuberculosis death rate reflects the recent government efforts to get it under control and is probably lower than in many settlements. Although the present Sallumiut are heavy smokers — I know only two adults who do not smoke — deaths from lung cancer appear to be nil. Other forms of cancer are equally rare among the Eskimos. Whether this is because of some constitutional factors or because few people live to a very old age, I do not know. In spite of the high fat content of the diet, the incidence of heart trouble is also very low, probably because of the very active life that the Eskimos have led until now.

ECONOMY: DIVERSIFICATION

The annual migration cycle of the Eskimos has been severely truncated in the past two decades. There are more people living in the Sugluk area than before, and the previous resources, even if they had not declined as have the caribou, could not possibly support this number. Therefore, other sources of livelihood have come to be increasingly relied upon.

Annual cycle. During the winter, from November to April, all the Eskimos live at the settlement itself. There is little wage employment, and most of the men spend the greater part of their time inland trapping. They leave their families at Sugluk for days or weeks at a time and stay out as long as their food and dog food last. The people left in the settlement spend their time visiting, doing chores at home, and doing some carving. Some people go seal hunting at the tuvak edge but most prefer to trap.

In spring, April to June, most of the families move out to Sugluk Island by sled, and a large tent camp is set up. The number of families that moves out varies from year to year and is gradually declining. Since the Eskimos have recently got permanent housing, the trend is for fewer and fewer people to move out into tents. Those who do not move include people who have permanent employment in the settlement and those who are aged or infirm and cannot hunt. Because in recent years, 1963–1964, the prices paid for sealskins have risen enormously, some of the more active families have begun to disperse again during this season of good hunting. Bearded seal hunting on the ice near the island is quite good but there are too many people trying to subsist on the same resource to make it really profitable. Those families that go farther may hunt on the tuvak near Deception Bay or even beyond Cape Weggs. Some single and young married men with small families travel even farther to the better hunting areas near Ivujivik and

Wakeham Bay. These patterns will hold only so long as sealskins command a high price (between $15 and $30 each, as opposed to between $1 and $5 in the 1950's).

The breakup of the ice at Sugluk Inlet takes place in late June and can be said to signal the beginning of summer. Most of the people stay out at the Island or at their spring camps, although some return by sled before this. During breakup itself, which lasts two weeks or so, there is no travel to and from the Island, so provisions have to be laid in for the duration. Travel overland is still possible even after breakup as the snows in some valleys may not melt until July. As soon as the ice has cleared from the Inlet, most people come back to the settlement by boat. Those who have been out hunting by sled return while there is still snow. If the eastern Arctic patrol ship, the *C. D. Howe*, is not due for some weeks, there may be extended hunting along the coast by those who have large boats. Those who have smaller boats try to hunt within one day's journey from Sugluk. Generally the shipping season starts in July.

As has been described, all the Eskimos have to be at the settlement for medical inspection and the *C. D. Howe* and other ships provide employment for many men when the time comes to unload the year's supplies and any construction materials they may have brought. With the considerable amount of government activity in the past few years, new buildings are built every summer. Although white construction crews may be flown in, there is usually plenty of manual labor for a number of the Eskimos. After the *C. D. Howe* has gone, the men either engage in wage employment or they go hunting. For those who are not employed, every possible hunting opportunity is taken while the good weather lasts. For those with small boats (for example, outboard canoes) hunting is restricted to an area fairly close to Sugluk. For those with Peterheads — now three family-bands — longer trips may be taken as far as Wakeham Bay and beyond. These larger boats are better able to catch whales and bearded seals and this meat is the basis of the winter supply of dog food.

In September the first real snow falls, and autumn may be said to start. Everyone who is not out hunting lives in the settlement at this time. There is little wage labor, except perhaps for finishing the construction of new buildings, and trapping cannot start until the fox pelts are really white — sometime in November. This is one of the poorer times of the year. The weather is often too bad for hunting in small boats and there is not enough snow to build igloos. Until recently all or most Eskimos lived in snow houses, but since 1957 more and more wooden houses have been built, and by now no one has to suffer the dripping and cold igloos all winter. In October the annual walrus hunt at Nottingham Island takes place. Only those groups with Peterhead boats can go such a distance and in such bad weather, and even they cannot go if they do not have enough money or credit for the considerable fuel required for the 250-mile journey. After the hunt, the boats hurry back in order not to be caught in the sea ice, which begins to freeze over and form a new tuvak in November.

It can be seen that in recent years there has been a trend toward a more static and concentrated population than ever before in the area. For most of the year, the Eskimos live in the settlement crowded around the buildings of the white agencies. Although the men go hunting as before, they generally leave their families in the settlement and since the coming of the school (1957) they have been supposed to leave the children in the settlement for nine months of the year. Apart from the actual economic and technological changes, the very size and density of the settlement itself has had profound effects on the lives of the Eskimos.

In the last fifteen to twenty years hunting and trapping have contributed less and less to the livelihood of the Sallumiut. At the beginning of the 1950's these two sources were the mainstay of Eskimo life, and when they were insufficient the Eskimos had to go "on relief." This involved applying to the company manager for "rations" (essential supplies), the cost of which would then be reimbursed by the federal government. I have already noted that by 1950 the Eskimos in some areas received as much as 50 percent of their money income from government sources. However, a large proportion of this was in the form of a family allowance. These monthly payments were of considerable importance to Eskimos who had few other means of earning money and who had large families. For instance, a man with a family of four children would get nearly $30 a month from this source out of a total money income of less than $100 per month for the average household.

Hunting, however, supplies a large proportion of the food consumed, more than 50 percent at certain times of the year, and also provides essential raw materials for such things as sealskin boots. It is impossible to estimate the value of these products, as they are not traded and there is no price on them. We cannot even estimate the equivalent value in store goods that would be needed to replace them, for such items are just not available.

As I have described, most summer hunting is done within one day's journey of Sugluk, either by boat or by sled, and only with Peterheads can long journeys and extended hunts be undertaken. Hunting is generally done only when the weather is fair because in anything but calm water it is very difficult to see the head of a sea mammal as it comes up to breathe, which further limits the amount of hunting that can be done. The methods of hunting described are still in vogue, but more and more sophisticated rifles (e.g., .222's), which allow accurate shooting at increasingly greater distances, are coming into use. This allows for easier hunting but it also increases the number of seals lost by sinking. Seals used to frequent Sugluk Inlet itself during the summer, but recently the increase in the number of motor boats has frightened them off. This has increased the need for more extended hunting expeditions, which has favored those with the larger boats and forced the poorer people to rely more and more on other forms of livelihood. In addition only those Eskimos with larger boats can hunt white whales, which are rare in the area. Fortunately, these whales are easier to see than seals in choppy waters and do not sink when killed; therefore they may be left floating while the hunters in the boat make sure they have killed the whole school. Then all the bodies are gathered up and the process of cutting up, loading, and later caching may proceed. Polar bears are very rare and are never intentionally hunted except when they come near the settlement or a camp.

154

Caribou have all but disappeared from the area, but the thought of caribou hunting still excites those who remember their flesh and skins in their traditional uses. In 1954 two of the best sled men in Sugluk set out to hunt caribou. Although they traveled more than 250 miles to the south, probably as far as Payne Lake, they only managed to shoot two of the few caribou they saw. The meat of these two was used up for food and for the dogs by the time they arrived back in Sugluk and all they were left with were the skins. However, in the most recent years the caribou population of Ungava seems to be on the increase. The people of Fort Chimo and Povungnituk are killing more than they can remember having killed for many years. During the spring of 1964 a few men saw some caribou tracks while they were some one hundred miles inland tending their trapping lines. When they got back to the settlement and spread the news, a number of men started to prepare their sleds and collect provisions for the hunt. They were only persuaded not to go by the lateness of the season which would have meant very poor conditions for sledding — melting snows and fast-flowing spring streams. If the trend in the caribou population continues, it is quite possible that men will include caribou hunting in their spring trapping excursions, adding their most welcome meat and skins to the Eskimos' diminishing resources.

Birds are still hunted, and the land around Sugluk is often a favorite place for ducks and geese during their long flight south in the late summer. Sometimes they are so tired after crossing the Hudson Strait that they are easy marks for shotguns and .22's. Eider duck used to breed in large numbers on the islands and cliffs along the coast near Sugluk; however, the raiding of their nests has driven them to more distant places. Ptarmigan are a welcome addition to the spring diet and are eagerly hunted when there is little else around. Both men and women hunt them and some may get back to Sugluk after a day's hunting with as many as a hundred in their bags. The murres, which are so abundant in the Ivujivik area, are found along the sea coast near Sugluk but are hunted only as a supplement to the more important seals in the area.

Fishing is still an important part of the Sugluk economy but now weirs and fish spears have almost disappeared, and it is carried on almost exclusively by the use of nets. Fish are quite abundant in the inland lakes near Sugluk and in the spring may be caught by men jigging with metal hooks. At the time of the fish migrations to the sea in the early summer, net-fishing near the river outlets at the head of the bay and in tidal water is quite productive. Farther from the settlement, similar fishing is even better at the mouths of other rivers and bays. Fishing in shallow coastal areas could be quite productive during the summer but many men prefer to hunt seals and leave the fishing to the women and the infirm.

Other natural resources in the area include the late summer berries which are still gathered in quantities by the women and children. These gathering excursions are usually of less than a day's duration and many farther areas are left untouched. Mussles and seaweed are still gathered and eaten, although both are falling out of favor as a food source. Mussles are becoming less common in the area because of overharvesting and can supply only a minute proportion of the diet in any case.

The fastest growing and steadiest aspect of the Sugluk economy is wage labor. Permanent wage employment, however, is still only for a few. In 1964 there were only six men and four women who had full-time employment and most of them belonged to one rather prosperous family. These permanent employees probably contributed more than 30 percent of the total money earned in wages, the other 70 percent coming from various forms of irregular employment.

Most such irregular employment is found outside the settlement. For instance, in the summer of 1959 nineteen men were flown to Frobisher Bay to work on construction projects. In the past decade mining exploration and development have consistently employed a few men for various lengths of time. Recently there has been initial development of the mineral resources found at Asbestos Hill, some 25 miles inland from Deception Bay. Although this project requires large numbers of manual laborers, the administrators have, perhaps wisely, decided that not all the employment should be given to the men of any one settlement. So, although Sugluk is the closest labor supply, men have also been flown in from other settlements in Northern Quebec and even from across Hudson Bay. Furthermore, to prevent whole families from settling as "squatters" near this huge development, men are employed for only three-month periods at a time. The majority of the employees are young unmarried men and, so far, no form of settlement has developed in the area.

I have already mentioned the ten or so permanently employed people within the settlement. However, there are other forms of seasonal labor, much of which is used as a substitute for relief and given to those who cannot hunt well on account of infirmity or age. Among this type of labor are such things as cleaning up the settlement after winter and digging the essential drainage ditches. Unloading ships and transporting and storing goods are jobs requiring able-bodied men, even though a caterpillar tractor (Snowmobile) has recently been imported to handle the major tasks. Construction work also employs a number of the able-bodied or skilled, but the majority of the jobs, among which rolling oil barrels is the most common, demand very little training or skill. Although the Eskimos do not enjoy wage labor as much as the various forms of hunting, they realize that hunting has become comparatively unproductive as a full-time occupation and gladly try their hand at wage labor even though they may not wish to work more than a few months at a time. In addition to these forms of employment, a few families are hired every year as janitors at the weather stations at Nottingham Island, at Resolution Island, and even as far as the one at Coral Harbour. These steady jobs are usually given to family men and last about a year. Some men, however, if they are good workers and wish to save considerably more money, may be allowed to work for longer periods and one man worked for seven consecutive years when saving money toward his family's Peterhead. Wage employment, then, is here to stay. It will probably increase as more and more agencies are concentrated at Sugluk and displace other forms of activity by the 1970's.

The outstanding feature of the economic activity in the eastern

Canadian Arctic during the 1950's was the sudden growth of soapstone carving (Martijn 1964; Graburn 1966) as a major occupation. Commercialization was started at government instigation and carvings were test marketed in 1949 and 1950. The project was a success, and by 1952 the people of Sugluk were beginning to make and sell carvings for money. The Hudson's Bay Company was the purchaser and the carvings were sold down south through the Canadian Handicrafts Guild and have become famous all over North America. By 1956 carving was contributing over $33,000 to the money income of Sugluk and this was more than 50 percent of the money earned or otherwise acquired. In 1957 the market appeared to be saturated and the Hudson's Bay Company suddenly ceased to buy carvings at Sugluk. By this time many men had become dependent on carving for a major part of their incomes and this was a great blow. As one man said to me, "I was not even able to afford a cup of tea before going hunting in the morning." The government administrator realized the plight of the Sallumiut and began to buy carvings again. Some months later, the Company also started to buy them again and since then carving has contributed between 15 and 20 percent to the total money income.

In traditional times the Eskimos had carved small objects of ivory (Payne 1888–89:217), and soapstone had been used only as the raw material for lamps and for clumsy cooking pots. Carving in soapstone was an innovation, but the Eskimos took to it with some skill and a few of the men became really good carvers. Not just these few began to carve: more than 80 percent of the adult population have tried carving as a source of income, though some have made only a few pieces. Most of these Eskimos are not particularly skilled and the flood of small and poor carvings has tended to spoil the market. Some carvings bought in Sugluk, I am told, were unsalable and still reside in warehouses in Ottawa. I interviewed most of the adult men about their carving activities and all but one of them, including those who might be considered "artists," said that they loathed the activity as an occupation and that they only carved for the money it brought them, which was very little in terms of the long hours needed to make a carving.

Most of the men would rather go hunting even with a smaller return whenever the weather was good. Carving has become the activity of the disabled and infirm and in times of bad weather. The supply of soapstone is well known to the Eskimos for they had mined it for its former uses. It occurs in veins up to 6 feet wide at many places along the coastline and mining the stone has become an additional activity during summer sea mammal hunting. In addition to this, in the last few years the government has had large quantities of stone shipped to Sugluk so that there will always be a supply even during the winter months. This stone is sold to the Eskimos at ten cents a pound, which barely covers its cost.

Carving, although subject to an unstable market, filled an economic gap during a period when hunting and trapping were not too productive and there was relatively little wage labor. It contributed considerably to the economic health of Sugluk and reduced relief expenditures (see Figure 4). It will probably never contribute so heavily again but it will not completely cease. It may become the occupation of those few people who are good at it. Other Eskimos will only put much effort into carving during the shipping season when there are plenty of visiting whites who are prepared to pay higher prices than the store, which pays a wholesale price only 25 to 30 percent of the market price down south — handling, breakage, distribution, and profits account for the rest.

Men in their twenties and thirties are the major supporters of their families in Sugluk. After that age, their hunting efficiency decreases and they are less suitable for the heavy manual labor that is demanded of most temporary employees. Boys begin to hunt and trap in their early teens but do not become really proficient until their twenties. Peak efficiency in hunting is reached in the late twenties. However, the most successful trappers are in their middle thirties because trapping is an occupation requiring great skill and experience but not demanding so much quickness of eye and speed of reaction as hunting sea mammals with guns. The minor forms of hunting, such as of birds and hares, are usually the occupations of teenagers and considerably older men. Such hunt-

FIGURE 4   TOTAL INCOME AND COMPONENT PARTS; SUGLUK 1950–1964

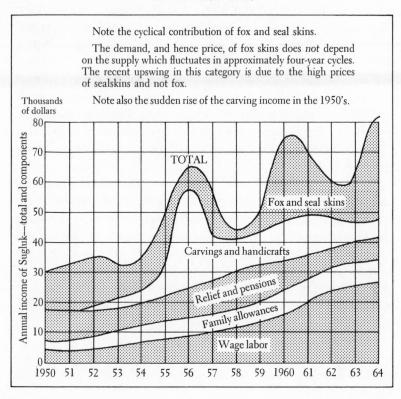

Note the cyclical contribution of fox and seal skins.

The demand, and hence price, of fox skins does *not* depend on the supply which fluctuates in approximately four-year cycles. The recent upswing in this category is due to the high prices of sealskins and not fox.

Note also the sudden rise of the carving income in the 1950's.

Thousands of dollars

Annual income of Sugluk—total and components

TOTAL

Fox and seal skins

Carvings and handicrafts

Relief and pensions

Family allowances

Wage labor

ing is not considered "real man's work" and can be successfully prosecuted with much lighter weapons. Fishing, generally, is seen in the same light. However, during the early summer when the char first swarm around the river mouths and tidal waters of the coast, fishing is a very productive occupation and the more able-bodied men concentrate on it for a few days at a time.

The expenditures of the present-day Sallumiut are divided between the equivalents of traditional items, such as guns and boats, and new items that have been introduced by the white man, such as tobacco and radios. A limited analysis of expenditures from a few families shows the major characteristics. Unless the Eskimos are particularly saving for some "target goods," the order of preferred expenditure, agreed upon by a large number of Eskimos, is as follows: (1) food; (2) tobacco and cigarette paper or cigarettes; (3) clothing; (4) hunting equipment, ammunition, guns, gas, and boating necessities; (5) furniture and luxury items, such as record players and radios.

For the modern Eskimo this is an expected and probably sensible order: from the earliest days of white contact tobacco has been a "necessity" for the Eskimos. (In fact, it formed 17 percent of the expenditures of these families.) Of the food bought, 90 percent is what is classed as staples, that is flour, lard, canned milk, and the like. If certain luxury foods, such as candy and soft drinks, are available, they form a high proportion of the foodstuffs bought. When ships' canteens are open, these sweets are sold in large quantities. For instance, when the *C. D. Howe* was in Sugluk for two days in 1960, the Sallumiut spent more than $500 on such items.

TYPICAL PATTERNS OF EXPENDITURE

(AVERAGE OF THREE SMALL FAMILIES WITH NO EMPLOYED MEMBERS)

Items	Average $ per family per month	Percentage of total expenses
A. Food: staples	$12.05	22.2
other	1.35	2.4
B. Clothes	10.40	19.4
C. Household	6.33	11.0
D. Hunting equipment	10.80	25.0
E. Luxuries: tobacco	9.00	16.6
sundries	.05	0.0
radios, records	1.80	3.3
Totals	$51.78	99.9

More of the material equipment owned and used by the Sallumiut is store bought every year. Kajaks were gradually abandoned as a hunting boat during the 1950's and were replaced by various forms of manufactured boats. The total number of all boats owned by the Sallumiut was fifteen in 1959 and had increased to twenty by 1964. This is still less than one for every two households, so considerable sharing is necessary and this will be further discussed in the next section. Most of these boats are small dinghies and canoes, the majority with outboard motors. It is not uncommon for one man who owns a motor and another who owns a boat to cooperate in hunting with each other, although by no means exclusively. There are only five large boats, Peterheads and whaleboats, suitable for extended hunts. Not all of these are in good repair but the costs of new items often force the Eskimos to use equipment that is both antiquated and unsafe.

Until recently there was an abundance of sled dogs in Sugluk. Numbering almost as many as the human population, they were generally in very poor condition, especially during the summer when they were rarely fed but lived by scrounging for scraps. In fall and winter they were carefully fed with meat and store bought cereals by those who were concerned about having good teams for the trapping season. Because of lack of game in the Sugluk area, many teams never got really well fed and the output from trapping may have suffered. Since 1963 small motorized snow vehicles ("Ski-doos") have been available in the area. Though they cost $600 to $1,000 new, the Eskimos have made every effort to buy these for winter travel, claiming the following advantages: ability to average 15 to 25 miles per hour versus 4 to 10 miles per hour for dogs; no need for harnessing and unharnessing in mornings and evenings; no need for feeding at night and all through the unproductive summer and fall; a headlight for night sledding; greatly reduced physical effort required; probable lower direct cost of fuel and oil compared with the hunting required to feed a dog team; and greater prestige value. Often left unsaid are the disadvantages: costs of $200 to $1,000 per year in maintenance and depreciation; higher incidence of frostbite due to greater speed and lack of physical exercise; the machine cannot smell its way home; it cannot be eaten in emergency; greater frequency of serious "traffic accidents"; great frequency of breakdowns requiring the driver to walk home; and relative inability to pull heavy loads in very steep or rough places, to negotiate dangerous ice, and to operate as an emergency pack carrier in the summer.

The first Eskimo-owned Ski-doo was bought in 1963 and by the winter of 1967–68 there were over twenty-five in Sugluk. Conversely the number of households owning dog teams dropped from over thirty-five to one. Some other households owned one or two dogs each mainly to eat scraps, the men claimed. This changeover has had serious consequences. Rarely are more than 70 percent of the vehicles in good repair so many men are unable to hunt as regularly, though two men often go with one vehicle. Because of the high incidence of breakdown, usually two or three teams accompany each other on long trips. Many men are financially insolvent through trying to pay for the parts to keep their machines going — many in fact fail and the remains of machines are scattered round the settlement or are cannibalized for the few that remain. The annual fall walrus hunt is no longer undertaken because there is no great need for supplies of dog food and in turn the walrus population has increased greatly. The Eskimos rely more and more on store bought foods for their own consumption. The extended range of the vehicles has enabled those with working machines to extend their trap lines and in 1968 most with working vehicles went together on two caribou hunts which were successful in getting caribou more than 300 miles south of Sugluk. Compared with the abortive 1954 attempt, most of the shot animals arrived home without being eaten and some of these were put on sale to the rest of the population at the local co-operative store.

There are approximately two guns per hunter in Sugluk, if one includes the teenage boys. Most of these are various forms of .22's or 30-30's and .303's, the larger guns being used for the final killing of large sea mammals and the smaller for smaller game and for initial shots at larger game. There are also a number of shotguns, used not only for killing birds but also as the larger rifles are in killing seals. Although some hunters take good care of their equipment, most guns are not nearly so well looked after as they are in other communities, such as Lake Harbour and Wakeham Bay, where hunting is still the most important occupation.

In the past decade the whole appearance of the Sugluk winter community has changed. At first, in 1958, the Hudson's Bay Company interpreter was given lumber to build himself a wooden winter house, and soon after this a number of other people copied the idea, using scrap lumber. For the poorer and older Eskimos, the government in 1959 sent up some prefabricated houses which were put up by the Eskimos themselves. Although these houses were well insulated and better than igloos many of the Eskimos thought they were too cramped. Soon after this the government started sending a larger type of "Eskimo Unit" house to Sugluk and other settlements. These were more expensive and, although they were subsidized, the Eskimos were expected to pay about $1,000 for each. As almost no families could raise that much money, the houses were built and the Eskimos allowed to pay when they were able, with no interest.

These houses had a large sleeping-living-cooking room and a very small "bathroom" with a chemical toilet and a bath but no water supply. The toilets were rarely used and the baths were generally used as storage places for clothes or meat. Since 1963 larger houses with two, and more recently three, separate bedrooms have been made available. The first few were bought by those in permanent employment but those erected in 1967 were rented ($27 to $42 per month, including oil and electricity) on the basis of need to those with large families and poor previous accommodations. In other settlements this same type of house is sold to those showing need and the ability to keep up the regular monthly payments. As the houses cost more than $8,000 (gross) the Eskimos have to pay $100 to $150 per month for rent and fuel even though they do not have to pay the full costs. More such three-bedroom houses will be built in all Arctic settlements but whether they will be rented or sold will depend on the policies of the local administrators.

Thus permanent igloos have disappeared from the lives of the Sallumiut. The interiors of the houses are no longer arranged along the same lines as the traditional igloo, for the simple reason that there is no snow in a wooden house to form the traditional sleeping platform. Beds, raised off the floor, are in common use; most of them are constructed of wood but some are cast-off white man's cots. The beds are covered with the same mixture of caribou skins, blankets, sleeping bags, and odd clothing that covered the sleeping platforms of the last decade. Many of these are distributed by the missions at Christmas time and are collected in the south as charity. Under the beds and on the floors are sacks or plastic bags of clothing not in use. The Eskimos still make very little use of chairs and tables and most families eat squatting on the floor around the communal pot. Cooking equipment, however, has changed almost as drastically as housing types. The *qullik* went out of use in Sugluk because it was too troublesome and took too long to cook things and to dry clothes; its place was taken by a variety of oil-burning stoves. Most of these are Primus or Coleman stoves, both of which are suitable for summer and winter use and are portable enough for a man to take along on a trapping expedition or in a boat. In some of the summer tents, oil drums, cut in half, are used for burning wood scraps and brush. In the newer government-supplied winter houses oil-burning cooking ranges are used and there are a few space heaters which are large and more than the Eskimo needs but they certainly heat the houses well. Most of the Eskimos complain that the oil they burn costs them too much and they would like a smaller type of stove. In these government houses electricity is supplied from the community generator and there is electric lighting, but in most houses Coleman lamps and various wick-lamps are still used.

Summer living conditions are a little more traditional. Canvas tents completely replaced the sealskin kind and nearly all families own them. There are a few people, mainly the aged and disabled, who have never moved out of their winter houses since they abandoned igloos. However, most people, those who make some attempts at hunting and go out to the island in the spring, move into large, low, white tents. Much of the furniture of the houses is transferred into the tents, but some people use sleeping platforms because they do not want to have to move beds around with them when they travel. Generally, summer tents are smaller than the houses and are therefore just as messy and cramped. Food is left out in the open, as ever, in both tents and houses and the interiors of some of the dwellings look and smell like those described by the most disgusted early missionaries! On the part of the younger people there are serious attempts to keep neat houses and to emulate the appearance of white man's dwellings. I would imagine that in the next few years more and more of the houses will become more orderly and sanitary and fewer and fewer people will move out of them during the summer.

Clothing in present-day Sugluk is almost entirely store bought. The outer garments are often made by the women according to the old patterns from material bought from the store, but even the familiar Eskimo-style cloth parkas are giving way to manufactured clothes. Only in footwear are Eskimo articles still common: winter boots are as warm as anything purchasable and a great deal lighter, and Eskimo waterproof boots are equally efficient, although they wear out quickly on rock and concrete. In the last few years the stores have sold tanned cow and moose hide which the Eskimos are increasingly using for the soles of winter boots. Such materials are said to be warmer than the traditional ujjuk skin soles and are very much easier to sew. The upper legging parts of the boots are increasingly being made of canvas which is easier to work than the traditional sealskins, dries more easily, and releases more good pelts for sale for cash. Summer waterproof ujjuk skin boots are disappearing even faster and are being replaced by rubber hip-waders. The latter are more practical in deep water, are less subject to cuts by sharp rocks, and are relatively cheap compared with the amount of skilled labor needed to make the sealskin boots. The rising prices of sealskins sold to the stores is a major factor accounting for the decline in Eskimo-style footwear: in the winter and spring of 1964 sealskins went up fivefold in price and very few new boots were made. But an increasingly important consideration is the complete inability of the young women to sew the traditional waterproof seams.

It may not be very many years before all the Eskimos are dressed like the laborers in our own society. In matters of material equipment and taste, it is obvious that for most Eskimos the models are the seasonal laborers who are annually brought in for construction work and other blue-collar jobs. In the eastern Arctic, as opposed to the McKenzie Delta (Clairmont 1963), the Eskimos have not yet taken "middle class ideals" and aspirations to heart; this, however, may soon come with the increasing amount of schooling they are beginning to have.

166

As noted above, four distinct family-bands have arrived at Sugluk over the last forty years. Three of these were originally independent groups who wintered together in small camps along the coastline and who pursued most of their summer boating activities together. After decades of wandering along the coastline, coming back to winter camps, and splitting and re-forming, these groups have finally come to rest at Sugluk. The fourth group was not an independent, integrated economic and social group: it was a group of families from Ivujivik who had originally been in different camps although related by kinship. One of these families had the structure of a small band but other households were headed by widows whose husbands and camp leaders had died. These latter groups from Ivujivik have tended to consolidate, owing to their ties of kinship, but for all intents and purposes they are leaderless. In addition to the four entities described, there are a number of other families who arrived independently and who exhibit little solidarity except within their immediate families. Thus, the population is divided into four groups each of which is (1) co-residential, (2) economically cooperative, including corporate ownership, and (3) kinship based. For comparison's sake, I have called the additional fifty to sixty people at Sugluk who lack these three characteristics the fifth "band" or the "Others."

A major function of each band is to own and operate a large hunting boat (the Peterhead), which is used for the extended expeditions that are now necessary for efficient hunting. In 1959 two of the four bands owned and operated such boats, and a third family was well on the way to saving enough money to buy one. Since then this third group has obtained, from the Catholic missionary, an old boat that had been out of use for many years. They have replaced the motor and some woodwork, repainted it, and can now stand on equal terms with the other two umialiit. Each boat costs from three to five thousand dollars secondhand, is expensive to operate (about forty cents per mile), and requires a crew of seven or eight men to operate and hunt from it. Thus, among the major requirements of each band are adequate economic re-

167

sources for capital investment and operation, and an ever-ready supply of manpower to make use of all suitable hunting opportunities. To allow for members who may be ill or in wage employment a pool of ten or more able-bodied adult men is necessary. Thus, as there is rarely more than one adult male per household, the sizes of the bands range from eight to twelve households (i.e., from forty-five to sixty-five people).

At first glance, the kinship structures of the Sugluk bands seem to be bilateral (see also Graburn 1964:132–145). They may be compared with Steward's "composite hunting band" (Steward 1955:143ff), which he states is the social consequence of the type of ecological situation of "traditional" Eskimo society. However, comparison of the present structure of bands with Steward's ideal model shows a tendency to patrilinearity. Somewhat similar groups have appeared among Eskimo populations under acculturative influences in, for instance, Povungnituk, Quebec (Balikci 1960a), Point Hope, Alaska (Valentine 1952), and St. Lawrence Island, Alaska (Hughes 1958).

I shall outline the forms of these bands presented in 1964, commenting on changes that have taken place since 1959. The residential associations of these people are seen in the plan of Sugluk settlement (Figure 5). Because the Eskimos have been living in houses provided by the white man they have less choice of residence, and the winter association of the members of these families is less clear than it would be for the summer groupings.

A. The Kaitak Band. This group is directly descended from and includes many of the members of the camp group that was in Sugluk in 1927 (see Figure 3, p. 133 above). Since then S has died and the leadership has been taken over by his oldest son K(aitak). The effective core of this group is K's large sibling group and their spouses and children. The group has also been enlarged by the addition of the many children of J, who are now married adults. This band has remained very solidary and has few links with other groups. Its main characteristics are (1) residential and social isolation from other groups, (2) tight ingroup social control, (3) cooperative ownership and use of a Peterhead boat, and (4) an unusual and continuing high rate of in-marriages between first cousins.

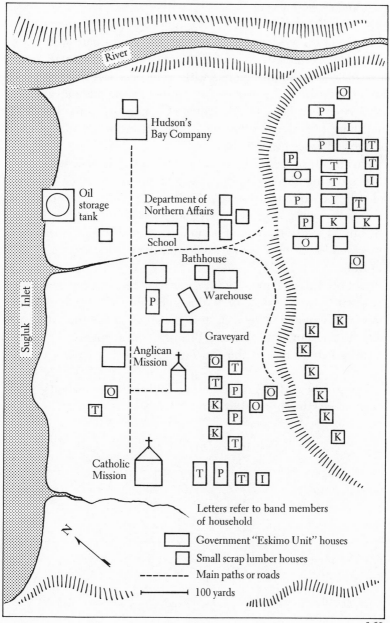

FIGURE 5 SUGLUK: COMMUNITY PLAN AND
ESKIMO HOUSEHOLD GROUPINGS MAY 1964

River

Hudson's
Bay Company

Oil
storage
tank

Department of
Northern Affairs

School

Bathhouse

Warehouse

Graveyard

Anglican
Mission

Catholic
Mission

Sugluk Inlet

N

Letters refer to band members
of household

Government "Eskimo Unit" houses

Small scrap lumber houses

Main paths or roads

100 yards

One or two other families whose extended ilagiit reside in other places have attached themselves to this band through ties of marriage and economic cooperation.

B. The Papigatuk Band. This group has recently obtained an old Peterhead, replacing their ancient and inadequate whaleboat. This group is similarly composed of the descendants of male members of a large sibling group, with some less fortunate families having attached themselves for various economic advantages. Leadership has been in the hands of Papigatuk since his older and more respected brother died from starvation during hunting on the winter ice near Quartak.

This band is exceptional in that (1) it is the largest, with more than sixty members, (2) its men hold the majority of full-time jobs in the community, and (3) it is generally more oriented toward the white man in material and social culture than any of the other groups. In spite of a number of solidifying in-marriages, the group less often acts as a whole and there is less internal social control.

C. The Taiara Band. (See Figure 6) This group is the most "respected" social group in Sugluk and probably the most traditionally orientated. However, this does not mean that they are poor by the standards of A and B. In fact, this group was the first to get a Peterhead and the less fortunate vie for a place in this group.

Groups (1) and (2), two brothers and their descendants, form a very close-knit core to this band. The leader (T)aiara is said to

FIGURE 6   THE TAIARA BAND

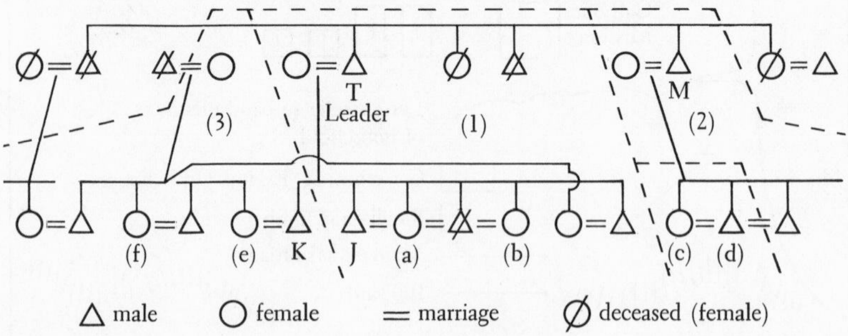

△ male   ○ female   = marriage   Ø deceased (female)

170

have been one of the greatest hunters along the coastline in this century and is very highly respected by whites and Eskimos alike. The leader's eldest daughter (a) married a man from a subgroup of band A, and for summer hunting purposes this man was incorporated into band C. However, for trapping and winter residence he rejoined band A with his mother and brothers. The widow (b) of one of T's sons has remarried and rejoined the band of her father (O). She comes from the lowest social stratum of the community, and everyone wonders how she was able to marry so "high." (c) and (d) married a brother and sister and (d), being young, resides in the camp of his wife and his wife's father. However, in both hunting and trapping ventures he is definitely a part of band C, having paid for part of their Peterhead. Group (3) is only related through marriages. The woman (e) was widowed from another band, and remarried a son of Taiara who is much younger than she and who is said to be the best hunter in contemporary Sugluk. Her brother had previously married a distant relative of this band and, as a very able hunter and the contributor of a considerable sum toward the Peterhead, he has been successfully incorporated. His wife's brother, who is slightly crippled, is the catechist for the community and a fairly important man, as well as being a fair hunter. Hence, this whole group (3) has been upwardly mobile through its achievements rather than its kinship connections.

D. The Ivujivingmiut. The members of this band are those who have recently arrived from Ivujivik in response to the greater economic attractions and available services at Sugluk. They were, however, already related in many ways to the Sallumiut and have made use of these ties. They are a less cohesive band and, in fact, the relation between their two major groups is not so close as that with other bands.

A large sibling group is the core of this band; the deceased leader's son and daughter married a sister and brother of the Taiara band — who still sometimes shares his money with this group. This group also owns a medium-sized boat for hunting, but it is too small to benefit all the adult males at any one time. A distantly related group composed of a widow and her adult unmarried sons tries to make use of its ties to both this group and band B, rather unsuccessfully in the latter case. The core sibling group has similarly tried to make use of its affinal links to band C through the leader's son and daughter, again with limited success. Another family consists of an older man and his children. This man was polygynous until a few years ago, when the Royal Canadian Mounted Police removed his second and third wives and their children. He had a full-time job for many years but now lives by hunting and trapping.

Since 1959 the leader of band D has died. Although the group is still reasonably cohesive in residential and social patterns, they are no longer economically cooperative and are splitting into smaller subgroups, each of which tries to ally itself with some other band. In economic matters they tend to operate as a number of one- or two-man units for both trapping and hunting seals from their small boats. They have no ambitions toward becoming a Peterhead-owning integrated group.

E. The "Others." These people are in fact from five different families not related to each other. They comprise eleven households, each of which has for economic and other reasons tried to align itself with one or more of the four major bands. Almost always they have attempted to join the band to which they are most closely related. Where an association has been successful there is an almost complete break with the family of origin, and where it has failed the "Others" are almost outcasts. Some of the members of these households are the butts of many jokes and some are called "crazy." These particular family groups follow no traditional pattern. However, their attempts to achieve incorporation into one of the four big groups symbolize their wishes for social and economic achievement.

Bands and Visiting Patterns. In addition to the more obvious phenomena of economic cooperation and household groupings, other data show the solidarities of these groups. In 1959 I recorded and analyzed some 1,154 visits between households. People visit households within their own band considerably more than households of other bands, even though many members of the other bands may be close kin (e.g., out-marrying sisters).

Each band is approximately one-fifth of the total population of Sugluk. If each group were randomly chosen, we might expect visits *within* any one group to be 20 percent of the group's total visits. A percentage in excess of this would indicate that the group was not a random entity. That more than 44 percent of the visits to band E were from within E, in spite of the demonstrated fact that it is not socially integrated, is explained by the fact that no one else usually wants to visit them very much! In truth, members of band E visit *out* three times as often as members of other bands visit them. This excess of outgoing versus incoming visits is unapproached by any other band.

One aspect of recent community life is the need for social groupings smaller than the total community itself (cf. Hughes 1958). In the traditional katimajut camps and restricted ilagiit, the number was small enough so that all people could enjoy face-to-face interaction. However, since the emergence of this larger present community of Sugluk, now comprising over three hundred Eskimos, such patterns of interaction are no longer possible. The band has therefore come to be the subgroup of intense social interaction within which most economic and social transactions take place. The numbers of visits indicated in Figure 7 show this well. The bands are by now considerably larger than the original restricted ilagiit from which they originated, sixty as against from twenty to twenty-five people. They have become larger because (1) the Peterhead requires the cooperation of about ten able-bodied men, (2) the rate of natural increase is much higher than before, and (3) the annual cycle nowadays no longer demands the constant splitting and separation of groups. It is probable that in the future one or two of the larger bands will break up into more manageable groups and develop new leaders.

The Eskimos do not have any special names for these contemporary groups in Sugluk. If you asked a Sallumiut, he would probably say they were so-and-so-'s ilagiit. But this would be ambiguous, for ilagiit would also mean all that person's relatives, whether they lived together and cooperated or not. In traditional times the people of any camp were called "so-and-so-*kut*," (-*kut* meaning "at his place," like the French *chez*). So it is in Sugluk

FIGURE 7   VISITING PATTERNS BY BAND (1959)

		Visitors are members of band				
		A	B	C	D	E
Visitees are members of band	A	181 (76.5%)[a]	6	22	8	20
	B	16	171 (46.5%)	86	44	49
	C	16	52	105 (43.5%)	43	29
	D	6	49	19	72 (36.4%)	52[b]
	E	16	8	18	19	49[b] (44.5%)

[a] Each percentage indicates the proportion of intraband visits out of the *total* number of visits that that band receives.

[b] It is interesting to note that the members of band E visit band D more than they visit themselves. This does not apply to any other group of visitors and visitees. It tends to show that band E is less an integrated group than any of the four main bands.

today. One would, for instance, identify the members of band A as *Kaitakut* — the people of Kaitak's group. This could also mean, in another context, the people in Kaitak's household.

These bands tend to be entities in a more real sense in the summer than in the winter because the use of the Peterhead boat, a major cooperative function, is a summer activity and only the summer hunting involves decisions about when to move camp from one place to another. In the winter the economic cooperation required by trapping involves only small groups. It is quite possible for each individual to have his own trapping line and to go off by himself on his sled, but most men prefer to go with someone else because it is not so lonely and it is safer if one gets lost or is ill. The fifty or so regular trappers are organized into twenty groups, each with its own set of traplines. Ten of these groups are composed of two brothers, some with an additional distant relative; five are father-and-son teams; and three others involve the cooperation of more distant relatives. Only two people regularly trap alone, although others may do so occasionally or for traplines near the settlement. Even women may set a few traps within a day's walk of Sugluk when foxes are very abundant.

Most households are composed of a married couple and their children, some with one or more distant relatives living with them. Ten households comprise widows and their families. Less than 10 percent contain two or more nuclear families. These figures are for summer residence arrangements. There are fewer houses in the winter than there are summer tents and houses so that more families have to share households in the winter, at least until the government supplies more winter housing. There are a few families who change their affiliations or re-group during the winter. For instance, they may share the boat of one band and hunt with its members during the summer and then for housing and trapping in the winter get together with their brother(s) who may have been affiliated with some other band during the summer.

Some young married men are affiliated with their wives' families most of the year. This was the majority pattern for the traditional Eskimos of this region (see Graburn 1964) and is still followed. If the husbands come from a large and economically cooperative family, however, they usually keep their ties to it rather than throw in their lot with their wives' families. An examination of the structures of the bands shows that a number of people have joined their wives' families, but this is usually because they have no brothers to join forces with or they come from a relatively poorer family.

Economic cooperation within each of the three boat-owning bands is most marked in the summer, when the large boats are used for hunting. In every band a number of men have contributed to buying the boat and so all have rights to use it and responsibilities to maintain and run it. The boats were originally bought through the savings of these men, which were put into a joint account at the store. All families have individual accounts for their regular activities and for the most part individual families are economically independent with respect to money. Joint accounts are a reflection of the traditional camp sharing patterns, expressed in the new medium of money and credit. These traditional sharing patterns are generally still carried out in the distribution of large sea mammals or when there is an abundance of smaller animals. During the last two decades the people of Sugluk have come to recognize the permanent nature of their solidarity. Although originally the various bands arrived at separate times and still spend their summers hunting separately, the trend has been for more and more people to spend most of the year in the settlement. Thus Sugluk has become a permanent katimajut (coming together) of a number of restricted ilagiit. It is, in fact, an enlarged version of the traditional winter camps which used to gather at the good tuvak seal hunting sites.

The scale of the groupings has changed considerably. In the old days an ilagiit might be comprised of three or four households and some twenty-five people at the most, such as the band that was first at Sugluk in 1927. Even the largest and most temporary winter katimajut never exceeded one hundred in the Hudson Strait area. According to the rules of sharing, the products of large sea mammals and numbers of small seals and caribou should be shared with the whole katimajut. This is still the ideal in Sugluk, and more than 90 percent of the families subscribe to this notion. However, it may not last much longer. In 1959 when the men of one band returned from a hunt near Charles Island with thirty-six large bearded seals some of the younger members did not want to share these with the other more than two-hundred Sallumiut, but the will of the older men prevailed and every household received considerable amounts of meat. A similar disagreement also took place over the products of the annual walrus hunt and ended the same way. Now that the older men are losing their influence and some of the younger men are having a larger say, especially in the new community-wide organizations (see next chapter), the whole pattern of community-wide sharing will break down and give way to a commercial attitude toward the products of hunting, which until recently were generally kept separate from the money part of the economy and the products of trapping. The former were shared according to the principles of reciprocity and the latter, apart from the joint accounts for boats, were individual matters and conducted in terms of market exchange. In other words, after they began to trade regularly, the Eskimos created two separate "spheres of exchange" — one for the traditional economy and the other for the white man's economy. This lasted many decades but, as with nearly all peoples under the pressures of acculturation and world markets, it is finally beginning to break down. This may very well hasten the decline of the importance of the family-based bands and increase the independence of the nuclear family.

One problem that is not yet clear is the question of selection for and succession to leadership within the bands. In band A, the original leader was S, who is now dead, and leadership has since passed to his oldest son K, who consults with his brothers on most matters. However, for important decisions, such as undertaking a year of wage labor elsewhere, his younger siblings have had to get his permission or, at least, his advice. At all periods, the leader of this very tightly integrated band has been the oldest brother of a large sibling group.

Band B is somewhat different. In the past both P and his older brother O were rivals for group leadership. Both lived with their families in the Diana Bay/Quartak area. O, who was a respected catechist, was lost when he and his kajak were taken out to sea by the ice in Diana Bay in 1943 and P has been the leader ever since. He is now an older man and someone will soon have to succeed him. His oldest son K is a rather shy man and is permanently employed as a generator mechanic. A younger son is an interpreter and administrative assistant for the Department of Northern Affairs and is therefore a very important man in the whole community. It is he who may well become the leader of the whole group.

When band C arrived in Sugluk, the leader was the famous hunter Taiara who was also an umialik, an office he inherited from his father. His older half-brother went to Cape Dorset and ceased to be a member of this group. Taiara was still the leader in 1959 and he was the man to throw the harpoons, which is the final act of seal hunting from a boat and usually accorded to the leader. Unfortunately, one time he missed a seal which the group had been hunting for over an hour and it sank. Taiara thought he had hit the seal but the others said he had thrown the harpoon too late and perhaps he was getting old — he was at least 68 at the time. From then on he never threw the harpoon again and perhaps that was the end of his effective leadership. After that he had a stroke from which he very nearly died. In 1964 he walked with a stick and spent much of his time in bed; however, he still acted as leader and used his powerful personality and authority at every opportunity until he died in 1965. His oldest (living) son J should have taken over by the normal procedures, but he is a widower and a man of few words. However, the other Eskimos were already beginning to speak of the Peterhead as "J's boat" as though he were already the umialik. He had always been the chief mechanic on the boat and was the one who spent seven years doing wage labor to save the capital to buy it. Taiara's younger brother M was traditionally the steersman but will never assume the leadership: his sons have married into other bands and the whole group may separate from band C.

The Ivujivingmiut, band D, were led by the oldest living brother of a large sibling group. Since he has died the group has been somewhat leaderless, although the older women still congregate socially and the dead leader's son is a minor isumatak. However, the group has no Peterhead and has no ambitions of getting one, and so may break up through lack of an umialik.

The norm for succession to leadership of a restricted ilagiit was from oldest son to oldest son, assuming that the men had the requisite qualities. We have seen that this rule was followed by these groups at the time of arrival at Sugluk. Since then, the rule has been followed as far as possible.

A further possibility is the formation of new groups under new leaders by fission. For example, the oldest son of J, the oldest of a large sibling group in band A, may split his group from band A and assume leadership. Until the 1960's, this sibling group associated with their wives' families in the summer and with band A in the winter. However, J's son is now the headman of a group that finally managed to save enough to buy a Peterhead from the Hudson's Bay Company through an account in his name. They now form a fourth major boat-owning group. This would be part of the normal processes of fission of large ilagiits, which will continue as long as such groups and their Peterheads are important and as long as the population continues to grow.

A typical summer tent at Sugluk. The woman in front wears a traditional parka made of store bought material. (1959)

At 1:00 A.M., the unmarried people meet in Tunu's tent to chat and make dates. (1959)

The interior of a government supplied 3-bedroom house.. Notice the modern furniture, the raw seal on the floor, and the Ski-doo motor in for repair. (1968)

CHAPTER SIX

*The Present Community
and Some Problems
of Change*

MORALITY AND DELINQUENCY

In traditional Eskimo life children were welcomed and brought up under the close and loving guidance of their parents and camp-mates. Physical punishment was very rare for younger children, although violence was not uncommon among adults. In this small world the children were almost continually supervised and they learned their adult roles by observation rather than instruction. Both boys and girls strove to grow up and join their adult kinsmen in the activities and pleasures of manhood and womanhood. When learning new tasks children were rarely reproved for getting them wrong, but they were scolded for antisocial behavior. Such conditions lasted while the restricted ilagiit or camp group was an independent entity. Since all these groups now live most of the year round in Sugluk and the children are spending more and

181

more of their time in school, the factors making for ordered and integrated group life have diminished.

Life for the Eskimos is not as hard as it used to be, and there has been a reduction in the number and urgency of essential tasks to be performed by family members. Also, there are far more children together in one community than ever before (over 150) and this allows the more idle ones to get together without supervision and encourages antisocial activities. These peer groups comprise children in the eight to fourteen age group, and the greater proportion of them are girls. With no housework to do and very few recreational outlets outside school hours, they roam around the settlement finding mischievous activities with which to pass the time, often carrying on late into the night. These activities are rarely large scale or serious but they are definitely antisocial and in contradiction of Eskimo standards of behavior. They are the results not only of increase in population size but also the consequent increase in opportunities to be away from adults who feel direct responsibility.

The following story is typical of the mischievous type of behavior that is becoming more common:

One afternoon I was sitting in the tent of an old widow, who had just come back from the hospital where she had been treated for tuberculosis. She lives alone in the smallest tent in Sugluk and is very poor. Her only surviving child, a son, had been in the hospital for two years. Three girls, aged nine, eleven, and twelve, came in while the old lady was scraping a skin. After chatting with her they went to the other side of the tent where there was an open can of molasses on top of an old oil barrel. Crowded together with their backs to the old lady, the girls silently tipped over this can and spilled all the contents into the drum. Then the three went over to the old lady and told her the can had fallen over. She did not even look up from her work but told them to put as much as they could back with a spoon. Again crowding together, they scraped up the molasses alternately into the can and into their mouths. When they had finished they wiped the oil drum clean with grass, proudly told the old lady what a good job they had done, and then went out, giggling all the time.

Later the missionary told the leader's step-father about this and other bad behavior. The events were stoutly denied and the same sort of thing happened many times again after that. The girl who was the leader in the story above seems to have suffered from not having a father during the seven-year period her mother was a widow. She used to be very bright and pretty and much attention was paid to her when she was about five, but she is no longer the center of attention. Her talent seems to have been misdirected. Since 1959, when the incident described occurred, this girl has become one of the leaders of those girls who hang around the white man's quarters. True to the type she wears lots of lipstick and "flashy" clothes.

Perhaps her case is understandable, but what is more puzzling is the complete command she has of many girls her own age and older who come from very "normal" homes. The parents of many of these girls do not know what is going on and find it hard to stop when they do.

In recent years some of the children who have had a year or two of schooling quickly learn to pick up English phrases that the seasonal white laborers use. They get great joy from shouting them at their parents and other people who cannot understand English. Two of the more extreme cases were two small boys who would continually shout "Shut up!" or "Get out!" at their parents and refuse to obey them to the point of exasperation. One feature of Sugluk society is that if parents get angry at a child or threaten him, the child can easily hide or go to another household and the community is too large to keep tabs on where one's children are.

In present-day Sugluk the boys seem much less involved in spiteful or antisocial behavior than the girls, even though they have just as much spare time. Their activities are limited more to wrestling, fighting, throwing stones, and chasing small animals — typically "proto-male" behavior. Whether the situation will take a turn for the worse, as it has in Frobisher Bay according to T. Yatsushiro (1958–1960) and by my own observations (1960), remains to be seen. However, even in the much larger and more acculturated community of Frobisher Bay the delinquent behavior may be a temporary phase, for Honigmann (1965), who was there in 1963, reports little of the kind of "gang" and deviant behavior previously reported and observed.

During their adolescent and young-adult phase it is again the girls who cause most of the trouble, although it is not of such an antisocial kind. For instance, during the summer of 1959 when the Department of Northern Affairs had some builders living temporarily in the schoolhouse, girls from the ages of twelve to twenty-nine paraded themselves in varying degrees of exposure in front of the windows; only the older ones went further than that. The Northern Service officer did his best to stop this behavior, and the R.C.M.P. was called to give the girls a special talk and warning, but to no avail — in fact the policeman was regarded by some of the women as a good prospect himself.

Summer, of course, is the period for much of this kind of activity, for this is the time when the ships come in and there are the most visitors and laborers in the settlement. However, since the inception of regular air travel, such visitors are more frequent all year 'round. In addition, there is an increase in the resident white population, many of whom are young men without wives. I am assured by my friends at the Hudson's Bay Company that similar activities take place continually, usually at the instigation of the girls and women. The Hudson's Bay Company itself has a policy of removing staff who are known to have had sexual relations with the Eskimos, and this has happened at least three times in the last ten years.

Of course, as we have seen previously, sexual relations between white men and Eskimo women for gain have a long history. Today, although the element of gain is still present, to have such a relation with a white man has become a mark of prestige among a certain group of women. At Frobisher Bay, where things seem to have gone even further, one Eskimo man said: "Eskimo women seem to prefer white men to Eskimo men — even their own husbands." Needless to say, without some evidence of a demand there would be no supply, but most of the Eskimo population deplores such activities whether or not reward is involved. It is considered "un-Eskimo" for the women to be the aggressors.

Sexual activity between the males of a "dominant caste" and the females of a lower "caste" is found in societies all over the world. At Sugluk there was one case where the opposite was true. One young Eskimo, only nineteen years old, had been very active sexually among Eskimo women older than himself. This was very much disapproved, especially since all the women were married. The young man then befriended the white daughter of one of the teachers and used to take her for sled rides over the hills, affording great entertainment to the Eskimo children who would hide and watch from the other hills. When the adults heard about the nature of these rides, the young man was given a plane ticket to the next community and his father told him not to come back until he was married. He returned on the next plane! Such cases are very rare, and even in our own society men continue to be hypogamous and women the "social climbers."

Gambling has always been a traditional amusement of the Eskimos of this area. Nowadays it takes the form of playing cards. In 1959 cards were played by young and old Sallumiut alike. Generally the games were modifications of well-known games and the Eskimos were very quick and clever at them. Usually the stakes were small: ammunition, tobacco, and cigarettes among the adults and barrettes and candy among the children. These games would be played by a crowd of people sitting on the sleeping platform or floor and playing for hours on end, with very little gained or lost. Often the games would go on late into the night. Since the Hudson's Bay Company started trading in cash instead of tokens, the stakes have been changed to cash. There was a period, coinciding with the introduction of drinking (see below), when the stakes went remarkably high. I have heard that some men won and lost as much as an outboard motor in an evening — the equivalent of four months' average income for a head of household! Moreover, the games ceased to be friendly and many fights broke out, something that had been very rare in Sugluk before.

In 1964 this gambling was still going on. There was one house where one would be sure there would be a game going on all night long. Very occasionally the lady of the house, a widow, wanted to sleep, so the "scene" would be moved elsewhere. Generally the stakes were from about twenty-five cents to a dollar and a few people would win or lose more than ten dollars a night. However, the hostess had become an expert player and her daughters followed her in that occupation. One of the daughters, who was given a job as a teacher's assistant in the Government School but appeared inept and was fired, managed to make a good living at cards. Her mother was given a job because she was a widow and the local administration thought she would be better off employed than on relief. She often failed to show up and when questioned she said that she could not work as bathhouse attendant unless she was given a pay raise because she was losing so much money by not playing cards all afternoon!

Generally the crowd of players sits on the floor, hiding their money and throwing their stakes into a hat or the middle of the cards. A cloth is used as a table and the game proceeds silently and very fast. This provides entertainment for the many bystanders who wander in and out at all times of the night. Among these are young children whose parents are too engrossed in the game to care what is happening at home. But the Eskimos say it is good fun and all friendly and no one worries too much about losing. This attitude is in contrast to that in the period from 1960 to 1962.

In 1959 there was no drinking at all by the Sallumiut; there was no demand for liquor and no supply, although it was quite legal for Eskimos to drink. A few men had tried intoxicating liquor when working for mining companies or the Department of Transport and most said they did not like it. When the men returned from a summer's construction work in Frobisher Bay, the thing they criticized most was the drinking there. However, the following fall or spring one of the Eskimos returned from a year's work at the D.O.T. station, where he had learned how to make home-brew out of raisins, sugar, yeast, and water as well as how to distill, which was illegal. He abandoned the latter activity when his still exploded, blowing his house apart, but fortunately injuring no one. Home-brew was easy to make and not expensive; many families started making it and drunkenness became rife, with unhappy results. As I have said, card games grew more serious and fights broke out. There was more and more extramarital sexual activity — even postmenopausal women were committing adultery. Some people "lost their senses" and ran around in the snow without clothes; one of these people nearly died. One girl is said to have given birth to her father's child.

Finally, the production of home-brew was stopped. The Eskimos say that some of the older men went to the store and asked that raisins no longer be sold. It is also possible that the Hudson's Bay Company manager, by himself or at the request of the government official, decided not to sell them. In any case, the only people who have raisins now, and hence the only people who can brew, are those Eskimos who have permanent jobs with the government. Their annual supplies, "rations," always contain raisins, but drinking is no longer a problem.

All the activities described above, including those of pre-adults, are group activities. In addition, there are some individual delinquents, as well as some persons who have become seriously disturbed and have been taken out for treatment, diagnosed as schizophrenic. Living in the community at Sugluk are two adults, a brother and sister, who are said to have been mentally disturbed for a long time. The man, the Eskimos say, is *isumairksijuk*, "crazy," from time to time. He has been known to attempt to rape women and he has assaulted men of whom he was jealous. When he was caught stealing a number of small items he claimed that the spirits had put them in his pocket and that he did not know how they got there. Once he stole some beer from the N.S.O.'s house and got drunk by himself and then became violent. His sister has been accused of loose sexual behavior both before and after her marriage, and in consequence she is judged to be a very poor mother.

Some of the adolescents are said by the adults to be "crazy" because of their frequent and unrestrained sexual activities, but usually the accusers admit that they also were probably "crazy" at that age. Eskimos allege that a certain sort of mental unbalance goes with these activities, causing the individuals to become preoccupied and even melancholy, but that usually they get over it when they marry and have children. Perhaps these phenomena account for most Eskimo suicides, such as the recent one at Ivujivik (Turner 1894:186–187; Balikci 1960b).

It is interesting to note that nearly all the more pronounced deviants are found among band O, or if they belong to other bands they are those members without close ties. Thus antisocial behavior is confined, except for the general spread of drinking and gambling, to a relatively small proportion of the Sallumiut. As yet little of this behavior in Sugluk is of the "visible" kind that has been directed at the whites in some more acculturated and disorganized areas such as the western Arctic (Clairmont 1963).

MARRIAGE AND AUTHORITY

The Traditional Pattern. Until recently Takamiut patterns of courtships had changed very little from traditional times. Marriage was a necessity for Eskimo life, and my older informants said that all able-bodied people were married. Formerly, prior to the coming of the white man, men married between eighteen and twenty-five and women between fifteen and eighteen, although there were always a few married earlier or later. Eskimo life was very open, and children learned all about sex from babyhood. Among boys sex activities were initiated at puberty or a little after. Informants say that parents of girls tried to have them marry before they were long past puberty, but even so very few were virgins at marriage. If a girl became pregnant, the man responsible usually married her, although the marriage might not last long. The Eskimos never considered premarital sex a problem, although extramarital affairs were the cause of much violence.

The two most usual procedures for first marriage were:

1. Infant or child betrothal by the parents, usually to solidify relationships between friends. The children were considered husband and wife from their early years and had little to say in the matter.

2. When no prior arrangement such as this had been made, the young man usually told his father which girl he liked, and the parents then made the arrangements. If the boy did not decide on his own and was of marriageable age, his father might suggest that "so-and-so" would make a good daughter-in-law, and encourage his son to marry.

However, the families of a couple did not always agree. A man might go to another camp and try to take a woman in the middle of the night, and sometimes the man and the woman's parents fought about it. Sometimes the woman might already have a husband, or she might resist and be tied to a sled and carried off.

When marriage was of either of the two usual types, the young couple lived with the girl's parents for a while, first, to see if he would be a good son-in-law and provider, and second, to see if the girl would get pregnant. If she did not, the man might leave her to seek another; barren women rarely kept a husband for long. The trial marriage period usually ended when the girl became pregnant, after which the couple were considered married. There was no formal ceremony.

The Modern Pattern. Today all young Eskimos are expected to marry, although the age for women has risen somewhat to about twenty. The old people believe that the younger generation puts too much emphasis on looks when seeking a marriage partner and that they do not care enough about whether he or she would make a good worker or parent. This, however, may be one of the exaggerations old people all over the world often make when speaking of the younger generation. For instance, I recall, one girl, very attractive to both whites and Eskimos, was of age in 1959 but remained unmarried until 1965. Most of those I asked about this said that this was because she did not know how to sew sealskin boots properly, and this is probably the most important task for an Eskimo wife.

When a couple decides to get married, they tell their parents and discuss the whole matter with them. Usually, before or after telling their parents, they begin to sleep together in a trial marriage as in earlier days and this is not generally frowned on by the parents. If the union seems satisfactory to them the parents give their permission, but they may add a condition or postpone the time of the actual marriage. For instance, the girl's parents may say that she can marry but that she will have to wait until her younger brothers and sisters are old enough to help her mother in her many tasks. Sometimes the parents may ask the couple to live in the tent of the girl's parents for a while, so she can still help

189

with the housework and children; but young couples usually refuse to comply with such a condition.

Today arrangements are discussed with the Anglican missionary, and he may have some advice before the date of the church wedding is set. During the engagement period the couple are said to be promised to each other, and no other man will approach the girl for marriage unless she shows strong indications of wanting to change her mind. During this period the couple usually sleeps together, in spite of the opposition of the missionary to this custom.

The sequence of events described above are ideal norms and in many ways similar to the traditional customs, save only for the church marriage. However, these older cultural patterns were adaptive for the traditional situation of a small population group, considerable adult supervision, and the absolute necessity of having a marriage partner. These conditions, of course, no longer hold, and the aboriginal pattern described is inadequate for the present situation. Today the patterns of courtship follow from the activities of earlier adolescence, which I shall describe. I will then attempt to analyze the situation in the light of other relevant features of contemporary Sugluk life. The basic problem is that the aboriginal customs are no longer functional, and, although the situation improved between 1959 and 1968, there is still a high proportion of adults who have never married. Both the white population and the older Eskimos admit worrying about this, as do the young people themselves when talking confidentially.

Adolescent Sex Life. As noted above, adolescents generally experience a full sex life. Although some boys are shy and do not join in, there are very few girls who do not. Most boys first experience sexual relations at about sixteen or seventeen, but the girls are said to start earlier, even as young as twelve or thirteen. Children of this age speak freely of sex and make sexual allusions; for instance, one of their favorite pastimes is the repetition in public of a series of questions to each other about their activities, real or supposed:

A. "Sua?"   "What did you say?"
B. "Ikpasak."   "Yesterday."
A. "Kinalu?"   "With whom?"

B.	"(name) . . . lu."		"With . . . (name)."
A.	"Nani?"		"Where?"
B.	"Avani/tupingani . . ."		"Over there/in her tent . . ."
A.	"Sutsuni?"		"What was it like?"
	etc.		

After having asked "Kinalu?" A may suggest the name of one of the oldest women in the community, and the whole crowd will burst into laughter.

Many teenagers have their first sexual experience with someone much older than themselves who undertakes to teach them. Many of the older men told me that this had happened to them as boys and that although they had not enjoyed the experience they could not resist the opportunity when it was presented again.

Promiscuity. Much of the sex-life of the teenagers and unmarried adults is not aimed at the formation of permanent unions. Many people are very promiscuous, and the older people say that the situation is much worse than it was in their day because the very large size of the community makes the choice of a mate difficult.

Dates, rendezvous, and overtures are made in two ways. First, a man may write a note in syllabic script asking a girl to meet him at a certain place or time, perhaps enclosing some small gift such as a cigarette lighter, a brooch, or a hair barrette. He will send this to the girl via some friend or give it to her himself. If she accepts, verbally or with another note, he knows she is willing to be his partner for the night. If she does not, he may try again later or turn his attentions to another girl. The second method is direct approach when the couple happens to be together. First the man jokes about the matter, and if the girl seems to enjoy the jokes the suggestions become more serious. He may then make some physical contact and if the girl does not resist he will ask her to be his partner for the night. All this may happen at a dance, or a movie, or when they are just sitting in a tent or walking outside.

Extramarital sexual behavior is much affected by the seasons. In winter the weather creates many difficulties and there are few comfortable places to go, almost the only ones being abandoned houses. Spring is the most difficult season of all, for snow remains on the ground until June and there is least darkness, forcing couples to go far from the settlement in order not to be seen.

Conditions are better as the year progresses and fall is the most cooperative season, with little or no snow on the ground, the nights still relatively warm, and many hours of darkness. In the fall couples do not have to leave the settlement in order to have intercourse but may go behind boats and oil drums.

It is said that some of the younger people are becoming much more blatant about their sexual activities, even taking along with them their younger brothers and sisters, or ignoring passers-by. Opportunity for extramarital sex rarely occurs inside a dwelling for those who still live with their parents. However, sometimes the household of a young widow or widower may become to be regarded as a meeting place for all those who wish a rendezvous away from their parents.

There is no such thing as actual prostitution in Sugluk, but some of the men complain that they cannot afford to buy the gifts required to get a woman. I think this is an excuse they make up because they have been rejected many times for other reasons and are bitter. Many Eskimos know of the existence of prostitution, especially those who have been down South, but the institution will not be established in Sugluk until there is a larger contingent of white men there or nearby.

Children of unions with white men are looked after by the mother, who may or may not marry later. Eskimo men say they do not like their women to behave in this way and would prefer not to marry such women, but with the great shortage of eligible and willing women in Sugluk the men have little choice.

The Marriage Problem. The great reluctance of many of the young people to get married and of their parents to give permission for marriage constitutes a problem. In Sugluk there are at least forty-five adults eligible for marriage who are not married and almost all of them would be married if they were living in smaller settlements under traditional conditions. Twenty-two of these people are women, and of these only one does not engage in some kind of promiscuity. This behavior is creating problems of illegitimacy and resulting in a very unstructured and uncontrollable community life. All the white residents deplore this reluctance to get married and most of the older Eskimos say they

192

do. Yet the problem, which has been significant for only ten to fifteen years, is growing. Some of these people are well past the expected age of marriage, and with their chances of marriage lessened they become more promiscuous. Promiscuity is conducive to adultery, which is perhaps more frequent than in previous times. People get used to having a series of different sexual partners before marriage and find the habit difficult to break afterward. Furthermore, former sexual partners of married people seek to continue the relationship.

More than 37 percent of the forty-five unmarried adults, seventeen people, were prevented from marrying by their parents in the three or four years before 1959. Many more have been prevented indirectly, for example by their parents' promising them to someone they do not want to marry, and thus halting the approaches of others. Prevental sanctions are strengthened by present-day "post-living," which discourages young people from marrying without approval and getting off to another camp or settlement for a time until the matter cools off. It is known that in the last ten years only two couples have defied their parents' prohibitions and gone ahead and married. For a time these couples and their parents were on very bad terms, but sooner or later the bad feeling was forgotten and they became friendly again.

I asked many of the young people why they did not disobey their parents and go ahead and get married, and a number of good reasons were offered. Some said they respected the decisions of their parents and many said that a marriage without parental permission is bound to be unhappy. Others pointed out that they could not live in the same settlement as their parents and be at odds with them and that they would rather wait than quarrel, a thought very much in line with the present Eskimo value system. Others said that one could simply not get married when one's parents did not want one to, it just was not normal Eskimo practice.

When many of the older people were interviewed on the subject, nearly all agreed that things were much better these days as far as quarreling and fighting were concerned. Christianity had taught them not to fight under any circumstances against their neighbors and kin. They claimed that by putting this value first, life was much happier, even though young adults no longer rebelled against their parents and married. The younger people cannot remember the former anarchic way of life, but they, too, rarely wish to become involved in quarrels and fights.

Let us now examine the motives of the parents for not wanting to let their children marry. More than half those who prevented marriages were fathers. Some of these may have been widowers with young children, who depend on their elder daughters to do the woman's job in the house. If a man cannot successfully use his daughter to bargain with in an exchange for a new wife, then he cannot let the daughter marry until the children are old enough to look after themselves. This is an understandable position, and the only alternative if he cannot get someone to marry him is for a man to allow all his young children to be adopted, which has happened once or twice. The women who prevent their daughters from marrying are usually widows who feel they need a daughter around the house to do a lot of the work for them in their old age. However, these old women are all getting pensions or rations, making them the most secure in the settlement where in the primitive economy they would have been the poorest. It is felt that many are purely selfish, and some of the young people are very bitter about it.

The former missionary often had all the parents of eligible young adults in and talked to them, as individuals and collectively, about the desirability of marriage for their children. They all agreed that the young people should marry, but when it came to their own children, they found reasons against marriage. A typical example is the following:

In July 1959, T, a girl, and Qa, her beau, decided they wanted to get married, and they told the Anglican missionary about their decision. However, Qa did not tell T's father, A. Qa then left the settlement to work elsewhere for six weeks. Meanwhile, when I was investigating the problem of marriage, A, not knowing of his daughter's desires, spoke to me about her marriageability. He said that he would not stop his daughter from marrying, but that his wife had four other smaller children to look after and still wanted T's help in the household. Therefore, if she got married, her husband would have to live in her parental household. Such an arrangement is not acceptable to

194

young Eskimo men, and this would effectively stop any forthcoming marriage.

In September, Qa returned to the settlement, but went off to hunt for a time. During this period T changed her mind. Now she wanted to marry P and he wanted to marry her. She was still getting letters from Qa, who was ignorant of her change of heart. P thought he had a better chance than Qa of securing her parents' permissions: he knew that A knew (unofficially) about Qa and T, and he thought that the girl's parents liked him better than Qa. Also, P and T were by now on speaking rather than letter-writing terms, a step toward intimacy to the Sallumiut.

P took T to see the missionary about their marriage plans, but when T got there she refused to talk because she was shy and thought that the missionary would laugh at her for changing her mind about Qa. P's elder brother K talked to A about the possibility of T's marriage to P and at first negotiations were agreeable. However, A and his wife made the same stipulations A had expressed to me and things were left hanging. K then said that if permission was not forthcoming he would himself take P and T to the missionary and ask for a private marriage with few people in attendance. The missionary was unwilling to do this for fear of arousing bad feelings in the community; he said he preferred to talk to the girl's parents himself.

After this K became rather reluctant about pressing his brother's marriage possibilities. He knew that T had sexual relations with at least three other men and that if P found this out he might not want to marry her. Thus the situation bogged down and nothing was done that winter. P became disillusioned and K did not help him any longer.

Many of the prohibitions of marriage by parents have been on the ground that the intended husband was undesirable, for example, that he was a very promiscuous person. By preventing marriage, however, they are only promoting this situation. Sooner or later there will be more men like this and their daughter will have to marry one anyhow. Only a few of these parental excuses have been fair and honest.

Willingness of the Young Adults to Marry. Most of the young adults interviewed on the subject of marriage were men; the women were less willing to talk about it, and seemed to feel guilty when the subject was brought up. Nearly all these men said they wanted to get married and were willing to marry almost any woman in Sugluk. There are a few men who are too shy to approach a girl for marriage, or who are now getting on into their thirties and seem to have lost interest, but it is mainly the girls who do not seem to want to get married. More than half of the parents do their best to encourage their children to get married, but the sanctions they had for this in the traditional culture rarely apply any more. In the old days the girls obeyed because a man was able to say to his daughter, "Marry that man or I will turn you out" and some fathers did. Nowadays such a threat would be useless because there are many households where a girl can stay if she wants to. This somewhat contradicts the values of obedience and not quarreling described above, but it seems that this value is more heeded with respect to the prohibition of marriages rather than encouragements.

There are girls who claim that they never want to get married and that they are quite happy living the promiscuous life they do. Many older people say this may not be true, that it is just an excuse because the girls are shy or cannot marry the person they want. They tell their daughters that they need not marry if they really do not want to, but if they do not marry they are not to run around with all the young men. But their warnings are not heeded. Another factor in the attitude toward promiscuity is the general belief the Eskimos have that a woman cannot have a baby if she has intercourse with several different men. It is said that even if a girl is pregnant, when she sleeps with another man she "bleeds again," and it is remarkable how few illegitimate children there are considering the amount of promiscuity. Few of the Eskimos at Sugluk know about contraceptives, and those who do say they would not use them. They are not available there in any case, which, as one man pointed out, may be a very good thing, for if they came into general use there might well be an increase in the amount of promiscuity among those people who fear having illegitimate babies.

To some extent this promiscuity among young people approaches the old trial marriage, but where this mechanism for getting married worked in the traditional situation, so much has changed that it rarely does now. A couple may have a "trial marriage" but because of the competition they may still change their minds many times. Many of the young men and girls just do not know how to carry out a successful courtship under present-day conditions. They are at a loss for what to do, and if they follow their parents' advice in some ways they may be thwarted in other ways. Girls have been prohibited by their parents from marrying even after they have had a child in a trial marriage, and nearly all of them refuse to disobey. Yet when it comes to their parents' telling them to marry they disobey time and again. Sometimes, as we have seen, a man wants to marry a woman and the parents agree on condition that he come and live in the house of his parents-in-law and help the father. Most men will not submit to this; they know the constant quarreling it may lead to and, also, that once they are "in the grip of" the parents-in-law it is difficult to get out again. There is only one such household in Sugluk now and the quarreling started before the marriage took place.

Some of the men have got around the problem by marrying girls from outside the settlement, for example from Ivujivik, Wakeham Bay, or even Nottingham Island, and bringing them back to Sugluk. The two former places have their marriage problems, too: in Ivujivik, almost everyone is closely related to everyone else through the family of a very prolific man, Adami I., and at Wakeham Bay there are few girls of marriageable age. Some of the Sugluk men wanted to marry girls they had met at Frobisher Bay when they went to work there in the summer. Since the air service started, others have gone to Povungnituk and found wives there. In fact, with the greater number of communities within reach, the situation seems to be improving. Also, some of the parents, seeing the gravity of the situation, have begun to exert more pressure. The older people are effective when a number of them get together and agree, but when each makes up his own mind little is accomplished.

It is evident from the foregoing that a major cause of the prevailing promiscuity is the inability or unwillingness of people to marry, and we have to look for the causes of this phenomenon. There seem to be two major causes of delays in marriage: first, as we have seen, there are some parents who do not wish their daughters to marry; and second, there are the young adults, mainly women, who say they do not want to marry. The majority of these young people are healthy and take a normal interest in the opposite sex.

Examining the first cause, the refusal by the parents, we find the changed basis of the economy of the older people the prime cause. Men with families cannot do without women, and if they are widowed and too old to remarry they wish to keep their daughters to help, whereas undoubtedly they would have married or given the children for adoption in the old days. Old women now have much more economic independence than ever before and can do without men. They are therefore no longer as dependent on bringing in a son-in-law as they were in the old days and can keep daughters working for them. The old women are now economically more powerful than the young unmarried girls, and sometimes more so than the prospective husbands. Yet when the parents try to apply positive sanctions to get children married, the post situation weakens their authority.

So we see that owing mainly to the changes in the economy and to some extent in the demography, the power of the parents over their children is now negative where it used to be positive. Perhaps in the future the power of the parents in these situations will be much reduced in both ways, the marriages they now prevent will take place, and some sort of balance will be restored.

As for the young people who claim they do not want to marry, the causes are more difficult to determine. Probably very few of these people really do not want to marry ever, but they say they do not because of new factors in the society that did not exist in the old days. In the first place, many of the young men did not know how to adapt to this new situation the old courting mechanisms that their parents used and taught them. Second, the abundance of choice that confronts both men and women is something they have no way of dealing with. Thirdly, they do not wish to disobey their parents, with whom they must live in the same settlement, especially because they have been taught not to quarrel as they used to. And fourthly, some young women may really derive all the satisfaction they expect from their life of promiscuity and do not wish to be tied down by a husband and responsibilities. So we see that the young people have problems to contend with that their parents never faced, brought about by changes in mores, economics, and, to some extent, demography.

The support that the white man's government gives to all Eskimos, married or single, is the major direct economic factor. Widows and old people get pensions and young unmarried women with children are supported. This situation allows Eskimos to remain unmarried in most of those situations where previously they would have found marriage necessary. Thus the present acculturated situation, although it cannot be said to have directly caused the present marriage and mating patterns, allows a greater variety of sexual arrangements than were ever before possible.

Some of the Eskimos say that when one or two of the more stubborn parents die, or are disobeyed, there will be a great rush for the young people in the family to "catch up." This actually happened in one instance. A group leader, who had often refused offers for his daughters, died, and his widow, who had not put up so much resistance, saw that some sons-in-law would be better than none. So, all at once, three of her daughters were married to three men of one other family. It was all arranged by the parents, who in fact were distant ilagiit and wished to ally the families closer. Thus in one stroke six people, or 13 percent of the unmarried Sallumiut, married. Most of the young people seem to be just waiting, hoping that "everything will be all right in the end," and doing nothing for fear of further hurting someone's feelings.

Some men plan to marry girls from other settlements they visit while working, and many more will do so. This is an old Eskimo pattern for relieving the pressures of marriage in one place.

When there is more wage labor, the power of the young people will definitely increase, and the sanctions of the old people will be reduced to the point where couples will get married whatever their parents say. This happened to some extent in the old days, but such a situation may not happen in Sugluk for some time.

Since 1959, of the 45 unmarried adults, 24 have married, four of them outside the settlement. However, during the same period another 20 or 25 have become "eligible" so the problem continues. In addition the rate of illegitimacy has risen from 14 percent of live births (1955–1959) to 17 percent. The missionary is worried that illegitimacy is ever increasing. One major factor is that children are still welcomed. Whether given for adoption or not, children bring in from six to eight dollars a month family allowance and are therefore no economic burden. This is not an insignificant amount of money to most Eskimos.

To summarize, we may say that economic and hence demographic factors have combined with changing authority patterns to produce a new situation. The previous adaptive patterns are no longer working and new ones will have to arise. Thus the Sallumiut are in a state somewhat approaching anomie here, and we could call this an example of "cultural lag."

EDUCATION, ECONOMY, AND THE FATE OF SUGLUK

There has been a Federal Day School in Sugluk since 1957, as part of a program initiated some ten years earlier throughout the Northwest Territories (Jenness 1964:78–79). This program, the result of reports of poverty and apathy among the post-war Eskimos, was designed to give the Eskimos a normal Canadian education and, presumably, to prepare them for a world somewhat similar to the world down South. Until this time the only schooling in Sugluk had been carried on by the two missionaries and was confined to reading and writing in syllabics and spiritual matters.

For the most part, the teachers, language, and instructional equipment of the government school conform to those of southern Canada. The policy underlying the methods of education is that the children should be taught the same subjects with the same grade levels as southern schools and that English should be taught as a second language. However, all instruction is in English because (1) it is the policy and is meant to get the children to practice talking English, (2) ". . . no white teacher in the Arctic . . . can speak the language fluently, and no Canadian Eskimo has yet reached the stage when he can pass the regular teaching examinations" (Jenness 1964:127), and (3) as one teacher said, "the children would refuse to use any English word when they knew I knew the word in Eskimo, so I felt it was defeating the purpose of teaching them English for me to learn Eskimo." (Quoted in Willmott 1961:107.)

One of the major problems of this school system is the constant use of English and the refusal of many teachers to let the children speak a word of Eskimo when in school. This is very uncomfortable for the children and some of the Eskimo adults are beginning to compain about the methods used:

> In one Takamiut area school the junior teacher forbade the children to speak Eskimo in school and she punished some of the children who did so. The Eskimo parents were very upset when they heard about this, as they do not believe in physical punishment of any kind, especially for speaking one's own language. One of the parents, who also happened to speak English and knows a lot about the outside world although he did not go to school, became their spokesman. He went to the head teacher who was also the husband of the offending teacher and complained. The head teacher, defending his wife as well as the system, said that such behavior was policy and would help the children learn English. The Eskimo was very indignant and said that he did not think children should be taught English by force or they might in a few generations forget Eskimo, their own language. He told the teacher, "How would you like it if your children were punished for speaking English in school and you knew that perhaps your grandchildren will forget English altogether and only speak Eskimo? If anything like this happens again we will all refuse to send our children to school."
>
> The teacher did not know how sophisticated the Eskimo was and told him that if they refused to send their children to school that was against the law; he would call the police and maybe the parents would be sent to jail or have their subsidies cut off. The Eskimo replied that he would love to go to court to be tried on this charge. He said that he would write to all the newspapers and tell them just how the Eskimo children were being treated — then they would send all their reporters to the court to hear the case and it would be in all the papers. . . . The offending practices were stopped and the teacher and his wife left at the end of the school year. [From a number of informants in the settlement involved]

It is interesting that after a few more years of contact with the white man this leader admits privately that he was wrong in his actions against the teachers. He says that he now realizes that Eskimos will not learn properly in school if they do not listen to the teacher and if they refuse to speak English. On this matter he is at odds with the majority of his less sophisticated friends.

After so many years of intensive acculturation and of being pushed around, some of the Eskimos are beginning to be conscious of what is theirs and what they may lose. A number of the younger adults now maintain that the government should pay rent for the use of land in the Arctic, for it is the Eskimo's land. Others, although well paid already, wish to be paid far higher wages. These perceptive people are not those who have been to school but those who bear the brunt of dealing with the white people — the young and middle-aged adults. They will not, of course, be able to extract money from the government for the use of their land because it could easily be proved that the Eskimos had no concept of land ownership and rent in their own culture. Many Eskimos, when they feel that they have been wronged, write letters in Eskimo to politicians down South. Some of these letters are taken seriously because the government is very sensitive about its image in the treatment of natives, and action is sometimes forthcoming.

The major impact of the school system on the Takamiut so far is the restrictions it places on their movements for eight months of the year. This applies far more in Wakeham Bay and Ivujivik, where schools were opened in 1961, than it does in Sugluk where the population was already more sedentary. All children are supposed to attend school through the school year, which means that their parents must either leave them behind or stay in the settlement all year themselves. The Eskimos, unlike the Indians, are very loath to leave their children in a hostel or in someone else's care, and so the migratory cycles of camp groups have been extremely truncated since schools started. The police are not brought in when parents take the children out of school, but the parents know that they are expected not to and that the children's absence will affect their education. Some families whose children do not go to school regularly are threatened with having their relief and subsidies cut off, unless they are hunting very seriously and have no other employment. All these factors, combined with the changing ideas of Eskimo livelihood, have combined to produce the static year-round communities that have grown up in the last decade or so.

A major question in educating the Eskimos is "Education for what?" Jenness notes that there are hundreds of skilled jobs in the North, such as teachers, nurses, radio-meteorological staff, and administrative assistants, that are held by whites. All these could be held by trained Eskimos, and the hunting could better be left to those few untrained people who do not want regular employment. However, at present or within the next few years, few of these jobs, especially nursing and weather-forecasting, could be given to Eskimos unless they were really thoroughly trained and made fully responsible (Jenness 1964:120–136). For all these jobs a knowledge of English would be necessary, as well as further training. Yet even after a number of years of schooling very few Eskimo children have learned English. After eight years of schools at Port Harrison (1950–1958) only one student could speak English at all fluently and about two have a similar command at Sugluk after the first seven years (1957–1964). Jenness points out that the major problems are (1) that the logic and order of the Eskimo language is so different from European languages that it demands entirely new thought patterns; (2) that the children are in a completely artificial environment in the day schools in their settlements and make no effort to practice or use English outside school hours, whereas if they were in a hostel or boarding school down South they would pick it up much more quickly; and (3) that there is very little desire for them to learn English and hence there is little encouragement on the part of their parents, who never went to school or learned English. However, Jenness is hopeful for long-term results and remarks that in a decade the progress made is remarkable considering the fragmented nature of the Eskimo social world and the previous total lack of experience with anything like the school as an institution.

Willmott, who studied the situation at Port Harrison, is more pessimistic:

[After eight years] only four Eskimos speak English. Of these four, only one has been to school, the other three learning their English during extended stays at TB sanatoria. . . .
The school is therefore primarily dysfunctional in an educational sense to Eskimo society. Its functions are limited, as stated before, to 1) freeing women from the care of the children for a few hours a day, and 2) caring for the health of the children by providing them warmth during the winter and one meal a day, as well as a constant check-up and the referring of all infirmities to the nursing station. (Willmott *op. cit.*, 107–108)

In the Sugluk area the Eskimos are ambivalent about the school situation. Most of them realize and admit that their children will probably never be able to get good jobs or compete with white men unless they learn English, yet few of them will encourage their children as much as is necessary. For instance, during the seven years of Sugluk schooling about ten children have reached the level where they should go on to further schooling. But there are no such schools in the area because there are not enough qualified students to fill one. The parents of less than half the children have been willing to give permission for their education to be continued at some distant boarding school, so their education has come to an end.

More successful than the regular school program has been the vocational training for young men in such fields as mechanics. For these intensive courses fluent English is not necessary and some nine men have gone out for a few months to a year for the program. Although not all of them have become fully qualified and obtained full-time jobs, a few have and so some of the available jobs are beginning to be filled by natives rather than outsiders. One other problem which, though not vital, is irritating to some Eskimos and some whites, is that the children are forgetting or not learning syllabics. Since the relative demise of the mission schools the Eskimos have learned to write Eskimo in a Latin orthography, if they have learned at all; thus, when away from home, they cannot write to their parents, who know only syllabics. Moreover, they cannot read the religious texts that are also in syllabics and the missionaries fear that the educational program will combine with other already present factors leading to increasing secularization of life. Jenness would consider this situation satisfactory if the children learned to become literate in English instead (Jenness 1964:121–123). This is not the case, however; until the coming of the schools at least 99 percent of the adult Takamiut were literate in Eskimo, but since then the proportion of Eskimos who are functionally illiterate in any language has been increasing.

The whole problem of the economy of this area has troubled administrators and others for two decades (Jenness 1964:99–119;

204

Cantley 1950). We have discussed some of the present problems in the previous chapter. One of the most significant factors in the economy of the area is that the average per capita income of the Eskimos is extremely low (about $25 to $35 per month), yet living costs in the North are very high. The other major problem is that a good proportion of this low income comes from one form of subsidy or another paid by the federal government. At present there are some 26 full-time jobs in the Takamiut area, less than half of which are held by Eskimos. Even if they were all held by Eskimos this would still leave more than 50 men unemployed. There are far more people concentrated around the settlements than ever before, and what hunting there is provides relatively little income. Even the best hunters in the area rarely gross more than $1,500 a year. This figure would be based, for instance, on the trading of 100 sealskins at $15 a skin (a high price). Yet MacLaren, the best authority on the subject, estimates that from Cape Weggs to Charles Island the whole coast could yield only 400 seals a year maximum without seriously decreasing the seal population (MacLaren 1958:30–31). At that rate the coast could support only four hunters! Income from trapping is likewise limited: even with a high average fox-pelt price of $25, few trappers ever get the 60 foxes that would be necessary for an income of $1,500, even in the best of years!

With all the available jobs filled by Eskimos and all the able-bodied men hunting as efficiently as possible, there would still be a population of which the vast majority were living far below the poverty level. Carvings and handicrafts have been a help but these activities can never support more than a few people for very long. Temporary employment in manual labor requiring few skills helps a few more families for a month or so each year. As most people admit, the problem is not unfamiliar in underdeveloped areas elsewhere in the world. There are too many people and too few resources. The population is growing at three percent or more a year owing to the recent health measures and the freedom from starvation. In theory there are many resources in the eastern Arctic but because of the climate few if any can be profitably worked. There was a nickel mine at Rankin Inlet which operated from

1954 to 1961, and employed a number of Eskimos. However, the ore ran out and the mine closed down, leaving fifty families with little means of support and material equipment they could no longer possibly afford to maintain. It is not that Eskimos cannot adapt to regular wage employment, although it was feared that the monotonous routine and year-round regularity demanded would be unacceptable to a population of "stone age" hunters. There have been problems with Eskimos getting to work on time and some would like more time off for hunting, but, although after a number of years many return to their less organized life, long-term employment is by no means impossible, even for those who had never gone to school (Yatsushiro 1960).

The major possibility of large-scale employment in the Takamiut area is at the asbestos mine and its harbor near Deception Bay. In 1964 and 1968 no one was sure whether the company was going to go ahead with the enormous project, the completion of which depended on the world market. In its early construction phase it already employed about four Sallumiut among its over one hundred employees. If this company were to go into full-scale operation at some future date, it might employ even more Eskimos. Although it would draw employees from all over the Eastern Arctic, to spread the benefits, this would still contribute a good deal to the six hundred or so impoverished Takamiut. Asbestos Hill is not the only possible enterprise that could be opened up in the area, but, as Jenness points out, employment without skills and education is of short-term value:

. . . should the iron ores of Ungava, or of the Great Whale River District, be exploited within the next decade, as seems not impossible, scores of Eskimos and their families will doubtless congregate there and earn good wages during the first few years; but unless they can be educated and trained in the interval, they will fall by the wayside again as mines enter into full production, and become an even heavier charge on the public purse than they are today. (Jenness 1964: 119)

But mining and employment are not the only features in the changing economy. The Eskimos' own ideas about the nature and rights of economic processes themselves are changing. Since the advent of the successful soapstone carving program in the 1950's, the idea of cooperatives has taken hold. In Povungnituk the

Catholic missionary started a "Sculptors Association" which the better carvers belonged to. These men set prices on their own carvings and then divided the excess profits from their sale down South. Thus there was a cooperative effort in part run by the Eskimos and definitely for the benefit of the Eskimos (Balikci 1959). This organization has since developed into a full-scale cooperative with a store competing with the Hudson's Bay Company and it does considerable business. However, it is still heavily subsidized and requires periodic assistance of Canadian whites for accounting up North and full time white agents buying and selling down South. In another area, fishing cooperatives have been started at George River (1958), Chimo (1960), and Payne Bay (1963), as well as at more distant places. These organizations, to which the local Eskimos contribute nominal capital, practice extensive net-fishing during the summers. The salmon and char are brought back to the settlement, cleaned, and stored in government-installed refrigerator units to be later picked up by ships and taken South for sale. The Takamiut Eskimos seem to have the idea that these enterprises are immense commercial successes and they hardly realize that they require large subsidies.

At Sugluk in 1964 there was a movement afoot to form a cooperative, as though this would mean riches for all. A number of the more interested men, particularly those on the Community Council (see below) got together to discuss the matter. The Quebec Government representative was present and one Eskimo and I acted as interpreters and helped explain things. The Eskimos did not seem to care what particular activity the cooperative was set up for; they wanted to run movies (see below), to get fish for the commercial market, to buy foods and store them in the government freezer for consumption in hard times, and to run a general store in competition with the Hudson's Bay Company.

The movies were already in trouble. In 1961 the Community Council had made its first large-scale decision in its three years of existence. From one of the construction companies they bought a small building for $750 and with credit at the store they bought a movie projector. They showed movies once or twice a week, renting films at the normal commercial rates, and managed to keep their financial heads above water. However, in the hands of the Eskimo projectionist the projector rapidly fell into disrepair and needed a complete overhaul, which would have cost more than the council had. In addition, the Eskimos were still flocking in large numbers to the Catholic missionary's movies: he had a better projector and seats in the auditorium, and he charged only ten cents a person. As a missionary, he could get films more cheaply than the Eskimos could, and they had to charge twenty-five cents to cover costs. After some debate, the Eskimos asked the Quebec representative and me to go to the missionary and ask him to stop showing movies or at least to show them free! I told them that it was not my affair, and that I was very sure the missionary would not stop showing films. So a delegation of Eskimos went to the missionary, but I do not think they actually asked him to stop showing films. He offered them a much lower price for their projector than they thought it was worth, but he could repair it himself and they could not. He planned to synchronize it with his own projector so that he would not have to stop and change reels. The Eskimos returned rather confused and did not immediately make up their minds. They continued to show movies, often the same one four or five nights in a row, in order to make more money out of each film so they could recoup their costs and have the projector overhauled. In 1968 they were still showing movies in competition with the missionary and had greatly improved the seating and timing of their operation, though attendance remained somewhat sporadic. "Racial" pride prompts some of the attendance, in that it is "the *Eskimo* movie."

A cooperative formed for large-scale commercial fishing would not be a success in the Sugluk area either. There are not enough large rivers and inland lakes to support a large-scale and hence economical operation. During the summers the visiting ships had for many years provisioned their larders with char, bought from the Takamiut for ten cents a fish, although it is $1.80 a pound in Montreal. As long as there was no freezer the Eskimos were not able to raise the price because if the crew did not buy the fish it would spoil. However, the people of Sugluk recently got the use of a large freezer belonging to the federal government. They started to stock fish for the expected arrival of the ships, planning to demand a higher price, maybe from fifty cents to a dollar a fish. They also radioed to Ivujivik and Wakeham Bay to establish an agreement that all the Eskimos of the coast should hold out for this price so that the general price was sure to rise. However, some of the ships got cheap fish at Cape Dorset across the Strait. When they arrived on the south coast they were furious and one captain said, "We have been good to you for many years and always bought fish for ten cents each. If you are going to try and do this we won't buy any at all!" The Sugluk Eskimos were bitterly disappointed and one man went out to the ship in his canoe when the others were not looking and sold his fish for fifteen cents each — at least he was going to make some money. Things were not too bad for the Sallumiut, however, for they had a freezer and could always eat the excess fish later in the year.

A few days after this the ship arrived in Ivujivik where all had agreed to stick to the higher price. I was there at the time, and although we had heard that the crew had bought some fish cheaper at Sugluk, we knew it was not much and that they would want more. When the crew arrived at Ivujivik we told them the price of fish had risen, and there were arguments and near fights. Two of the crew stole some fish from an Eskimo boat, but we got it back. We discovered that actually the crew did not want any more fish to eat on board but that they planned to take them back to Quebec, transported free in the ship's freezers, and sell them for a profit. Two Eskimos left the settlement and went out to the ship where they managed to get between thirty and fifty cents a fish. Most of the others were left with piles of fish they would have to feed to the dogs or try to dry, for there was no freezer in Ivujivik. That night the crew members went out on their own with nets and caught many fish, though netting sport fish is illegal in northern waters. Moreover, one of the better hunters went with them and showed them where the fish were, for which he was quite well rewarded; he explained to me that "the fish were there for the taking and would not be caught if the white men did not get them, so why not." This is another example of the Eskimo attitude that resources cannot be "owned." The following day some men and I went fishing and caught about forty large fish, which we took to the ship where we tried to bargain with the mate. He said "We have enough and our freezers are full. We could only buy them for charity." He bargained us down to about seventeen cents a fish, since it was no good our keeping them for we had plenty and even that price was a 60 percent increase over the year before! About four days later another ship, the *C. D. Howe*, came in. The crew was of a better class, and they were quite willing to pay one dollar a fish, knowing even that was a bargain. But by then most of the fish had spoiled and there were very few still to be caught. This tale illustrates the great difficulties the Eskimos face even when they have an abundance. The white men are very hard bargainers and nature is often fickle with her supply of game. Nevertheless, for the first time in their history, the Takamiut banded together and tried as a unit to engage in a profitable enterprise. Next year, they said, things would be different!

In proposing a cooperative store, the Sallumiut had very little idea of what was involved. They planned to use the small "movie house" as both store and warehouse and expected to get all supplies on credit. Having heard that there was some white assistance at Povungnituk, they asked me, who seemed to be a friendly and intelligent white man, to be manager — at no pay! I had to decline the offer, and even the Quebec representative, who was strongly against the Hudson's Bay Company monopoly, thought that having a full-scale store was too ambitious an idea.

The really significant idea brought up at the meeting to discuss cooperatives was the buying and selling of native foods. The men asked the area administrator if they could have part of the freezer kept for this purpose, free of course, and then have someone on hand from time to time to buy the seals, fish, and birds as they were caught. They suggested a price of ten cents a pound for meat or ptarmigan and twenty-five cents a pound for the resale back to the community. This was enthusiastically agreed on and everyone thought of the huge profits to be made — fifteen cents a pound on the thousands of pounds of edible animals caught every year. However, at the time they did not think about who was going to buy this food. In hard times, most of the population would not be able to afford it unless they were subsidized. It seemed obvious to me that the bulk of the purchases would be made by the white

210

community, especially of the delicious birds and fish, and that the rest would probably be bought by the five or so Eskimo families who had permanent jobs. These Eskimo families would in fact be subsidizing their poorer brethren, which might not be a bad idea considering that in the past they joined in the general sharing of all large catches, like all the Sallumiut, yet contributed little of their earned income to the rest. I left the community before this idea came to fruition, but I was in Ivujivik during the summer when it did. The prices were those chosen earlier and many men were daily selling to the cooperative during the good summer's hunting. The Quebec officer had raised a small loan that enabled the cooperative to start by having enough capital to buy the meatstuffs. I did not learn who was buying from the cooperative or whether it had finally killed the old community-wide patterns of sharing.

Whether this cooperative was a commercial success or not, its significance to the long-term aspects of the social and economic system is enormous. Until this time the Eskimos had two major spheres of exchange: (1) the white man's goods, money, and wage labor, which were individually owned and shared only with the close family; and (2) the native products, which were shared as far as they could reasonably go, ensuring that all, even the least productive, benefited. This arrangement has been part of the Eskimo culture ever since regular trading began. Willmott calls these two categories respectively money economy and subsistence economy (Willmott 1961:24–29). For Port Harrison he states:

Traditional patterns of sharing appear stronger in the camp than among the settlement Eskimos. This varies directly with the proportion of commodity production. This shift from communalism to household can be viewed as a result of the shift from subsistence to commodity production. (*Ibid.*:26–27)

This used to be true in Sugluk, but we can see that a breakthrough has come about. As far as I know this is the first community among the Canadian Eskimos where a cooperative has started on the basis of the commercialization of the subsistence economy for consumption in the same settlement.

If the cooperative is a success this will mean a quick end to all the felt obligations for sharing beyond one's family. Kinship will increasingly become a basis for whatever distribution remains. Thus kinship will be emphasized, but I expect that the effective cooperating ilagiit will become smaller, as has happened at Pelly Bay (Balikci 1960a:144). The band organization will continue to provide the larger solidary grouping as long as Peterheads are efficient hunting vessels, but it may lose its significance except in the summer, a trend which is already visible.

Although the subsistence economy of Sugluk is disintegrating, the political solidarity of the community is beginning to emerge. Soon after the Northern Service officer arrived in 1958, he suggested the formation of a community council made up of an elected headman and two assistants. Monthly meetings were organized for all interested men, and whites were discouraged from attending. A headman, one of the band leaders, was duly elected. The council continued to meet from time to time with very little effective power. It had few functions and most of these involved delegating the headman to go to the government official and complain about small matters; for instance, some of the men felt it was unfair that they should carry whites back and forth from the ships that visited in the summer without being reimbursed for gas and oil. The council did little except to deal with small problems like this and others concerning the dogs that had become hungry nuisances during the summer. Various men were elected as headman from time to time, but none seemed to be satisfied that any good was being done and most thought it was rather a bother to be a "carrier of complaints." At one point the elected headman was the least respected man in the community and, incidentally, the head of one of the small families in the band of "Others." Some of the whites thought this was a joke at the expense of the Northern Service officer to show him how little they thought of his council.

The council, however, has survived, although it has gained very little power and does not exercise delegated police functions as do those at Great Whale River and Fort Chimo. Its first major action was the creation of the movie business described above. It seems that some of the younger men are now taking more interest and

212

that the council will apply itself to more strictly economic pursuits than previously. In one way participation in the council is a channel through which young men may achieve authority before their time and direct the organization into the area that interests them most — money. Most of the men interested in the council also said that they would become subscribers to the new cooperative by buying a nominal $5 share. The formation of this cooperative may be the most important thing the council has undertaken.

From 1964 to 1967 the infant cooperative limped along, buying and re-selling native foods and performing some buying of furs as an outpost of the well-established Povungnituk cooperative. In 1967 the Eskimos of the eastern Arctic sent representatives to a meeting in Povungnituk with government and other officials to discuss the future of cooperatives. It was decided to federate the cooperatives in the Canadian Arctic into three regions, Eastern, Central, and Western. As Povungnituk was and is by far the most advanced cooperative in the whole area, in organizational and ideological terms, its leaders, Eskimo and white, decided to go ahead and form a federation of the cooperatives of northern Quebec. Partly because this deviated slightly from the overall plan set forth in the conference, they were denied federal subsidy; but they went ahead anyhow, getting a loan from the provincial government and setting up headquarters at Levis across from Quebec City. At first the federation comprised the cooperatives of Povungnituk, Great Whale River, George River, Fort Chimo, and Payne Bay. That same year cooperatives were started through both local Eskimos and the agents of the federation in Sugluk and Ivujivik.

The full-blown Sugluk cooperative inherited the individuals involved in the previous attempt, some of whom had been to Povungnituk to be trained in the store there. The enterprise is housed in a large pre-fabricated building donated by the Quebec Government, comprising store, warehouse, and office under one roof. It is stocked with goods obtained on credit and ordered by employees down South familiar with the Povungnituk experience. During the year four employees dwindled to two, because of personality clashes and the precarious financial situation. Occasional visits by white federation employees served to sort out some of the troubles, but many of the population, though proud of *their* store, continued to look on it as a source of debt while they sold their skins to the competing Hudson's Bay Company for higher prices. The cooperative bought carvings for high prices although they sold only slowly in the markets down South. Advice from federation officials and a change of Eskimo personnel stemmed some abuses in early 1968, but, like the Ivujivik enterprise (see below), the future is precarious without continuing subsidy. That it should function at all is a matter of great pride to the local Eskimos and to many whites considering the competition from the company, the sad state of Sugluk's economy, and the almost complete lack of training and education of the employees. Most of the Eskimos have bought $5 shares and some "shop co-op" out of loyalty but more sound business will be necessary for the store's continued existence.

SUGLUK AND THE TAKAMIUT AREA

Sugluk is now by far the most important and largest community along the south of the Hudson Strait. It also remains the least well endowed with game. The number of white men there and the amount of recent construction far exceed that of all the other communities put together. The government has declared it the administrative capital of the area and from here the area administrator conducts his business with a powerful two-way radio and regular schedules to Ivujivik and Wakeham Bay every day. Each of the latter two communities now has a one- or two-room school and a school teacher, who is also the government administrator, but the authority lies in Sugluk.

The population of Ivujivik has recently dropped to fewer than one hundred Eskimos, many of the former residents having gone to Sugluk. Ivujivik is still a good hunting area, where the Eskimos live much of the year in camps along the coast on the Nuvuk Islands, and its importance has been somewhat sustained by the recent arrival of a Quebec Government official. However, it is a threatened community and in its relationship to Sugluk are many aspects of the relationship between Lake Harbour and Frobisher Bay (Graburn 1963). The Eskimos of Ivujivik see that Sugluk is growing much faster than their own community. In material equipment they are poorer than the Sallumiut and since the arrival of a school in 1961 their annual migrations have been cut in duration and lessened in efficiency. Like the Sallumiut, they have abandoned igloos, replacing them first with scrap wood, canvas, and tar-paper houses and recently with Government prefabricated houses. Most of the people are deeply in debt at the store and however hard they hunt and whatever the prices only one man makes a reasonable living from hunting and carving. The Hudson's Bay Company ran a camp store with an Eskimo trader but the enterprise constantly lost money. In 1964 the Quebec official started to buy seal and fox skins as an "outpost" of the cooperative at Povungnituk, offering higher prices than Hudson's Bay Company, whose small volume of business declined even further.

In 1967 the Hudson's Bay Company sold its store and inventory to an Eskimo cooperative, one of the newly formed federation, which continues to use the former staff. The Ivujivik store is ambitiously stocked, but the economic resources of the area are so poor that the store can clear neither its inventory nor its debts. Unless subsidized by the government (through the federation) or directly by the Povungnituk cooperative, it will find it difficult to remain in business. One other problem, common to many small communities, is that there is a demographic imbalance with more than twelve unmarried men and only four unmarried girls. In the summer of 1964 many of the Ivujivik men went by trap boat to Sugluk looking for wives and women. When they returned they said they had had a good time but they did not like the attitudes of most of the Sugluk unmarried women, whose problems we have discussed above. If the store left, Ivujivik itself might disappear unless the cooperative is highly subsidized. As do many small hunting communities, it may disappear in the face of the glowing attractions of the civilized metropolis down the coast.

During World War II Wakeham Bay diminished greatly in size. However, the camp store and the mission kept going and the community has recently begun to flourish. One feature that differentiates it from other communities is that 25 percent of the total population are Catholic and therefore not supposed to marry Anglicans, and vice versa. This means that the problem of finding spouses in the community who are not close relatives is very difficult, and few of the younger men wish to leave the community, for as Catholics they would have even greater difficulty getting married elsewhere. Since the store at Diana Bay closed, the Diana Bay/Quartak area has no store at all and the people trade into Payne Bay which is 100 miles away. Members of this community are related to both the Kangirksujuamiut (Wakeham Bay) and the Kangirksumiut (Payne Bay) and some have already left to live nearer a store. Thus through natural increase and immigration Wakeham Bay has grown slightly and its population is now somewhat larger than Ivujivik.

There are two Federal School teachers at Wakeham Bay, and I am told that the volume of trade at the Hudson's Bay Company camp store has recently become enough to warrant a permanent white manager. Hunting is still very good but the people are only just recovering from their war-time poverty. When I was there in 1959, all the Eskimos lived out in camps and no one had any boat other than a kajak. Yet when I was there in the spring of 1964 there were a number of boats and canoes, some with outboard motors, and kajaks were fast disappearing. Since 1959, when everyone lived in igloos, the government has built "Eskimo Unit" wooden houses for most of the population. These are all lined up in neat rows along the shore and, combined with the coming of the school in 1961, have curtailed the winter hunting. Also, by 1964 drinking had become something of a problem at Wakeham Bay and gambling was rife, but neither of these reached the extremes they did at Sugluk, probably because of lack of raisins and money. In 1963 the Quebec Government sent in two representatives who have since opened a school, supplementing the federal one.

Relations among the Eskimo populations of Ivujivik and Wakeham Bay and Sugluk continue to be close, in spite of the disappearance of the hunting camps that lined the coast. Supplies to

216

the two camp stores are taken by sled or boat from Sugluk with Eskimo crews. We have seen that the men of each community often look for wives in the adjacent ones — "the grass is always greener." Family ties between these communities are close and some former restricted ilagiit are now split between communities because of recent migrations. The Sallumiut have members of their nuclear and extended families (defined as far as first cousins bilaterally) living outside Sugluk and distributed thus:

Takamiut		
Wakeham Bay	33%	
Ivujivik	23%	
Quartak	8.5%	64.5%
Akianimiut (Baffin Island)		10.6%
Itivimiut		11.7%
Ungavamiut		8.2%
Coral Harbour		0.5%
Total		95.5%*

* Others live outside this area.

Sugluk is sure to grow in importance and numbers even though it may never be an economically self-supporting community. Whether the smaller places continue to exist will depend upon whether a continuous demand for fox and seal skins keeps prices relatively high. It is a remote possibility that if Asbestos Hill gets under way there may be an unexpected and unwanted migration to this frontier community. This would result in a village of squatters living in scraps and shacks rather like the village of Iqaluit at Frobisher Bay. Another possibility, one that was hotly debated when I was in the area, is that the education and administration of the area might be taken over by the Quebec Provincial Government. If this should happen, some of the Eskimos have said that they would leave for the federal territories of Baffin Island, and some Quebec officials have said that they would open small communities at all the good hunting sites, each with a store and school to redistribute the Eskimo population. In the fall of 1968 five Sallumiut families moved by boat and airplane to take up residence in Cape Dorset, and more may follow.

217

CHAPTER SEVEN

Comparisons
and Conclusions

THE EASTERN CANADIAN ARCTIC

The eastern Canadian Arctic comprises the land and the coasts around Hudson Bay, Hudson Strait, Labrador, Baffin Island, the Foxe Basin, and, to a lesser extent, the islands of the High Arctic. All except the latter are inhabited by Eskimos, and all the Eskimos in this area have been subjected to approximately the same series of outside influences, though not necessarily in the same order or with the same intensity and thoroughness.

In previous chapters I have outlined most of the major factors of the history of the eastern Arctic, many of which passed through the Hudson Strait and hence influenced the Takamiut. Although the whalers and explorers did not penetrate to every area and the traders did not settle near every camp, the acquisition of metal and manufactured objects, the idea of trading, and the white-

Eskimo dichotomy became familiar to all Eskimos by the second or third decade of this century at the latest. It is since then that the major differentiations have taken place, not because the Eskimos have become different, but because the speed of change and the numbers and complexity of white agencies have been very unevenly distributed. In the past ten years there have been a tremendous number of community or acculturation studies undertaken in the eastern Canadian Arctic. Extracts from a few will illustrate the major characteristics.

Since the introduction of the white man's technology and trading, the most significant change in Eskimo life has been the gradual gathering of people into more and more permanent settlements. We have seen how this happened in the Sugluk area in the past few decades. There are two general stages: first, when residence in the settlement is for only part of the year, and second, and more recently, when the Eskimos live in the settlement all year round.

In the eastern Arctic nearly all the Eskimos have reached at least the first stage, where most families spend at least the winter in the settlement. The exceptions are few and include Pangnirtung, Igloolik (Damas 1964), and Lake Harbour (Graburn 1963), where their absence is voluntary, and Port Harrison (Willmott 1961), where police during the period 1957–1962 ordered all Eskimo families to live at least five miles from the settlement unless someone in the family had a job in the settlement. Since then the camp Eskimos have gradually taken up permanent residence in the settlement. In these few places the majority of the Eskimos reside most of the year in mobile camps composed of restricted ilagiit much as they used to in the past. However in all these places, as well as in permanent settlements, the Eskimos are dependent on white technology and trading for their existence. They are no longer independent groups, able to make their own living off the land. In addition, some, if not most, of them benefit from welfare and pensions and all of them are aided by the federal government's monthly Family Allowance checks.

Eskimos in many of the smaller settlements, such as Ivujivik and Wakeham Bay, as well as many groups in the larger settlements, such as Great Whale River, Povungnituk, and Chimo, spend most of the winters in the settlements. The men leave for days or weeks at a time usually in pairs or small groups to go trapping, but almost everything of social significance happens in the settlement. In the spring some or even most of the families leave the settlements to go hunting seals and other game at the well known breeding area or where seals are known to bask on the ice. All must return to the settlement in the middle of the summer to await the arrival of the ships, especially the Eastern Arctic Patrol hospital ship, except in those settlements where it does not call. Many families stay in and around the settlement for the whole summer, too, making hunting trips of rather short duration. These latter families often get relatively little game because the areas near the settlements are overhunted and the frequent use of motor boats and guns frightens the game away. Even in the most acculturated areas there are still a very few families who prefer to spend nearly the whole year away from the settlements, only coming in for trading and medical attention. They are the rearguard of the trend of change and are decreasing in numbers. Often they are led by older men and when these die or become too old to be effective hunters the whole family moves into the nearby settlement. A considerable factor in eliminating these independent families and camps has been the recent introduction of Federal Day Schools with supposedly compulsory attendance. The Eskimos know or feel that their children should be in school and yet are rarely willing to leave them at a settlement and travel around without them for large parts of the year. I feel secure in saying that the introduction of schools is the major factor in applying the death blow to independent Eskimo family groups.

For more and more of the Eskimos, in fact for almost all of them in some settlements, life is almost completely centered around the settlements and their white agencies. This applies not only to those with wage employment but also to those, the majority, who still try to make a living out of hunting and trapping. This is true for the larger settlements like Rankin Inlet, Frobisher Bay, and Great Whale River as well as the smaller settlements such as Payne Bay and George River.

We can see that Sugluk is fairly typical with respect to the trend towards more and more settlement-living. In 1959 more than half the families moved out to the camp at Sugluk Island for spring and summer hunting. Only a few went farther with any permanence; those groups with large Peterhead boats were able to hunt hundreds of miles away but did not take their families along. In winter all the families lived in the settlement although the men trapped far inland. By 1964 far fewer families moved out to the island and many preferred to stay in their government-supplied wooden houses all the year round. A few families did spend some weeks outside the settlement hunting seals on the ice because the price of sealskins at the store had risen tenfold. In the summer those groups with Peterheads made good use of them for the economically lucrative summer seal hunting but only the men were involved. I can certainly predict that any semblance of permanent residence outside Sugluk will soon die out and that distant expeditions during the summer will lessen in frequency as the prices of sealskins lower and the cost of buying and running Peterhead boats climbs. If these economic factors do not come about the summer hunting will still continue, but on a men-only basis as at present. Sugluk, perhaps, represents a more acculturated settlement with respect to permanent settlement residence than many others in the eastern Arctic because (1) no one has ordered the Eskimos not to live there, (2) there are a full range of white agencies and increasing wage employment, and (3) the population is far too high to be supported by the meager resources of the simple surrounding coastline. If Eskimo families seriously wished to hunt full time for their living they would move to the better-supplied areas around Ivujivik and Wakeham Bay as a very few have done, but the trend is overwhelmingly in the other direction.

In size and structure, Sugluk is a medium settlement. There are the large places such as Great Whale River, Frobisher Bay, and Fort Chimo, each with more than five hundred Eskimos and more than one hundred white personnel. These large settlements have all had or still have airbases or military installations and a greater proportion of their Eskimos are engaged in wage labor. There are, in Frobisher Bay at least, "Eskimo Townsmen," as Honigman (1965) has called them. This, of course, is equally true of those few places, such as Churchill, where the Eskimos are a minority

221

group marginal to a large Canadian town (Hughes 1965:16, 19). The rationale for the existence of many of these places is military or economic rather than the presence of the Eskimos. However, the large numbers of Eskimos who have gathered at them have caused concern and problems that were often unforeseen.

Sugluk is representative of that middle range of settlements which do or did depend for existence on providing trade and services to the local Eskimo population. These include Povungnituk, Port Harrison, Baker Lake, Eskimo Point, Cape Dorset, and other settlements in which the Eskimo population is on the order of a few hundred and rapidly increasing. They have a fairly complete range of white agencies, such as Hudson's Bay Company stores, Northern Service officers, schools, nursing stations, and missions. Sugluk is fairly typical of them and presents the same kinds of economic and social problems, though it is probably a little further advanced than most in the trend to permanent settlement residence, as explained above.

Smaller than these places and generally more given to hunting are a large number of settlements such as Lake Harbour, Ivujivik, Quartak, Payne Bay, Wakeham Bay, and Clyde River, with populations around a hundred or two hundred at the most. In many of these places the population is hunting oriented and spends many months of the year in camps following the game. However, there are often only one or two white agencies at such places, for example, a church and a school or a camp store and a mission. In some settlements there have been more agencies, but they have been shut down for reasons of economy (e.g., Lake Harbour); and in others the Eskimos feel that they have been neglected and have fewer services than at other nearby settlements, such as at Quartak or Ivujivik. In such places the Eskimos have moved or are thinking about moving to the larger settlements, and in fact these small places may just disappear as permanent habitations, as Cape Smith, Amadjuak, and Little Whale River already have.

The overall trend, then, is for smaller settlements to get smaller and even to disappear, and for the medium- and large-sized ones to get ever larger. This leaves large stretches of coastline uninhabited as never before — even areas that are abundant in game, such

222

as Cape Smith or Amadjuak. At the same time, the populations of the larger settlements such as those in Frobisher Bay or Ungava Bay have far outstripped the supply of available game, and growing numbers of Eskimos are bound to become more dependent on the white man for their very existence. It is hoped that wage labor may be available sooner or later (Hughes 1965:19–22; Jenness 1964:99–199), but this is out of the question for the next decade or more. Stop-gap measures include large amounts of relief, distribution of Eskimo carvings, prints, and handicrafts for the market, and the encouragement of cooperatives for the gathering and marketing of fish and other products. The opening of Federal Day Schools is seen as the long-term solution through which the Eskimos will be educated enough to allow them to take over most of the jobs now being held by whites in the North. In all these matters Sugluk is typical.

OTHER ESKIMO AREAS

Eskimos have inhabited Siberia, Alaska, Canada, and Greenland, and are still to be found there. In all these areas there are no Eskimos who are able to live without trading and civilized technology. In some areas, as I have pointed out for small groups of the eastern Arctic, the Eskimos are no longer dependent on hunting, trapping, or fishing: they make their living through wage employment, handicraft sales, and government subsidies. For the Eskimos in all areas the respective governments have made efforts to provide services, such as educational and medical programs, and, to some extent, to provide economic assistance or subsidy rather than allow the forces of the market to run their full course. I will not go into great detail as the whole area has been thoroughly investigated by Hughes in his excellent survey article (1965) "Under Four Flags: Recent Culture Change Among the Eskimos." Hughes points out the major differences between the agencies responsible for the Eskimos in each area:

In the extent to which there has been attempted an over-all, integrated approach to Eskimo problems, the programs of the Soviet and Danish governments are most similar. The United States has done much in Alaska, as Jenness points out (1962); but, as he also indicates, this has been somewhat haphazard, with an important area — economic stability — having been relatively undeveloped. The Canadian government has only recently entered the field of concerted efforts at development. This is not to say, of course, that a unified program of development necessarily solves all existing problems or avoids creating others. (*Ibid.*:47)

Both the Danish and the Soviet governments have more all-encompassing plans for the development of their Eskimos. In Greenland the government has fostered medical and educational programs but has discouraged private enterprise as a means for bringing the Eskimos into the modern world. In Siberia the Soviet government has, not without resistance, tried to collectivize activities and bring the Eskimos into the regular social and economic institutions of Soviet life. In Canada and Alaska the governments have tried to provide the basic services of life but have allowed private enterprise to operate relatively unhampered, even when this has led to near-monopoly as with the Hudson's Bay Company.

However, in all areas there has been the trend towards settlement living, with the consequent concentration of population, vacating of the coastline and inland areas, and greatly increased Eskimo access to white agencies, materials, and values. Even the remotest areas are less isolated, mainly because of the increasing use of air transport. Eskimos are given a greater awareness of the whole world and their small place in it; they are at the same time more mobile between large areas in the North and even between the North and various parts of "white man's land." In Alaska, particularly, Eskimos have tended to settle on the edges or in the lower-class areas of large towns and cities. This is less true of Greenland and northern Canada because there are fewer large cities there, though I have noted the example of Churchill above. Perhaps the population trends will continue throughout the area with the medium-sized settlements being abandoned in favor of a few large towns, though such a trend would not be completed within this century.

SETTLEMENT STRUCTURE AND THE WHITE MAN

In very nearly all areas the contemporary Eskimos live in settlements of various sizes where they are dependent on white agencies and in increasing contact with the white man. Even in those few places, such as Aberdeen Bay, Baffin Island or Leaf River, Ungava Bay, where a restricted ilagiit forms a year round camp and holds out against this trend, the individual members come into the settlements to trade, collect government financial aid, make use of medical services, and occasionally take temporary jobs. The size and structure of these large settlements is something completely unfamiliar to previous Eskimo ways of existence. The ordering and interaction of groups presents problems that the Eskimos never before had to face. In order to solve these problems the Eskimos at first draw upon cultural mechanisms with which they are familiar. In Sugluk the bands that have moved into the settlements have maintained their identity, based on kinship and former residence, and these bands continue to form residential and economic groups. The same was true of Frobisher Bay in the first decade of its vast expansion, and Hughes has analyzed a similar process three thousand miles to the west on St. Lawrence Island in the Bering Straits.

The existence and structure of these subunits of settlements vary from place to place according to the changing conditions that modify the demand for the presence of groups larger than the nuclear family household. Hughes (1958, 1960) has noted a change from patrilocal bilateral ilagiit to patrilocal patriclans or lineages on St. Lawrence Island, where the former bands have moved into the large village of Gambell and further solidified their structure. In comparing this rather extreme West Alaskan phenomenon with the more recent changes in the eastern Canadian Arctic at Sugluk and Povungnituk, Hughes notes the same tendencies but predicts that they will not be carried so far:

Whether in fact tendencies towards unilineality do develop will be open to historical determination. As noted above, however, very likely the tendency to assumption of more wage labor and decline in corporate subsistence activities based on kinship ties, confusion in marriage rules [as at Sugluk], decline in importance of the extended family, and neolocal residence upon marriage (often with geographic dispersion of relatives) will blunt the trends that may be developing in this direction. (Hughes 1965:26)

With this statement I concur, not only for Canada as Hughes applied it, but also for other places in the North under similar conditions.

To be more specific, I can see some overall trends. When Eskimos move into a settlement of a size far larger than their traditional camps (which in Western Alaska were themselves quite large villages) the traditional groupings, based on kinship and former geographical location, continue to provide the bases for interaction and economic cooperation where feasible. In the smaller groups, daily face-to-face interaction was possible between persons of all ages and both sexes. In the larger situation there has to be some new basis for selection and this is found in the already familiar mechanisms of kinship and co-residentiality. If anything, movement to a larger settlement may even enhance kinship ties for a time. This condition of settlement structure may last from a few years to a generation, depending on a number of conditions. During this period it is almost as though the Eskimos of a settlement were temporarily together, as they were on a trading trip, and were ready to disperse again into their geographically separate camps. If, as happens in some settlements, groups do leave for hunting camps for weeks or months, this structure will remain, at least implicitly, as long as such practices exist, as for instance in Ivujivik and parts of larger settlements like Fort Chimo. Even where the Eskimos rarely or never leave the settlement to reform independent camp groups, the structure may persist *if there is a need for strong cooperative groupings intermediate between the size of the whole settlement and the nuclear family household.* Bases for such a need are commonly the co-ownership of large equipment, such as Peterhead boats in Sugluk or Povungnituk where no small nuclear or extended family can afford to buy or maintain one alone. However, the maintenance of intermediate-sized groups may spring from the need for economic security, which was previously provided by the earlier sharing patterns in the camps. In a huge settlement, such as Frobisher Bay, no hunter can be expected to share his bag with *all* the members of the place, but the ethic of nuclear family "ownership" of large game has not yet arrived. Men feel their duties to provide for their relatives through the bilateral kinship network. Such obligations only diminish with high proportions of wage labor or a breakdown in the "spheres of exchange," as I have outlined for Sugluk. Generally speaking the older generation clings to the old values as long as it is an effective power; but younger men, who have spent most of their lives within settlements and who have undertaken much wage employment, are the leaders of the trend to slough off obligations to share beyond their nuclear families of orientation and procreation.

The maintenance of ilagiit ties described above is relatively temporary except where intermediate economic groups continue to be essential for economic efficiency and success — as in the need to hunt in Peterheads far from the settlement to obtain large numbers of sealskins that can be sold at a high price. Fox trapping, it must be noted, does not demand great cooperation and tends to break the larger units into their constituent nuclear family groups. In many settlements, and probably soon in most, the intermediate groups break down and the Eskimo families of a community re-orient themselves around other alignments. One possible and much evident alignment is the grouping of those who have wage employment as against those who still try to make a living off the land or government subsidy. It has been claimed that this pro-duces an emergent "class structure" (suggested by Valentine [1963]) dividing the Eskimos into what Vallee has well named Kabloonamiut (People of the White Man) and Nunamiut (People of the Land). This tendency has been noted in Port Harrison, Baker Lake, Frobisher Bay, Great Whale River, Fort Chimo, and elsewhere. Such tendencies have also been found in the western Canadian Arctic and parts of Alaska. Other intra-community divisions among the Eskimos have been based on "tribal" origin such as those at Frobisher Bay, Eskimo Point, Coral Harbour, Povungnituk, and Fort Chimo.

Such incipient class structures have much to do with the be-havior of the local whites. In all areas there are those Eskimos who speak more or less English, who look more or less "white" (owing to their mixed ancestry), and who have more or less permanent wage employment. If all three factors fall together, as they do in a government clerk who looks half, or more, white and speaks English well, such persons are bound to "stick out" among the other Eskimos. Furthermore, if an individual has a job that mediates between the white man and the Eskimos, such as an administrator who decides how much relief should be given or a store clerk who decides how much credit should be given, there is bound to be covert or overt resentment against him (or her) on the part of the Nunamiut. However, such phenomena last only as long as the individual has the job or the power. A class is formed only where there is a feeling of solidarity among such people, emphasizing their difference from any other group, passed on through their children, and this has occurred in some places. Willmott (1961) pointed out the rather derogatory attitude that the "settlement" Inukjuamiut (Eskimos of Port Harrison) had toward those who still lived in camps and did not have jobs. He added that there was an R.C.M.P. order forbidding those who did not have jobs to live in the settlement, and when "camp" people got jobs and moved permanently into the settlement they "changed classes." I believe that in a span of decades or a generation the intra-Eskimo "class" conception is only temporary and reflects achievement of life styles rather than long-term divisions.

A phenomenon of greater long-term importance is the development of castelike relationships between the Eskimos as a whole and the whites in the North:

In these situations there is instead [of a we-feeling among all participants of the community] a situation of community segmentation, and/ or — especially with white people in the community — a caste structure for the community as a whole. (Hughes 1965:26)

This model of contemporary community structure can be diagrammed:

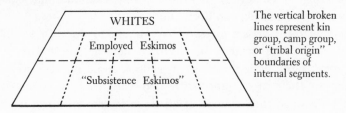

The vertical broken lines represent kin group, camp group, or "tribal origin" boundaries of internal segments.

With the passage of time and the decline in cooperative economic activities the vertical barriers are lost or replaced by those designating individual family units. The barrier between employed and "subsistence" Eskimos loses its force in the face of increasing universal education and job opportunities and gradual assimilation into the lowest rung of the national economy and society. Fewer and fewer Eskimos try to make a living from the land and, at the same time, many of the employed Eskimos who are able to afford the best equipment continue to take an interest in hunting and fishing, if only for sport.

At this point the "separate" Eskimo society ceases to exist. It has become part of the larger socio-economic system — the lowest part. I would amplify Hughes' statement on the presence of white/Eskimo caste differentiation in many northern communities by mentioning a few other widespread factors. Each group (Eskimo and white) tends overwhelmingly toward endogamy (inbreeding) — typical of a caste situation. In fact endogamy is almost one of the defining features of caste, which is a social system "of endogamous divisions in which membership is hereditary and permanent." (Berreman 1960:10) There are few white-Eskimo marriages (as opposed to concubinages) in the North, but generally men of the higher caste (whites) have sexual access to the women of the lower, and not vice versa. Even in those countries where there are intermarriages between castes (and this happens even in India), there "are unambiguous rules for assigning a child its lifelong affiliation with a ranked group on the basis of its birth." (Berreman 1966:280) In the Canadian North the child almost invariably belongs to the stratum of its father *where there is marriage*. Where there is no marriage the child remains "Eskimo." I might note that if, as has occasionally happened, the child (mixed) is adopted by a white family down South other rules apply.

Vallee attempts to show that for one community — from which he generalizes — there are very "un-caste-like" features, to wit: ". . . absence of . . . control over interaction on the part of the [white man]. . . ." (1962:124), and "[a few Eskimos whose] informal contacts with the [white man] may be comparatively frequent . . . determined by the fact that the Eskimo shares membership in the same work organization. . . ." (*Ibid.*:125) He goes on to define these relationships as "paternalistic" and not "caste-like." (*Ibid.*:126) I see no reason why they should not be both. Even in these, his strongest arguments against "caste," I find nothing that is incompatible with a particular kind of caste system, in spite of Vallee's emphasis on lack of the "myth of pollution" commonly found in India. On the other hand, I find great evidence, overt and covert, for the "myth of pollution" applying to the relevant cultural features of the North. Often those who fraternize on a friendly basis with the Eskimos — including anthropologists who live with them — are ostracized by most of the whites. Employees have been transferred to other places, slowed in their promotions, or even fired for having too close a relationship with the Eskimos — sexual or other. This may not have been true of the early trading settlements, where trader and even missionary had sexual access to the Eskimos and depended on them for company and friendship, but in the larger settlements it is often as though "suburbia" has moved North and the separation has grown rather than diminished. As Willmott points out:

There is no theoretical reason why [acculturation to caste rather than assimilation] may not develop between Eskimo and white in the Canadian [and Alaskan] Arctic. With the Eskimo providing the labor under white supervision, the entrance of industry into the Arctic need not lead to increased assimilation of the Eskimo. It may instead result in a strengthening of caste boundaries that are already evident between white and Eskimo in Port Harrison [and most larger Northern settlements]. (Willmott 1961:128)

This trend is present and will continue unless the current situation is reversed by superordinate factors, such as increased Eskimo-white intermarriage in both directions, equal or parallel access to economic opportunity, or really intensive and effective education. At present the trend appears all too familiar in comparison with other situations around the world, such as those of the Indians of North and South America, the natives of South and Southwest Africa, and the Aborigines of Australia.

SUMMARY

The story of the Takamiut emphasizes the extreme cultural, social, and technological adaptive ability of the Eskimos. In the first instance the Eskimos adapted, more successfully than their predecessors, to the rich yet unpredictable Arctic littoral environment. After the white man arrived the Eskimos treated the new resources thus introduced with the same realistic opportunism as they had the natural environment. They incorporated the new material and social conditions into their way of life in order to pursue those ends dictated by their unchanged value system.

The Eskimos, of course, did not realize for a long time that they were being hooked into a foreign economic system, but even if they had it is doubtful that they would have chosen a different path. Their willingness to seize new opportunities for the apparent immediate values overrode any cultural pride or conservatism, and is characteristic of many apolitical hunting and gathering peoples. Only recently, after so much has been lost, have new Eskimo political structures and cultural consciousness came to the fore.

The actual sequences of historical changes have been described with an emphasis on social and economic organization. It is to be noted that economic changes have usually preceded changes in social arrangements and that the former changes were usually directly or indirectly the result of white activities. Some of the major periods of change have been described as stages, but this does not imply any necessary or universal sequence. Each stage is a set of reactions to external (social or environmental) changes. They are therefore convenient markers for periods in the historical analysis. Balikci (1964) has demonstrated very neatly that comparison of various regions shows no such one-to-one relation between acculturative adaptation and white activities as Murphy and Steward (1956) proposed. The pre-existing culture and the environmental opportunities are also powerful factors. This last chapter, however, tries to demonstrate the over-all parallels that exist in similar situations all around the world.

Some of the major features illustrated by the historical analysis involve the changing social and cultural boundaries between the Eskimos and whites. After intermittent contacts and technological exchange for hundreds of years, the coming of permanent traders and the increased involvement in trapping weaned the Eskimos away from their economic independence and made them part of the world market system. Nevertheless, until very recently the Eskimos kept the money and subsistence spheres of their economic system separate. Recent economic and social pressures have, in Sugluk, caused a slow collapse of the older economic system. The Eskimos, therefore, have ceased to treat the market as a separate subsystem and have at last allowed themselves to become fully market dominated. They are no longer subsistence hunters but are professionals and, presumably, their actions will more and more be influenced by the factors of production.

After congregating in large settlements the Eskimos have recently been confronted with large numbers of transplanted whites and a caste situation has emerged. This has been accelerated by the recent influx of wives and children, who have tended to create "little suburbias" in the larger settlements (Fried 1966). The Eskimos of the Sugluk area are now facing this situation. Some clues as to what will happen in the future are found in a comparative examination of other Eskimo communities.

The old Eskimo way of life is no more. It has gone forever, just as have gone for us the days of the ox-cart . . . and the tallow candle. Civilization has caught both ourselves and the Eskimos in its dragnet, along with a variegated assortment of peoples in undeveloped Africa, Asia and South America. Two hundred, even one hundred years ago the Eskimos could easily have bridged the gap that divided their way of life from our own: but the dawning age of automation has widened the chasm, so that the bridge it now needs must be longer and stronger. Among ourselves the gap between grandparents and grandchildren is still narrow, and most of us can leap over it quite easily; yet it has already become too wide for thousands and tens of thousands of our young people, and many not only fail to cross it but fail even to make the attempt. (Jenness 1966:123)

Pirasualakpugut — we shall try.

Works Cited

Arima, E. Y.
1963 "Report on an Eskimo Umiak built at Ivujivik, P.Q."
Ottawa: *National Museum of Canada Bulletin*, No. 189
1964 "Notes on the Kayak and Its Equipment at Ivujivik, P.Q."
Ottawa: *National Museum of Canada Bulletin*, No. 194
Asher, G.
1860 "Henry Hudson the navigator; the original documents in
which his career is recorded; collected, partly translated, and
annotated with an introduction by G. M. Asher." London:
The Hakluyt Society, Vol. 24
Balikci, A.
1959 "Two Attempts at Community Organization among the
Eastern Hudson Bay Eskimos." *Anthropologica* 1:122–135

1960a "Some Acculturative Trends among Eastern Canadian Eskimos." *Anthropologica* 2:139–153

1960b *Suicidal Behavior among the Netsilik Eskimos*. Canada:
Northern Co-ordination and Research Center, Department
of Northern Affairs and National Affairs. Ottawa. N.C.R.C.-
60-2

1962 "Missionary and Shaman among the Netsilik Eskimo." Paper
read at the 61st Annual Meeting of the American Anthro-
pological Association. Chicago. November 1962

1964   "Development of Basic Socioeconomic Units in Two Eskimo Communities." Ottawa: *National Museum of Canada Bulletin*, No. 202

Ballantyne, R. M.
1857   *Ungava.* London

Berreman, G. D.
1960   "Caste in India and the United States." *American Journal of Sociology* 66:120–127
1966   "Caste in India and the United States," in *Japan's Invisible Race* (G. De Vos and M. Wagatsuma, eds.). Berkeley: University of California Press

Boas, F.
1888   "The Central Eskimo." *Bureau of American Ethnology, Annual Report* 6:604. Washington, D.C.

1901   *The Eskimo of Baffin Land and Hudson's Bay.* American Museum of Natural History. Bulletin 15

1907   *Second Report on the Eskimo of Baffin Land and Hudson's Bay.* American Museum of Natural History. Bulletin 15 (2)

1940   *Race, Language and Culture.* New York: Macmillan

Bohannan, P.
1955   "Some Principles of Exchange and Investment among the Tiv." *American Anthropologist* 57:60–70

Bohannan, P., and Dalton, G.
1965   *Markets in Africa.* New York: Doubleday, Anchor Book

Cantley, S.
1950   *Survey of Economic Conditions among the Eskimos of the Canadian Arctic.* Mimeo. copy in Library of the Department of Northern Affairs and National Resources, Ottawa

Chappell, W.
1817   *Narrative of a Voyage to Hudson's Bay in His Majesty's Ship Rosamund.* London

Clairmont, D. H. J.
1963   *Deviance among the Eskimos and Indians in Aklavik N.W.T.* Northern Coordination and Research Centre, N.C.R.C. 63-9

Damas, D.
1964   *Igluligmiut Kinship and Social Groupings.* Canada. Canadian National Museum Bulletin, No. 196

D'Anglure, Bernard S.
1964   "L'Organisation Sociale Traditionelle des Esquimeaux de Kangirsujuak (Nouveau-Quebec)." M.A. Thesis, Université de Montreal, October 1964

Davies, K. G. (ed.)
1963   *Hudson's Bay Record Society*, Volume 24 (1963), London

Dunbar, M. J.
1952   "The Ungava Bay Problem." *Arctic* 5:4–16
Erlandson, Erland
1834   "Journal and Correspondence," in *Northern Quebec and Labrador Journals and Correspondence, 1819–35*, in K. G. Davies (ed.), 1963
Finlayson, N.
1830   "Journal and Correspondence," in *Northern Quebec and Labrador Journals and Correspondence, 1819–35*, in K. G. Davies (ed.), 1963
Firth, R.
1951   *Elements of Social Organization*. Boston: Beacon Press
Ford, J.
1964   Personal Communication. Fort Chimo
Fried, J.
1966   Personal Communication. Berkeley
Gardner, G., and Wilmot, B. E.
1943   "Exploring in Labrador and Hudson Bay." Ottawa: *Revue de l'Université d'Ottawa* 13:78–117, 339–367
Giffen, N.
1930   *The Roles of Men and Women In Eskimo Culture*. Chicago: University of Chicago Press
Gordon, A. R.
1886   *Report of the Second Hudson's Bay Expedition . . . 1885.* Canada. Department of Marine and Fisheries

_____   1887   *Report of the Hudson's Bay Expedition of 1886.* Canada. Department of Marine and Fisheries
Graburn, N. H. H.
1960   "The Social Organization of an Eskimo Community: Sugluk, P.Q." Unpublished M.A. Thesis, McGill University, Montreal

_____   1961   "Eskimo Space-Time: A Preliminary Meta-linguistic Analysis." MS.

_____   1963   *Lake Harbour N.W.T.* Northern Coordination and Research Centre, Department of Northern Affairs and National Resources, N.C.R.C.-63-2. Ottawa

_____   1964   *Taqagmiut Eskimo Kinship Terminology.* Canada: Northern Coordination and Research Centre, Department of Northern Affairs and National Resources, N.C.R.C.-64-1

_____   1966   "Mixed Communities," in *People of Light and Dark* (M. van Steensel, ed.). Ottawa: The Queens Printer, pp. 120–128

Guemple, L.
  1962 "Innuit Spouse Exchange." Occasional Papers of the Department of Anthropology, University of Chicago
Hall, C. F.
  1865 *Life With The Esquimeaux*. New York: Harper & Brothers
Hawkes, P. W.
  1916 *The Labrador Eskimo*. Canada. Department of Mines. Geological Survey. Memoir 91
Honigmann, J. J.
  1962 *Social Networks in Great Whale River*. Canada. Bulletin of the National Museum of Canada, No. 178
Honigmann, J. J., and Honigmann, Irma
  1965 *Eskimo Townsmen*. Canadian Research Centre for Anthropology. University of Ottawa
Hughes, C. C.
  1958 "An Eskimo Deviant from the 'Eskimo Type' of Social Organization." *American Anthropologist* 60:1140–1147

  1960 *An Eskimo Village in the Modern World*. Ithaca: Cornell University Press

  1965 "Under Four Flags: Recent Culture Change among the Eskimos." *Current Anthropology* 6:1:3–73
Jenness, D.
  1962 "Eskimo Administration: I. Alaska." *Arctic Institute of North America. Technical Paper* No. 10

  1964 "Eskimo Administration: II. Canada." *Arctic Institute of North America. Technical Paper* No. 14

  1966 "The Administration of Northern Peoples: America's Eskimos — Pawns of History," in *The Arctic Frontier* (R. St. J. Macdonald, ed.). Toronto: University of Toronto Press, pp. 120–129
Kohlmeister, B., and Kmoch, G.
  1814 *Journal of a Voyage from Okkak, on the West Coast of Labrador, to Ungava Bay*. London
Lantis, M.
  1946 "The Social Structure of the Nunivak Eskimo." *Transactions of the American Philosophical Society*, 25
Low, A. P.
  1897 "Report of an Exploration in the Hudson Strait Region." *Geological Survey. Summary Report for 1897*, 10. Ottawa, 1898. Pt. A.

  1898 "Report of an Exploration of Part of the South Shore of Hudson Strait and Ungava Bay." *Geological Survey. Annual Report, 1898*, 11. Ottawa, 1899. Pt. L.

1902   "Report on an Exploration of the East Coast of Hudson Bay from Cape Wolstenholme to the South End of James Bay." Canada. *Geological Survey. Annual Report, 1900,* 13

1906   *Voyage of the Neptune.* Ottawa: Government Printing Office.

Lyon, G. F.
  1824   *Private Journal of . . . During the Recent Voyage of Discovery under Captain Parry.* London

MacLaren, I. A.
  1958   "The Economics of Seals in the Eastern Canadian Arctic." *Fisheries Research Board of Canada,* Arctic Unit, Circular No. 1

McLean, J.
  1849   *Notes of a 25 Years' Service in the Hudson's Bay Territory.* Publication of the Champlain Society, Vol. 19 (1932)

Malaurie, J.
  1964   *Le Nouveau-Québec.* The Hague: Mouton

Malinowski, B.
  1945   *The Dynamics of Culture Change in Africa* (E. Kaberry, ed.). Yale University Press

Martijn, C. A.
  1964   "Canadian Eskimo Carving in Historical Perspective." *Anthropos* 59:546–596

Munn, M. T.
  1922   "The Economic Life of the Baffin Land Eskimo." *Geographical Journal* 59

Murphy, R. F., and Steward, J.
  1956   "Tappers and Trappers." *Economic Development and Cultural Change* 4:335–355

Oschinsky, L.
  1960   "Two Recently Discovered Human Mandibles from Cape Dorset on Sugluk and Mansel Island." *Anthropologica* 2: (2):212–227

Payne, F. F.
  1886–87   "The Mammals and Birds of Prince of Wales Sound, Hudson's Strait." *Proceedings of the Canadian Institute* 5:111–123

1888–89   "Eskimo of Hudson's Strait." *Proceedings of the Canadian Institute.* Series 3, Vol. 6:213–230

1895–96   "The Seasons. Hudson's Strait." *Transactions of the Canadian Institute.* 5:104–113

Polanyi, K.; Arensberg, C. M.; and Pearson, H. W. (eds.)
  1957   *Trade and Market in the Early Empires.* Glencoe: Free Press

Pospisil, L., and Laughlin, W. S.
1963 "Kinship Terminology and the Kindred Among the Nuna-miut Eskimo." *Ethnology* 2:180–189
Prickett, A.
1860 "A Larger Discourse of the Same Voyage and the Successes Thereof Written by . . ." in Asher 1860:98–135
Robinson, J. L.
1944 "Eskimo population in the Canadian Eastern Arctic." *Canadian Geographical Journal* 29:128–142
Service, E. R.
1966 *The Hunters.* Englewood Cliffs, N.J.: Prentice-Hall
Steward, J.
1955 *Theory of Culture Change.* Urbana: University of Illinois Press
Stupart, R. F.
1886 "The Eskimo of Stupart Bay." *Proceedings of the Canadian Institute,* Series 3, Volume 4, Toronto
Taylor, W. E.
1964 "The Prehistory of the Quebec-Labrador Peninsula," in *Le Nouveau-Québec* (J. Malaurie, ed.). The Hague: Mouton, pp. 181–210
Turner, L. M.
1888 "Indians and Eskimos of the Ungava District, Labrador." *Proceedings and Transactions of the Royal Society of Canada* 15

1894 "Ethnology of the Ungava District, Hudson's Bay Territory." *11th Annual Report of American Bureau of Ethnology,* pp. 159–350
Tuttle, C. R.
1885 *Our North Land.* Toronto
Valentine, C. A.
1952 "Toward a Definition of Eskimo Social Organization." Unpublished M.A. Thesis, University of Pennsylvania
Valentine, V. F.
1963 Personal Communication. Ottawa: Northern Coordination and Research Centre
Vallee, F. G.
1962 *Kabloona and Eskimo in the Central Keewatin.* Ottawa: Northern Coordination and Research Centre, N.C.R.C.-62-3
Willmott, W. E.
1961 *The Eskimo Community at Port Harrison, P.Q.* Canada: Northern Coordination and Research Centre, N.C.R.C.-61-1
Wright, J. G.
1944 "Economic Wildlife of Canada's Eastern Arctic — Caribou." *Canadian Geographical Journal* 29:184–195
Yatsushiro, T.
1958–60 Personal Communications

Index

239

242